M000033290

CONTENTS

———

THE DEAL OF THE DOLLHOUSE

HOW TOXIC SELF-CARE
NEARLY DESTROYED ME

HOLLY HARPER

NEW DEGREE PRESS

THE DEAL OF THE DOLLHOUSE
How toxic self-care nearly destroyed me

ISBN   978-1-63676-560-0   *Paperback*
         978-1-63676-142-8   *Kindle Ebook*
         978-1-63676-143-5   *Ebook*

D, this is your daughter.
The message is: I finally wrote a book! I love you.

Love, H

* * *

This book is dedicated to Madeline, her best
friend Z, and their beautiful spirits, to my beloved
community for their enduring support, to my
family who always has my back, and to my uncle
Jim Gion and my dad Jeff Gion, who both left
us at the exact moments they were meant to.

BETTER THAN
I EVER IMAGINED

———

I sat down in March 2020 to write a business book about how being an entrepreneur and a woman is a thousand times more difficult if you are also a single mom.

When I separated from my spouse in 2017, I experienced what is called "a class slide," or decrease in socioeconomic status. In my case, I went from being a dual-income, health-insured woman with one child to a single-income, soon-to-be-uninsured single mom.

It was terrifying at first seeing insurance premiums go up and credit scores go down, but I was lucky to have safely landed at a "slightly lower class, but not impoverished."

As I was researching class slides amidst experiencing it, I felt irritated when I heard the story of a female entrepreneur who was wildly successful, but also married. She had a safety net to catch her if her new business failed. I felt jealous of women who had gone through divorce or separation but ended their memoirs with a new partner or a reaffirmed commitment to their husbands. I felt exhausted by women who had hit rock bottom but never had a child. They carried less risk and vulnerability by not being responsible for another human's life on top of their own.

At the same time, I felt set aside by some of my married friends. People who previously would have asked my spouse and I to join them for weekends at the shore stopped inviting me. People told me I should try to fix my marriage by taking one of their suggestions, without having asked what I had already tried. Some even suggested I had it good in my marriage, so they didn't see why I would throw it all away.

"Just apologize for cheating on him and *try harder,*" someone close to me said. "You had it so good before. He is a good man compared to most, and your daughter needs a mommy and a daddy."

The messages of "try harder and don't complain" combined with this new lower social and financial status were embarrassing and isolating.

I was so close to "having it all" just a few short years ago, and I had fucked it up.

"It was my own fault," I told myself at the time. "I broke the terms of the deal I'd made to just be grateful for what I've got—the house, the car, the vacations, the kid—even if something big was missing in my soul."

As I opened up about my sadness, confusion, shame, and fear, and started to bitch about how yucky it feels when people treat me differently when they learn I am forty and single, my friends and family stepped up to support me.

Some let me talk it out. Some suggested I go to therapy, which I did. Some just hugged me tight and opened a bottle of wine with me. Others challenged me to look at things differently. Many people gave me books, podcasts, articles, memes, and little slices of self-help so I could start to see I wasn't alone.

I began to really look deeper at what I wanted and needed from life, and what I discovered wasn't at all what I expected to find.

* * *

When I started to study the position of women like me—college-educated, middle-class, white, straight women—I delved right into how I experienced sexism and classism.

We want to be paid equally, treated equally, not be told to "smile more," and be respected for the qualities we possess, regardless of other people's gendered interpretations of us.

For example, we want to be competitive when it's warranted, and for that not to be held against us. We want to be bossy because we've earned the role of "boss lady," and for this attribute not to be a bad thing. We want our business ideas to be seen as valuable and not told, "That would make a great nonprofit."

I started talking to women in my community and my insights were reflected there. I came across loads of research about how college-educated, middle-class women are trapped in this labyrinth where we are told to work our asses off to find a way to "have it all"—careers, love, marriage, motherhood, financial security, healthy bodies, strong friendships—but we actually face a pile of dead ends and impossible choices.

Do we cut back at work to be a super mom? Do we put more money away for college and stay at home while she's young, or put her in daycare now so we can keep building our careers? When our husbands are offered an amazing opportunity, whose hopes and dreams do we put first? Why did our parents seem to already have this figured when they were our age?

Women are sprinting into dead end after dead end, running in circles in this maze. It's exhausting, depleting, and demoralizing for us, and I found the research to prove it.

We are in a pressure cooker, pushed to work tirelessly to "have it all," and are deeply ashamed of ourselves if we've either failed at "having it all" or we aren't happy with the end result. On paper the deal looks great, so if we say we want *more* or we're not fulfilled, we are either failures or ungrateful.

Many of us aren't in touch with, or we actively hide, our deepest, most traumatic feelings. We suffer alone and in shame, working harder than ever in our families, jobs, and busy lives.

But we are missing something in our souls. At midlife, we find ourselves constantly looking for outlets to bring us joy. The great capitalist marketing machine has caught on to our existential despair and is ready and willing to help us feel *great*!

Many savvy brands are disguising healing and self-care in a special sort of toxic corporate feminism, which does more to make influencers and motivational speakers rich than it does to actually help women or the world.

The result is women like me are paralyzed, stressed-out, and disconnected. When we speak up, we are often told to shut up lest we come across as ungrateful. When we do seek help, the help often ends up being superficial, a bunch of "quick fixes" designed to monetize our pain so someone else makes money from it.

The self-help industry largely falls short of connecting our individual needs to meaningful happiness, and it definitely doesn't encourage us to improve the larger societal context we are all a part of which got us in this situation in the first place.

What *is* this larger societal context we are a part of? It is called the patriarchy and it encompasses all of the ways this societal context entangles and inhibits our lives.

The patriarchy is shorthand for the history of the United States of America built on a male-dominated, European cultural foundation. It is majority Judeo-Christian in value and morality. It is predominantly white and heterosexual. It has adopted capitalism as its economic system and representational federal democracy as its legal structure.

The patriarchy is neither bad, nor is it good, but it does exist. The patriarchy shares a common set of values for what can be considered the "ideal of American society."

Americans value competition, winning, bravery, intellect, data, evidence, progress, proof, strength, independence, survival, land ownership, controlling and bending nature to our will, orderliness, family, hard work, and structure.

The history of women in the patriarchy is one of being second to men. Women have been historically infantilized and "cared for" by their husbands, for centuries were unable to own land, file for divorce, or work outside the home or farm. For decades women couldn't vote, choose what we could do with our bodies, or apply for credit without a spouse's signature. Women in the patriarchy were considered property of the men in charge.

Over time, women have fought for and died for equal opportunity to participate in the patriarchy and have the following rights: the right to own homes, start businesses, marry other women, identify as the gender of woman regardless of our biological sex, adopt or have children without a married partner, control our bodies, vote, be paid equally for equal work, perform jobs previously barred to us, attend schools and join organizations previously exclusive to men, among many, many other gains.

By the time I was born in 1980, women had made so much progress. We have been gaining ground in all the "metrics that mattered," and our social and legal values and structures are shifting to better support women's equality.

By the time I was in school, feminism had gone mainstream and women were told we *finally* could "have it all" if we worked hard enough.

* * *

As I write the above, retelling the history of women in America should put a gnawing, bad feeling in your guts.

What I just wrote is the dominant narrative regarding "the history of women in America." It's the textbook summary of the feminist movement: "Women came together with male allies, fought for rights, and won them. We still fight, march, and gain ground."

This story makes a good blurb in a seventh-grade history book.

But it isn't the whole story. I'm missing something, right?

Something massive, uncomfortable, and important is missing here. This fight was almost exclusively led by white women, and white women benefitted the most from its victories. We rarely dig deeper into how white feminism made gains for white women and often marginalized or excluded Black women, indigenous women, and women of color.

White feminism has been fighting so white women can gain access to patriarchal power structures. White women's feminism has largely been supporting, colluding with, and joining in on the patriarchy when we need it for protection, resources, power, partnership, safety, or because we have never been shown another way.

Read carefully again: white women have been working to access the power structures of the patriarchy to participate equally alongside white men.

White women have not been trying to change or eliminate the patriarchy itself. We have not been realigning the values of our society to value *all people equally.* White feminism and their movements have largely ignored the needs of other women and centered on our needs, and we have done this because of our power and relationship to white men.

We have bought into the patriarchy's definition of white womanhood and are working hard at climbing the patriarchy's ladder.

White women's power and treatment of Black, brown, and indigenous people is largely ignored because white people ignore it. As white women gain access to the patriarchy, we also gain access to write our version of the truth in those seventh-grade textbooks.

Yes, women—white women—have been fighting for equality *inside* of the American patriarchy. But we largely have not been fighting for humanity's liberation *from the patriarchy itself.* We have failed to fight for a new way of approaching the world, a new set of values, laws, economic priorities, and faith practices.

We also support the patriarchy by uncritically participating in it and perpetuating its racist, sexist, violent, and dehumanizing elements.

Now you're going to say, "Well, I am not like this! I am a progressive white woman! I know how messed up the system is and have been fighting for as long as I can remember. I've been to the marches. I voted for Hillary. I support Black Lives Matter. The problems are *systemic*. I want *all* people to have it all!"

If that's you, then you're exactly who I am writing these stories for.

The narrative of white women is one of individualism and exceptionalism (a patriarchal value), which causes them to react with, "I am not part of the patriarchy; I am fighting it. Those other women who voted for Trump are the ones who are hurting women."

We reject that we're part of the problem and assert that because we are a part of an oppressed group as women, we can hardly be called the oppressors. We're the allies!

Slowly, over time, I see "white privilege" more and more often rewritten as "white male privilege." We also see "white female privilege" relegated to the suburban and rural white women who secured Trump the presidency in 2016, or the Karens of the world who overtly use their white female privilege in aggressive ways.

But white female privilege and white women's position as part of the patriarchy needs to be examined much more critically. Especially the progressive, college-educated, white women who jump straight into wanting to fight without ever considering the violence of their own actions.

When I have, even gently, tried to examine white progressive privilege, my white progressive friends—male and female alike—are triggered: "We didn't *mean it that way.* We are voting for Biden. We donated. We are really trying to help.

We want to do the right things. We didn't know. We don't believe you. Who are *you* to lecture me about privilege? I was a victim of sexual assault. I married a Black man."

It can get ugly.

With my white female friends, I often can try and cut through the emotional part and stay with them in that moment.

"Yes, I am not trying to shame you. I'm not trying to question your intent. I am trying to point out the system you've internalized is fucked up, and that's why you're so triggered right now. You feel it, and you're scared," and what I hear next is, "I feel so guilty. It's so overwhelming. It's like I'm in a minefield. I'm so overwhelmed with work and kids and my spouse; how can I do anything about social justice or environmental devastation? I just don't know what to do."

Cue white lady tears.

Whenever our individual white lady privilege is pointed out to us, we are offered multiple escape routes. Those escape routes *are provided by the patriarchy.* Every time we opt to use one of these escape routes, what we're doing is keeping the patriarchy alive just a little bit longer.

The patriarchy defines white women as feminine, fragile, innocent, kind, maternal, patient, beautiful, delicate, and sweet. The white women *inside* of the patriarchy who often call themselves feminists or progressives don't really push back on those adjectives, they just add fierce, brave, strong, creative, powerful, mighty, and capable.

So, we run into the world as fierce, progressive warriors, fighting for our rights and marching on Washington. When someone stands up and points out we marched right over the top of a group less privileged than we are, we run out of the room broken, hurt, and embarrassed by what we've done, feeling misunderstood. Our *intentions were noble.*

When we're overwhelmed, white women are welcomed back into the open arms of the patriarchy who has told us for centuries he will protect us because we are fundamentally innocent and fragile.

When we are paralyzed by systemic problems or new, frightening situations where we don't have as much power as we're used to, we welcome the reassurance that fixing the world's problems are not on our small, delicate shoulders.

When we are called out for being a Karen—or committing a racist or aggressive act—we often withdraw to our white friends and their comforting words about how they know we "didn't mean it that way," putting our womanly, kind intent above the harm we caused.

In other words, white women talk about feminism, female solidarity, and fucking the patriarchy when we want equal pay, universal preschools, quality health care, free college for our children, and to stop being assaulted and raped.

But when we're called out by people with less privilege and power for making mistakes, abusing our power, putting our needs first, ignoring our privilege, ignoring the disadvantages of others, trivializing issues, talking about our intent over our harm, or pretty much doing anything "bad," we run back to that patriarchy and its values to protect our bruised egos.

Because we *mean well,* we want a pass.

We signed a deal that we get to be the ideal, perfect woman who, if she works hard enough and overperforms at everything, we get to have the picket-fence, dollhouse version of life. The kids, the car, the spouse, the career, the gym membership, the wine club, and the big backyard.

We've internalized the belief we are well-intentioned and deserve the benefit of the doubt.

We want our white privilege and our women's liberation at the same time.

It doesn't work that way.

* * *

The patriarchy in America is our dominant cultural ideal. It is so entrenched in how we see things, it's really uncomfortable when someone challenges the innate superiority or "goodness" of that American ideal.

The values of the patriarchy define what white womanhood is, and until white women reject that definition, own up to our historical violence, and work to change the definition itself, we're always going to be vulnerable to doing more harm than good.

But rejecting that definition and going against the dominant patriarchal system is painful and difficult.

When I rejected the "patriarchal" marriage structure because I was deeply unhappy in my marriage, there were wide-ranging personal and social consequences. When I rejected Christianity as my faith, among a predominantly Christian group of peers when I was an Air Force Officer's wife, I was isolated. When I embraced my sexuality and disclosed my infidelity, I was slut-shamed and branded "a cheater." Often this was *by other white women.*

I couldn't figure it out. Why are white women who are unhappy and stressed, alone and isolated, educated and progressive, all still largely embracing the patriarchal values that cause our pain in the first place?

I was so frustrated and pissed off I started ranting about superficial white lady privilege all the time. Stupid married people with their stupid SUV's and vacation homes. Stupid white ladies with their Brazilian blow outs and perfect white kids in perfect private schools. Naive white ladies whose husbands are climbing into bed with other women right under their noses.

"No one gets it. I am 'woke.'"

"Woke" is when you are first made aware of a particular form of injustice in society. I was "woke" to sexism, classism, and racism. "Woke" is most often used in reference to awareness of racism.

But then someone pointed out I was, in fact, *not* "woke."

I was just pissed off because I had lost privilege and was throwing a tantrum about it. This led me to my next level of engagement on my own privilege.

Yes, I was in pain and afraid. I was in a new social group with a new, lower status, and I was uncomfortable. But I was still relatively safe and secure financially. Healthy and employed.

My tantrum was not about other white women at all.

My tantrum was me being pissed off at someone else because I had lost privilege, and losing privilege sucks. It's frightening. It's painful. It's embarrassing. People simply do not want to lose any of the privileges we have. Who would? No one. Privilege is so great, that's why it's called "privilege"! Of course we're scared of losing it.

Anyone who has experienced poverty, sexual violence, a physical disability or injury, or are of a different sexual orientation or identity knows what it's like to lose and gain privilege. We want to *gain, gain, gain* and keep. That's a normal human reaction.

The stress over losing and winning is ingrained in us as a core value from the moment we're born into the patriarchy and branded "Americans." Americans are competitive, capitalist winners who want to *win, win, win* and keep winning.

This book is about how I came to understand the fear of losing privilege, which is—in most cases—manufactured to keep us afraid. Yes, you may lose a patriarchally defined status or privilege, but you're also gaining a new, potentially even more valuable privilege or perspective.

We are brought up in a culture, the patriarchy, that tells us our privilege must be protected and hoarded. We should prioritize those measures of success—winning, houses, cars, money, health, beauty—which grow our privilege so we will be safe and secure.

My story is about how, as I began to lose privilege, I realized my position in the patriarchy, my dependence on it, my idolization of it, my full buy-in, and the contract signed with T's crossed and I's dotted, was the problem.

I started to critically assess my actions, my values, my privilege, and my role in the patriarchy. I wanted to learn how I could hold myself accountable and take more responsible and meaningful steps in my life to bring happiness, joy, and connection instead of houses, pedicures, and six-pack abs.

For my daughter, my friends, my family, and myself, I wanted to stop perpetuating patriarchal myths and values. I wanted to dig deeper into my own version of feminism and Karen-ness. I wanted to press my white progressive friends about their discomfort about even *having conversations about our privilege* with me.

What dawned on me through this exploration is I have a ton of privilege and power, and my individual privilege doesn't diminish my pain and suffering. My privilege and power gave me time to open up and understand my role in the patriarchy so I could ask more questions and speak up.

When I spoke up, some people yelled, "Hell, yeah, Girl!" and others yelled, "Shut up and sit down, white lady!"

When people yelled, "Shut up and sit down," I could have done just that. I had done it before, and I share those times in here, too.

But in 2020, something felt different. I wanted to know who was telling me to shut up, who was telling me to sit down, and *why?*

* * *

The working title of this book was "I Am Racist?" I was exploring my privilege thoroughly for the first time and had a new understanding and definition of racism, which I explore in detail in this novel.

I use the phrases "Black and brown," "Black, indigenous, and people of color," and "BIPOC" interchangeably as I write. I use Queer or Q to talk about the LGBTQIA+ community. I will talk about cis-gendered, meaning your sex at birth aligns with your expression of gender. I will use the word womxn, meaning humans who gender themselves as women, even if their biological sex is not female. You might not understand a term, but Google does. Have it handy. I also had a new understanding of feminism and intersectional feminism.

Intersectionality is how the different elements of our identities expressed in a given society result in different types of treatment. These elements combined with our society shape our opportunities and experiences in individual settings.

For example, imagine how it would be if you joined the military as a man. Then what about if you were a gay man. Then what if you were a gay Black man? How might each of these three men experience their military career differently? Well, that also depends on if he is a college-educated gay Black man, and so on.

Essentially, every individual has somewhat different opportunities, experiences, fears, joys, and levels of violence in their lives based on the intersection of their own personal characteristics and the social settings they live in. Our lives are at the "intersections" of complicated things.

After all of this exploration and study, I had finally felt I was "woke" to intersectionality and wanted to help other white women like me explore our whiteness, the struggles between our various characteristics, and the trappings of living under the patriarchy's Rules.

I thought saying out loud "I am racist" would be bold or something.

I was wrong.

This wasn't the first time I had derailed on my never-ending journey to becoming "woke." Sometime in 2014, I had enrolled my daughter in a predominantly Black elementary school. I was learning about racism in education, and I asked my twenty-four-year-old former babysitter who was in graduate school to help me understand white guilt.

Selena might have stopped by to drop off a birthday gift for my daughter or just come by for dinner. We often talked about very personal things, and I was grappling with gentrification and white privilege in my neighborhood school.

Selena and I met in 2012 when she was looking for summer babysitting work after college, and I was looking for a summer babysitter. It was love at first Skype.

We have stayed in love ever since, and this random afternoon she was recalling a story from her time in college at a swanky liberal arts school, largely bereft of people of color, where she often found herself living in an episode of *Dear White People.*

"Can you help me understand this better?" I asked Selena, who is multiracial. "Like teach me about what I'm missing, and why do I feel all of this white guilt? What do I do about my white lady privilege?"

Selena is whip-smart, sensitive, and soulful. She has wells of empathy and intellect. She feels the world as well as she sees and understands it, and was a young woman emerging and already born of trauma, pain, love, and joy. I loved her instantly and never want her to leave my life. She's a liberal-arts-educated, progressive, lady-powered, *fierce* person by all accounts.

"No," she said. "No, I won't teach you. We can talk about it, but the first thing you need to hear is that it is not the responsibility of people of color to educate white people on this topic."

"Whoa," I said. "That is solid information."

She said this without shaming me. She just said it.

I wondered later how many times she had said that to clueless white people. She's so brave and true to herself. I was so lucky she trusted me enough to interrupt my white lady demands that a person of color to educate me, and I *listened.* She put herself at risk. I could have gotten huffy and triggered. I'm so glad I didn't. I'm so glad I didn't fuck that up because Selena is important to me.

"It shouldn't be on Black people, or any people of color period, to educate white people about what it's like to be a person of color," echoed Laura Wilson Phelan, a white woman whose career is centered on antiracist work in public education through her organization Kindred Communities. I interviewed Phelan for this book, and she echoed Selena's message six long years later. "That is what is challenging about Kindred in some ways because there should be no responsibility of the people of color in any dynamic that is about 'educating' white people."

Kindred is a nonprofit organization in Washington, DC, that supports parents, staff, and school-based and educational system leaders in partnering to codesign equitable, antiracist schools that advance collective well-being.

"[Kindred] is very intentional about building a reality associated with how stories move people and how personal relationships move people. Kindred isn't 'story circle.' We are framing a conversation where groups are working to find equitable solutions to shared problems. That stories result from that conversation is naturally a part of the process," Phelan said.

There are two key lessons here.

One: as white people, we must take this journey without demanding help from people of color who are not *specifically in the field of helping white people.*

Two: we need to listen to the stories of humanity, of many people. We need to be in a community *with people* to help find and connect with our own humanity.

"For example, we're talking about why a person was late to a session, and the person of color who was late just told you the police stopped them on the way in, and why, and how it felt," said Phelan. "You just hear about one another's lives in a safe, productive context and it's very different than watching a documentary about race. It activates a different part of your brain, the unconscious part where emotions are held, and relationships are held. If we want to get to the root cause of bias, that's where we have to go."

I am here to share my story as a white person, making tons of missteps with regard to sexism, shaming other women, blaming women, being racist, being a general person in crisis, and try to help you understand my personal intersectional life experience so you can learn. Then, hopefully, you will understand a little better what to do next.

So, don't go ask your one Asian friend to read your book draft *because you want a person of color's point of view.* Don't ask your babysitter to "teach" you about white guilt and white savior complex. Don't ask your daughter's best friend's Black mom to give you a pat on the back because you're writing a book for white people about something she's sick and tired of having to talk to white people about every fucking day because it's 2020 and *Jesus Christ Black and brown people are still getting killed by the fucking police every day and Black women are dying in childbirth at rates three times higher than white women and coronavirus is killing Black people at higher rates than any other group.*

Instead, we must engage in a community where we are humans helping humans. Reading, showing up, listening, and when we are triggered or confused, go back to a white friend and hash it out before bringing an apology, mea culpa, or fragile, triggered "you know I meant well" statement.

White women are dangerous to BIPOC and Queer people. White women have a patriarchal identity rooted in the ability to call the cops and be believed, tell someone they've been raped and have a man lynched, and claim someone did something and have a person removed from their job.

Of course, white women are diverse and have different levels of privilege than one another. You probably want to believe you are not one of these white women I'm talking about.

But it is time, today, for you to take a look at who you really are, examine the values you've been holding, what you do and have done with your power, and what type of world you want to live in.

It is time for critical assessment, accountability, and hard truths. My story is an example of *how to* undergo that self-assessment

When I finished writing the first draft series of stories, I was in a place of white urgency. My lens of privilege had been shattered, and I wanted to fix racism now, atone for my white woman mistakes, and be a part of the solution.

I thought it would be interesting to see if white women would read a book that is essentially a "Hi My Name Is Racist" name tag. We are all racist and can be antiracist at the same time! It was a revelation to me. I was being clever, intellectual, centering myself, and, ultimately, wrong.

Guess who told me the title of my book was a micro-aggression? Selena.

She writes, "I felt kind of frustrated or shut down by the posts about your book. Probably part of my discomfort or response is just because *I* am simply not the target demo and can't really connect with some of the content, but I think I'm also just confused about your and other white peoples' role in general in this moment. I get it's often more effective for white people to speak to and/or organize other white people, but that still feels shitty because there are so many other Black and brown voices right now I wish were further amplified and accepted as worth. Also, I think it's just a delicate thing to write this memoir and tell this story of your journey that (by nature of the title) is centered on race in a way which does not center on whiteness/white feelings in its discussion of systemic racism.

"Not sure if I'm explaining that well, and still taking some time to sit with and understand my response and feelings, but also know I can't really do that until I have more emotional capacity."

I cried because I felt ashamed. I hurt her.

She was gracious to reach out and tell me how she is sitting with and understanding her own feelings, and that became the source of my own next action. I moved through shame and did my best to repair and correct.

* * *

Because of her interruption of my racism, the final step in this book was developing an understanding of how my voice fits in so I don't hurt people like Selena or center a conversation about racism and antiracism on my needs.

Selena was right. I do need to shut up and sit down when it comes to the BIPOC experience of racism. I need to shut up and sit down when it comes to that topic and work to amplify voices that have been shouting for centuries.

When I talk here about racism, antiracism, and other forms of discrimination I have not personally experienced, I will cite my expert sources.

But the other people telling me to shut up and sit down? They were mostly white women and white men.

It's funny because I'm going into my life story and talking about the patriarchal values I've embedded in my body and brain. I've talked about how I signed a deal with the patriarchy—in marriage, in business, in values, in hoarding resources, in centering myself—and how I've used the patriarchy when I need it for touch, sex, escape, money, and protection from shame.

A pretty significant number of white women keep asking me why my voice matters. Why aren't we listening to BIPOC people? Why don't I shut up? How am I different than every other white lady memoirist out there whining about privilege? Why am I not letting BIPOC women take the lead here?

Well, read what Selena said. Read what Phelan said. Listen to BIPOC and Queer people: they're tired of teaching us about our white privilege, toxic culture, violence, hypocrisy, and *our own fucking history*. They're tired of talking about antiracism. They're exhausted, depleted, sick, angry, and just want reprieve.

So, this isn't about antiracism or racism, this is about college-educated, progressive, white women and our privilege. It's about the sinister messages we get about our innocent, maternal, innate "good white lady" selves who need self-care and empathy, but somehow, we're surprised when one of our sisters pulls out a cell phone and threatens to call the police on a Black man because he dared ask her to follow the park rules.

Yes, Amy Cooper is our white sister. She is one *us*. We need to know her and understand her to understand ourselves. We don't get to say "us and them" when it comes to white women. We need to say, "our sisters," and work from that frame.

Yes, we do need to read Dr. Ibram X. Kendi, James Baldwin, and Dr. King. We need to read Alice Walker and Audre Lorde. But white women need to learn our own history, too.

We need to do *both*.

I've started with my own history.

I've become an expert in seeing us, the cis-gendered, heterosexual, educated white women. We are mothers, sisters, wives, daughters, divorcees, single women, and single moms. We are often in bed with the patriarchy, literally and figuratively, which results in a ton of intersectional messiness.

We are struggling, often isolated, hardworking, and overwhelmed. I see us reaching for Glennon Doyle and Rachel Hollis. I see us reaching for a massage and a bottle of rosé. I see us being great moms and good friends. I see our fear and have seen us being shamed and hurt. I see my sisters on Facebook, too, doing something heinous.

Then I see us in my neighborhoods, progressive and fierce, yet continuing to avoid hard conversations about our own whiteness, our power, and our privilege, because we're not "that Karen on Facebook." We're somehow an exception to the rule.

No, we're not.

I see you, and I know what it feels like to be a white woman enjoying life in the patriarchy but having mixed feelings, caught between toxic corporate feminism and playing by the Rules of white, middle-class marriage while also facing financial and emotional stress.

We signed a deal somewhere along the way that requires collusion with the patriarchy in exchange for our comfort and safety. When we are forced to come to grips with the reality that people are dying all around us while we remain disproportionately well and privileged, we are often triggered and paralyzed by our shame.

We're experiencing this all during the same time as the era of Donald Trump, climate disasters, and COVID-19.

I'm an expert in my version of white lady anxiety, shame, loneliness, and moving up and down the socioeconomic ladder.

I am an expert in my journey, and I'm dangerously close to putting myself at the center of the conversation about racism if I don't course correct.

Yes, Black and brown voices need to be heard about racism and antiracism. LGBTQIA+ people need to be heard about intersectional gender bias and violence. Indigenous people need to be heard when it comes to the trauma of stolen land and bodies. People who dedicate their time and lives to shouting at this patriarchal wall of power need to be treated with utmost care, paid for their time, given room to heal, given space to feel safe, and be amplified.

Holly Harper needs to speak about her own experience.

Treading lightly, in solemn acknowledgment of my privileged position, I start the process of naming our collusion. I name my violence, my mistakes, my racism, sexism, ableism, and privilege so I can be held accountable to myself and to the people I love.

I must hold I am always at the dawn of "woke." I am always dangerously close to behaving and thinking in racist ways that cause others pain.

I'm trying to burn up the deal I signed with the patriarchy and build a new set of values I can be proud of, and I am trying and failing every day.

This book is about how I crashed through a lived version of Feminism 101, Sexism 101, Capitalism 101, History 101, Psychology 101, and finally had enough life experience credits to dip my toe into the Introduction to Antiracism for White Folks.

My go-to tool for understanding antiracism in practice (i.e., the answer to the question: *what do I do?),* which my friends and critics constantly pepper me with, comes from the teachings of EbonyJanice Moore, an educator and founder of The Free People Project. Moore is a womanist scholar, author, and activist. In her writing, media, and workshop series, Moore reinforces how important it is that—as individuals—we take the time to study our ancestry (i.e., the history of our people and their relationship with power) and our lived experience (i.e., your life story full of traumas, abilities, privileges, social pressures, etc.).

Moore teaches we must:

- Develop our Theory, or evidence of what is true in the world derived from learning, study, and living.
- Embody our Ethic, a belief-faith system grounded in our souls and bodies.

Only then can we be effective in our actions, or what she calls our Praxis, which is the practiceo of action.

Moore's Theory, Ethic, and Praxis is something I will get into more detail about later, but it's important to think about what you believe, why you believe it, how it feels in your soul, and *then* whether the actions you take are grounded and aligned.

The feeling of white guilt is a result of knowing something to be true (accepting a Theory that white privilege is real) and knowing it's wrong (accepting an Ethic that white privilege hurts people of color), and then sitting on your hands when you see the painful results of the system.

Our mass Praxis of inaction, avoidance, and exceptionalism (you know, "except me because I'm different than all the bad white ladies") is just as big of a problem as a group of white people carrying Nazi flags marching through Charlottesville, and we know it in our Ethic and in our hearts.

White silence is violence. But we still get defensive when someone asks us to own our privilege and our violence.

We feel guilt for our inaction and are paralyzed by our guilt. Our Praxis is the practice of doing jack shit and feeling bad about it, fragile about it, or triggered when someone brings it up. We rush back to white comfort where people are "nice" to us and don't go back to repair our harm.

Or, even worse, we want to rush to *do something, join the fight, end racism.* That is what most of my progressive critics have been shouting at me about.

"Shut up and sit down, focus on the *fight*," they say.

Well, if you've logged into any antiracism webinars led by BIPOC women lately, you'll know that is *not* what we should be doing. So maybe *you* need to hush up, sit down, and read this first and then start from a new understanding.

This book is about learning to overcome the guilt, fear, and paralysis and learn to *do something* from a Praxis or practice of joy, love, and confidence. Our Praxis must be centered in the teachings of a human who has less privilege than we do.

As Moore so beautifully said, "When Black trans women are liberated, we will all be liberated. "

We must lean into embodiment and let ourselves feel the trauma before we act on it. White women have so much power in our society that it is very easy for us to commit aggressive and violent acts, sometimes without even realizing what we're doing. We have to learn to just listen, hear what someone is telling us, be vulnerable, and breathe.

Your shame and your mistakes likely aren't going to kill you. Amy Cooper hasn't been murdered by police.

White women need to stop fighting so hard to gain power *inside* of the patriarchy because the patriarchy thrives on the consolidation and co-opting our power. White women need to start fighting to dismantle the patriarchy itself.

We have to learn to build community based on matriarchal values of collaboration, love, patience, empathy, curiosity, and honoring the wisdom of experience. Once in community, we will be given gifts of lessons, opportunities to fail, and pathways to joy. In community, we feel safe and loved. In community, we will feel in our bones, know in our minds, and be able to practice humanism, antiracism, anti-sexism, defying ableism, and dismantling the patriarchy. It blooms inside of us.

I share from the perspective of my deeply personal path, and I am aware as soon as I finish this sentence I will have continued to transform, make mistakes, and learn. But here is how I took those first steps in connecting my beautiful strength to my very real power, so I can live a life truly guided by feminist, humanist, antiracist values—and a huge amount of joy and love to support me.

CHAPTER 1

FUCKING THE PATRIARCHY

———

My neon yellow posterboard sign said, "Well, the patriarchy isn't going to fuck itself."

The electric energy of the Women's March in Washington, DC filled my Capitol Hill neighborhood in January of 2017. Tens of thousands of women streaming through the grand, brick house-lined streets, radiating a type of bittersweet joy.

I moved to DC in 2013, to Capitol Hill to be exact, just steps from the US Capitol itself. I'm in love with DC and the federal government oozing with intellectual and political history, grand marble buildings and historic Victorian mansions, the grit and energy of a city pulsing with love for its resurgence and loathing for its gentrification.

People come to DC from around the country, and around the world, to be at the center of global power. It's a city defined by its monuments and un-city-like short buildings. Everyone is interesting and thoughtful and progressive and empathetic. By everyone, I mean everyone I have collected and placed carefully in my inner circle.

So, of course my friends and I all got together on January 21, 2017, put on our hand-knitted, pink "pussy" hats, and walked down to the March arm-in-arm.

We were a big mish-mashed, intergenerational ladies club. A bra-burning, activist, lawyer mom linked arms with a practical, hardworking, Star-Wars-loving mom who works at NASA. A biracial, "inner-city-school," first-grade teacher in her twenties with no kids linked arms with an Air Force Officer's wife whose spouse voted for McCain in 2016. A single, thirty-something woman with Chinese heritage who took the train in from Manhattan linked arms with the most maternal of moms who was a white, progressive midwife with two biracial sons.

We had our sensible shoes, our snarky signs, and a collective terror about Trumpism, our daughters' future abortions, and why there were military vehicles in our neighborhood park.

The March was beyond describing without sounding trite. As we converged en masse in front of the US Capitol Building, we joined hundreds of thousands of beautiful people squished together so tight it took two hours to walk five hundred yards. The pressure of bodies could feel suffocating if it weren't so patient, safe, and friendly.

As we wedged ourselves into the center of the crowd, we could just barely hear the speakers, so we tried to march. No one could march by this point because we were packed in too tight. We inched our way across the Mall, trying not to lose the fingertips of our protest buddies, connected in front and behind in a human chain threading through a mass of other bodies. It was colorful, emotional, loud, hilarious, and undeniably womxn-powered.

Since that day, I began to see the world bloom in rose gold.

Maybe things have been pink all along, but for the first time in my life, womxn were ascending in a way that felt a lot warmer and more empathetic. We wear "Nasty Woman" t-shirts. We demand "me time." We unapologetically have zero fucks to give. We support one another.

The intense feeling of that collective womxn-identifying power began to fade as time passed, but the rose-gold tint stuck around.

It was in Target on a white coffee cup with a pink rainbow I saw rose gold words in *that* calligraphy, the ubiquitous one we know now as the "inspirational lady quote typeface," which said, "Wake up and be awesome."

It was on a Wayfair pillow demanding someone to, "Bring me coffee and tell me I'm pretty."

It was on Etsy, at the craft market, in the bookstore, and overwhelming my Instagram—rose gold "fempowerment" from every direction: "Be this, do this, believe this, don't give up…"

Then my very good friend gave me a book called *Girl, Wash Your Face.* Like many women before her, Melanie had found the author, Rachel Hollis, through her own supportive friend network. Hollis' message echoes the sentiment of, "Girl, you can do anything! Link arms! Be a queen!"

Like me, Melanie craved to embody that kind of freedom and confidence so she could transform her life into joy. She bought *Girl, Wash Your Face,* and now she was giving it to me.

I soon found out it was the rose-gold Bible.

Since its release in February 2018, *Girl, Wash Your Face* has held a consistent spot in the top twenty-five best-selling books in the country (until 2020 when Hollis' brand took a major hit, but more on that later). It sold more than a million copies and has thousands of five-star reviews on Amazon.

The book is a collection of stories and advice written by Rachel Hollis & Co. whose namesake spokesperson is Hollis herself. She's a perky, blonde California girl with a Horatio Alger-esque story of her own, bootstrapping her way from a heritage of cotton-picking Okies to becoming a Hollywood mama with a brand as a "lifestyle influencer."

Hollis structures her book around "the lies" that held her back from her version of women's empowered enlightenment.

The chapters, "I Am Bad at Sex," "I Should Be Further along by Now," "I'm Not a Good Mom," "I am Defined by My Weight" and so on, are about "recognizing the lies we've come to accept about ourselves," so we can grow into our best versions.[1]

I immediately knew I hated this book before I even read it. I just didn't know why I hated it so much. It was the same gut feeling I had about *Eat, Pray, Love,* which is Elizabeth Gilbert's memoir about taking a year to travel the world, eat pizza in Italy, meditate in India, and bask in the sun in Bali after her divorce.

I didn't know why Melanie liked Hollis's book so much. I love Melanie and her big, progressive heart and her resilience in the face of some really shitty cards she's been dealt. She has a demanding, soul-sucking job, a child born with severe allergies to almost every substance on earth, and severe anxiety.

Hating books like these sparked a spiral of confusion about why in the holy hell were we empathizing with rich white women who are jetting off to Naples to binge-eat their divorce woes away, or why we are still listening to Gwyneth Paltrow give advice about any fucking topic at all.

---

[1]   Rachel Hollis, Girl, Wash Your Face: Stop Believing the Lies About Who You Are So You Can Become Who You Were Meant to Be (Nashville: Nelson Books, 2018), ix-x.

That revulsion, over and over, came from a loose thread of thoughts dancing in my mind: "Yeah, but you're *a rich white lady. Yeah, but you're a dual-income household. Yeah, but you've got a college degree. Yeah, but you don't have any children.*"

But then there is Melanie. She's aware of her privilege, and she's progressive and generous: "*Yeah, but I'm suffering. Yeah, but I am in pain. Yeah, but I need help, and Rachel Hollis helped me.*"

* * *

It all came together late one night watching season two of *Shrill*, a Hulu comedy series. *Shrill* hilariously explores norms around traditional "feminine" empowerment, overcoming body shaming, gender and sexuality, relationships, and creates a platform through the main character Annie, our sincere, flawed heroine.[2]

The episode that tied it all together for me, called "WAHAM" (Women are Having a Moment), is about Annie (Aidy Bryant), a journalist for a fictional independent liberal weekly paper in Portland, Oregon, covering a women's empowerment conference. The conference is led by a white woman, author, and motivational speaker, and modeled after an amalgamation of the hundreds of real-life Rachel Hollises who make money shilling empowerment, self-care, and carpé-ing the diem.

There's a brilliant scene in the "WAHAM" episode where Annie asks this fictional "Rachel Hollis" about WAHAM's

---

2   Shrill, season 2 episode 6, "WAHAM," directed by Natasha Lyonne, written by Sudi Green, aired January 24, 2020, Hulu.

efforts to include marginalized populations—women of color, single women, women with limited means—into its folds of empowerment.

Annie sits across from Fictional Rachel, who is all dazzling white teeth, perfectly coifed blonde curls, and—I shit you not—a rose-pink pantsuit. Fictional Rachel is at first delighted to have the plucky young reporter's attention.

Discussing writing and fashion, Annie uses "that word"— fat—in reference to herself and the challenges she faces trying to find fashionable clothes for fat bodies. Fictional Rachel immediately clams up. The discomfort of bringing up something so clearly off-brand—fat, fatness—is acted out perfectly.

"Wow, I love how you say that word—fat—I-I don't know that I would say *that*," the stick-thin guru says uncomfortably.

Annie senses the change in her subject's demeanor and is simultaneously being hounded by the celebrity's pushy handler to get this interview over and done quickly.

A little less assuredly than before, Annie bravely asks Fictional Rachel her one and only interview question: "So, I was surprised to see tickets to this event *start* at $300, and I know part of WAHAM's mission statement is 'lifting up every woman,' but can you really do that if the price point is so inaccessible?"

"So, I've thought about this quite a bit, and we offer sponsorships for low-income women, so they can attend, free of charge. So, we've kind of already got that all figured out," replies our ladyboss in a clearly condescending tone, delivered as sweet as any a sugarcoated talking point ever has been. Fictional Rachel excuses herself quickly, escaping from Annie and any further uncomfortable topics.

Annie thinks about walking away, too, but presses in, asking Fictional Rachel's handler, "Would there be any way, I don't know, I could possibly meet with one of the low-income women who was sponsored?"

"Ugh. It's such a bummer actually," the snarky handler replies. "She couldn't make it because she couldn't get off work but enjoy the day!"[3]

She couldn't get off work. The comedy in that one statement encapsulates nearly everything I feel about this episode, the Rachel Hollises of the world, and all of toxic corporate feminism. She—the one woman they half-assedly tried to include—couldn't get off work because she doesn't have the privilege to take time for herself.

The *Shrill* episode was written by *Saturday Night Live* writer Sudi Green. Green and Bryant gave an interview with *Vulture* in February 2020 about the episode's "[smart exploration] of the complexities of corporate feminism and what that world has in common with patriarchal society."[4]

"Because so many feminist narratives are widely accepted, the advertising industry has caught on to say, 'Well, we don't want to say we want to make women thinner. We want to make them well and healthy,'" Green said to *Vulture*.[5]

The group of women I fall in, the Xennial gap sitting squarely between the Gen Xers and the millennials born between roughly 1975 and 1985, have been force fed the "you can have it all" message our whole lives.

We can be president. We can be doctors. We are Title IX. We can, and must, have *it all, and on our terms, and in our language.*

---

3   Ibid.

4   Elena Maria Fernandez, "Why Shrill Took Aim at 'Sinister' Empowerment Conferences." Vulture, February 10, 2020.

5   Ibid.

Fat is out. Wellness is in. Weight Watchers is out. WW is in. Retired people are out. AARP is in.

We are well. We love ourselves. We make time. We self-care. We "mom so hard." We slay. Fifty is the new thirty.

There are a ton of books, conferences, blogs, memes, and Instagram accounts to help us get fitted for our sparkling crowns of ladyboss, momboss Queenhood.

"I think for a lot of young women you feel very conflicted about it, and it feels like a very surface-level approach to women's issues," Bryant said to *Vulture*. "*Wear pink! Be loud! Go off, queen!* That's not reality, you know?"[6]

Yes, I'm conflicted, too. On one hand, it feels good to feel good, and be loud, and be supported, and be heard. So, we buy the books, attend the conferences, repost the memes, attend the Women's March, and go get drunk on champagne with our girlfriends where we cry about our mom's cancer, our spouse's depression, or our own unsatisfying careers.

But we also know something is off, too.

"It's harder to dissect. What am I really absorbing and being told? That is what 'WAHAM' is about. We have these big pink letters telling you to go off, but there are layers behind it, and that's even more sinister in a way," Green said.[7]

Green's word resonated with me. It is *sinister*.

In the "WAHAM" episode, one woman stands up and thanks the rose-gold leader for *helping her* traverse through pain to healing. One character is being "helped" by another character who is offering "help" as a way to earn a living, which seems okay on its surface. That's what therapists do, right?

---

6   Ibid.

7   Ibid.

But the sinister questions ignored are: *Is this person's help really the sort of help we need? Where are the voices of the shamed and silent who feel hurt and lost, and then confused because this "cure" isn't working for them? Where are the people who can't afford this stuff? Where are the non-white, non-middle class, or otherwise "non" conforming voices who have different stories of pain and trauma who can bring a dimension to this conversation which is clearly missing?*

The problem is corporations like Hollis & Co. churn out surface-level fixes with a few substantial solutions, making it difficult to figure out what is so sinister about it all while making a killing off of mostly white, middle-class women's suffering.

There has been a surge in the self-care, wellness, and "life coaching" industries. These industries sell products centered on the values that individual empowerment and wellness are paths to happiness as women seek ways to self-actualize and achieve happiness in our "have it all" culture.

Although personal empowerment and wellness are essential, no one is stepping up to say, "Wait, is this superficial or a quick fix? Am I better or just temporarily indulged?"

Even fewer self-care, wellness, and empowerment brands are sending out the message that once we *are* feeling better, we should take a breath, turn around, hug our sisters, and hold out our hands to help the next woman get *here.*

Instead, a group of brands with mostly white, mostly middle-class women as their namesakes or founders are monetizing feminism, creating a sparkly, rose-gold glass ceiling, which is just a new, pinker version of the patriarchy.

"Now I feel *great,* don't you?"

* * *

Looking back at my joyous memories of the Women's March on the National Mall with hundreds of thousands of womxn and allies in 2017, I saw the dark cloud hanging over us. It was an aching sadness we had to be there at all.

We knew we were lost. We had just lost our country to Donald Trump's misogyny and racism, a cruel personification of capitalism, and we were together in a mass of people dying to be found. We physically were in community together, but we had no clear path to merge into one powerful coalition.

The Women's March sparked a protest, but it didn't transform into the next wave of female activism.

Leaders of the March faced intense criticism for taking up issues primarily important to white, cisgender women while ignoring intersectional issues of BIPOC and LBGTQIA+ women.

In 2018, three founding members of the Women's March stepped down following allegations of antisemitism. The organization's engagement declined from hundreds of thousands of marchers around the world in 2017 to tens of thousands of active participants in early 2020.[8,9]

The Women's March ended up being a symbol of how white women tend to dominate the conversation about women's equality, and how intersectional issues can implode attempts at creating a big-tent movement.

When white women do show up, like they did to organize the first Women's March, we are often harshly (and rightly)

[8]   Mabinty Quarshie, "Is the Women's March More Inclusive This Year?" USA Today, January 20, 2018.

[9]   Isabella Gomez Sarmiento, "After Controversial Leaders Step Down, The Women's March Tries Again in 2020," NPR, January 17, 2020.

criticized for bulldozing over others with our power and privilege.

Often, we don't even know we are causing harm because we're just so used to being seen as "well-intended." So, when we are called out, it can be horrifying and shame-inducing.

What I do know is I loved that moment in time. It was soul food getting to join a broad female, female-identifying, womxn, Queer, and allies' coalition. We had hope, and that felt amazing.

But ultimately, the March as an organization lost its sparkle because of how white women engaged in intersectional spaces.

The hard lesson many white women got was to sit down, shut up, or you're going to step in some shit.

So many of us sat down and zipped our traps. We didn't know how to *not* center ourselves, so we became afraid to move.

If the leaders of the biggest, most amazing, safest and cleanest protest in our nation's history are called out for racism and antisemitism, then how can the everyday white, middle-class, well-meaning, college-educated, working mom dare to make a move?

When we are triggered, we try to protest we didn't *mean* to be racist. Our hearts are in the right place. We didn't know. We have *feelings*. We then just shut up, trying not to make a bad situation even worse.

White women are scared of the same things everyone is scared of: being poor, alone, and unloved, being seen as a failure, being thought of as person who hurts others, being minimized, being in pain, and being unseen.

Most of the time, in that fear, we are consciously or unconsciously holding tight to our privilege. We sit down and shut up because it's frightening, and we don't want to make a mistake and be publicly shamed when we actually do mean well. We also feel paralyzed and trapped.

But sitting down and shutting up or using "overwhelmed" as an excuse to do nothing *is a privilege in and of itself.*

We are told by the patriarchy we "have it all" now, so we have no right to complain. We have internalized that because we mean well, we deserve the benefit of the doubt.

We tell ourselves too many people are depending on us to work hard and not rock the boat because, as individuals, it will make little difference anyway, so we don't take real risks.

We believe any wrong move will result in our being labeled a Karen, our lives and reputations ruined, so we don't move.

As white women, our privilege is when we are afraid or ashamed, we can simply stop putting ourselves in the cross-hairs of any important fights for justice and equality, go back to our safe rose-gold existence, and feel no negative conse-quences in our daily lives.

Trapped by our privilege, isolated in fear, and encouraged by larger American cultural forces derived from the patriar-chy, we end up passively contributing to the very inequalities we so loudly marched to end.

American culture claiming "womxn today can and do have it all and shouldn't complain" is a bad bill of goods. It's snake oil. It's an illusion.

You know how I know? I lived the perfect, picket-fence life. I came from blue-collar, "white trash" America, clawing to become the first of my cousins, parents, and grandparents to get a bachelor's degree. I wanted to be the first to have the flowing, beaded, white wedding gown, to marry before babies, to own a home, and begin building wealth. I wanted to be the first to "make it" as the embodiment of an American dream.

I ended up sick, a failure, unloved, in pain, unseen, and completely fucking scared and alone.

I was told, verbatim, I should feel grateful because other people had it worse than I did.

But the more sinister message I was given from my white progressive, supportive community was "I'd been through a lot" so I deserved to "relax, self-care, and heal."

Sit down and shut up or go get a pedicure. No one told me to stand up, speak up, find a new way, you can do this…. and then go get a pedicure.

Over time, I came to realize the function of white female privilege was to distract me into self-help or self-indulgence cycles that enriches companies, not lives. These books and conferences and pillows and sitcom narratives about self-care and tropical island escapes and dopey, lovable husbands are pushing us into a circular pathway where we superficially feel good.

I did "have it all." I had the cool job and the big backyard, the newest iPhone and a mom's weekend in Austin. I have an adorable, well-attached daughter who saw me sacrificing everything for her protection and happiness, all while gently ignoring the deep suffering inside of me and in those around me.

The whitewashed woman's middle-class self-care, personal empowerment, feel-good industry is sinister and superficial, and simultaneously helpful and transformative, which makes it difficult to critique.

At the March, I was inspired but not transformed. Reading *Girl, Wash Your Face,* I was entertained, not empowered. Going to Austin for a girl's weekend, I was relaxed, but not connected in community.

I still voted blue and put my daughter in a "good school" and continued on in my life, largely unchanged. The only difference was I could give myself a pat on the back for my progressive activism as I wore my "Pussy" hat to school drop off.

It boils down to this: a coalition pushing back on toxic American cultural values is being actively fractured by white women who embrace the frills of the patriarchy when it serves us. We can always dip into the candy jar of the patriarchy's privilege to ignore social injustice. We have permission to stay stuck, busy, overwhelmed, and/or too fragile to help anyone else when we are in such pain ourselves.

White women who are legitimately in pain and struggling with the fear of survival continue to buy into the patriarchy's "have it all" machine. We are trained to turn to a tokenized empowerment self-help cycle when we realize we actually don't have much of anything feeding our souls.

The patriarchy, which is imbedded within our socialization, history, and cultural norms continues to use implicit and explicit messages to push us into this mindset that we are invincible queens and also fragile princesses.

This cycle can be summed up by the mantra of "put your own mask on first (and then pop on your AirPods and listen to my podcast, Girl!)."

We remain uncomfortably aware of, but only casually uninvested in, our seatmates, who literally still can't breathe.

CHAPTER 2

PLEASE DON'T TAKE MY PRIVILEGE

———

I read Claire Dederer's coming-of-age memoir *Love and Trouble: A Midlife Reckoning* right when it came out in 2017. I don't even know how I knew I needed this book, but I knew instinctually, like how a monarch knows to fly south.

I read a review in *The Atlantic* or *The Washington Post* and preordered the hardcover. It came in a perfect-fit cardboard sleeve, which protected my pristine first edition. It arrived months before my husband found out about my affair, but also months *after* I'd found out about his.

In 2017, I was deep in crisis. The epitome of isolated, struggling with my shame, feeling like no one would understand or forgive me if I were to cry about my unhappiness, bemoan my sweet (now-faithful) spouse's depression, or confess my affair. I had pinned myself into a corner through bad decisions, and yet I understood I had a seemingly perfect life to everyone else.

"What an idiot I was for cheating," I thought they would say.

"What a selfish thing, to throw away your perfectly good life like that for *sex*," I thought they would say.

"She's a huge, lying, cheating whore," I thought they would say.

In 2017, I knew I was failing so hard at marriage. I also thought if I could get my spouse to see things differently, maybe we could get through this rough patch. Maybe if he saw I was scared and alone, if he recognized he was depressed and passive aggressive, we could communicate our truths and reconnect.

I thought I could wait him out, see if either one of us would hit rock bottom, and then maybe become the phoenix-from-the-ashes of marriage stories.

I needed help figuring out what to do next, and since I had few people to talk to, I turned to books.

I read infrequently in the early years of parenting and would write even less frequently. I was too busy balancing my daughter's preschool calendar, the playdates and dinner parties, the holiday travel, our on-the-calendar marital sex, my freelance ambitions, and my illicit relationship with Craigslist personals and the fascinating cornucopia of men the internet was delivering to me.

Dating while parenting, working, and being married makes for quite a Google calendar.

But as my isolation grew more intense, I turned to memoir to help me understand my own path.

When I added *Love and Trouble* to my cart in 2017, I had no idea what to expect, but I could sense this book was going to be something revelatory.

I wanted Dederer to answer the hidden questions I had about myself: who is this carnal, porn-loving, flirtastic, woman who wants to fuck trapped inside of me? Is it strange

I crave love and intimacy, but can't figure out how to get that from my spouse? Is it bad the object of my desire is not my spouse, but I wish it were? Is my experience and craving of physical pleasure outside of marriage wrong? Am I irredeemable?

I *needed* Dederer to answer these questions. I was lost.

From the first sentence of *Love and Trouble*, Dederer was ripping into my brains and writing things down I knew were inside of me, too.

The opening chapter is a biting, congratulatory note to her present self for all of her domestic and professional accomplishments, "You did everything right," she writes to herself. The first book, the husband, house, the two lovely children, the romantically overgrown garden, the hard work, and so on.[10]

The book is an incredible feat of style and storytelling, hopping around like a guidebook to Dederer's life. In her work, she reveals to me exactly what I came looking for: I am not broken. I am not irredeemable. I am a passionate, carnal human who is complex and quite simple at the same time. I'm stuck in a narrative created by a toxic, patriarchal culture. The only way out is to turn inward, invest in understanding myself, and be brave enough to step forward into my imperfection and say, "this is me."

I came to Dederer for help understanding what was inside of me, and her memoir delivered.

As she questions her own place in society as a Gen Xer, she critiques how women are raised to view ourselves and our sexuality, how we struggle to reckon with our souls and

---

[10] Claire Dederer, Love and Trouble: A Midlife Reckoning (New York: Alfred A. Knopf, 2017).

our next steps at midlife and ends by offering an expanded horizon of what's possible. But we have to be brave enough to be as radically transparent and introspective in our personal lives as Dederer was in this book.

As I was researching Dederer, I came across a 2017 recording of a book reading she participated in at The Strand in New York. Sitting alongside Ada Calhoun, another author whose work explores the middle-class, female midlife crisis in America, Dederer and Calhoun appear confident in their expertise around middle-class, middle-aged women.[11]

Calhoun has done loads of statistical and anecdotal research on middle-class, middle-age women, while Dederer approaches the topic via memoir and discusses how she personally "made it through" her midlife crisis.

Dederer did what I am trying to do, which felt validating to hear. I process my experiences and feelings through reading and writing, so I know, above all, writing my story will be powerful *for me.*

But there was still something triggering about what Dederer and Calhoun were saying—or not saying, actually.

Both of these women had come to The Strand to validate millions of other women, like me, who were mired in midlife shame and isolation. But there was an elephant in the room, too.

Dederer's midlife crisis ended in a beautiful collection of wrenching stories bound together in a mint-green hardback book that rocked my soul, and led to her being asked to sit on a panel in a world-famous bookstore talking about hating my future coming-of-age memoir, and then getting

---

[11]   Strand Book Store, "Claire Dederer + Ada Calhoun | Love and Trouble," May 19, 2017, video, 46:30.

to authoritatively speak about marriage and the women's midlife crisis.[12]

She is redeemed, healed, transformed, and remains happily married.

It's like she got to expose all of her unapologetic, complicated humanity proudly, while all-the-while knowing she kind of still has "done everything right."

I wondered, "Is she at The Strand in part because she's found her way back to a non-threatening, patriarchy-accepted version of midlife womanhood, where tomorrow she will hop on a plane with a perfectly imperfect husband to go home to?"[13]

In 2017, Claire Dederer exposed me to a new way of thinking about myself trapped in a marriage, which was transformative to me at the time. She provided a narrative that was

---

[12] Author's note: During the interview, Dederer said these words and my heart stopped: "I hate, I just hate coming of age memoirs. I mean there's maybe three that I've read that are good, into [sic] my mind. I'm just not a fan of the genre because I feel like it's really, it's very rare that the writer is able to situate herself in dynamic to that younger self and find a voice that is functional, you know, and yet authentic. It just doesn't work." I was mortified. How could she know my memoir will suck? How come she's discouraging me, writing a review before she even sees the draft?

[13] Author's note: Suddenly, I feel small and pathetic. Dederer sees right through anything I'm ever about to even think about writing. I hate Claire Dederer for being on the side of my imposter syndrome, and I hate writing. But this isn't hate, this is shame. This is fear. I'm projecting onto Dederer what I most fear about myself: that I can never become a real writer, so I should give up trying. I realized quickly that my "how could she" exasperation and defensiveness was insecurity. I envy Dederer's talent and success. She brought out from the darkness my own insecurity around whether I should even call myself "a writer." Luckily, I was listening to this book reading in 2020 and not 2017. By 2020, I had been through too much for anyone, even one of my literary heroines, to tell me I couldn't write a coming-of-age memoir. Dederer could hate it, but my writing is about me and for me, and that makes it valuable.

affirming and gave me hope I, too, could come around and save my own partnership:

But in 2020, with the ashes of my relationship now cooled, not even smoldering anymore, her memoir looked a bit more like *Eat, Pray, Love* with the happy ending and Prince Charming.

Dederer has joined Glennon Doyle, Jen Hatmaker, Brené Brown, and truckloads of other coming-of-age, white, female memoirists in zeroing in on something important: midlife crises are definitely not unique to men. Women experience our own version of midlife crisis.

Today at midlife, Gen X (and Xennial) women still carry most of the domestic burden, are working more hours than ever, have loads of pressure, expectations, debt, and overwhelm haunting us (not to mention our angst over politics and climate change and racial justice). We are married to men who rely on us to care for them as they attempt to "grow out of" their own histories of toxic masculinity and attachment issues.

But come to find out as I dug a little deeper, Brené Brown, Glennon Doyle (post-divorce, remarried), Jen Hatmaker, and Elizabeth Gilbert and Claire Dederer are all married women.

Good for them, I guess. They are making it work, and I will not hold that against them. I must own my envy and dig deeper into understanding *why* their marital status was so triggering.

Then it was revealed.

I no longer identified with these women, so my loss of status being unmarried made me feel shame and loneliness all over again.

I was dying to find validation somewhere. I wanted an authority on midlife crises for women who fucked it all up, don't know what to do next, but are still brave and worthy of having her story heard.

Where is Elizabeth Gilbert *without* the zillion-dollar book deal and Prince Charming at the end? Where's the single mom version of barely making it paycheck-to-paycheck because the deadbeat dad is, well, a deadbeat?

Yes, there is a midlife crisis for women. Yes, mental illness is real and cannot be downplayed. Yes, we are financially, emotionally, ecologically, and socioeconomically in a vise grip of panic and stress.

But with middle-class, married women as the voice of the midlife crisis, the recipe for a cure seems to be to deliver a tell-all, give yourself carte blanche grace through self-care and a glass of chardonnay in the bathtub after a long day, and then kiss your sweet, evolved spouse goodnight.

Looking through my bookshelf, my eyes were open now to my *former* level of privilege. I used to be a woman seen. I was a woman in a heterosexual, dual-income, married household going through a midlife crisis. There are so many books for that.

But then I became a divorcing, adulterer, single-mom, financially unstable, who has no clue what comes next. I was no longer reflected in the happy endings of the stories lining my bookshelves (with the notable exception of Anne Lamott, whose book *Operating Instructions: A Memoir of My Child's First Year* was my only guidepost for the possibility of broadening the conversation).

Through my loss of privilege, now acutely aware women talk about their lives without acknowledging their own privileged positions as the "societally accepted" narrative of women who are redeemed because they settled back down in marriage, I began to understand what privilege—and losing it—feels like.

Not being privileged looks like being left out, with no voice to represent you, validate you, or hold you close and tell you you're brave and worthy of love and belonging.

Losing privilege is the experience of becoming invisible and no longer valuable.

Losing privilege is traumatic, and it makes sense now why we try so hard to hold onto it.

CHAPTER 3

EVERYONE IN THE ROOM, PLEASE BE UNCOMFORTABLE NOW

———

"I am not a feminist," said Andrea decidedly.

I'm not sure how feminism came up during a night out with a large group of my husband's coworkers and their spouses, especially considering the crowd.

A group of a few dozen couples and some of the "single dudes" were all at the pub, enjoying cask ale and camaraderie on a cold, rainy British Saturday night sometime in 2009. I remember the twinkly warm lighting of the streetlamps, pleasantly blurred through the windows by the falling rain, the buzz of conversation, and the comfortable feeling of knowing everyone there.

Andrea, like me at the time, was an expat Air Force Officer's Wife. We were all in our late twenties, stationed in the bucolic Suffolk countryside, living in cramped row houses or thatched-roof cottages, and taking the Chunnel to Brugges on weekends.

I write "Air Force Officer's Wife" in title case because it sort of felt like an actual job title, or how marrying into the royal family might feel. You have no choice in holding the title once you tie the knot. You have some odd, strange powers, like having people call you ma'am all the time. You are saddled with a load of unspoken obligations, like attending awkward "Spouse Coffees" and "Spouse Getaway Weekend" events that resemble sorority life.

It is a very insular social circle, especially when you're stuck overseas together.

I almost always enjoyed my time with my husband's coworkers. I loved their cleverness and the bar banter. I admired their sweet, grown-up-frat-bro affinity. They, as a whole, always were welcoming and smart, irreverent and good partners, hardworking and faithful men and women who married people with shared values.

The men were like most of the men I had grown up with in my rural mountain town in Oregon. They were my dad. They were my friend's dads. They were my brother. They were my childhood friends from the 4-H club, the track team, and the student council.

In fact, my husband and I were high school sweethearts for all intents and purposes, so I understood and felt comfortable with these men.

They are very white, very earnest, very hardworking, and very self-assured the world will reward them for those afore-mentioned qualities, even when they occasionally call one another pussies or they complain about reverse sexism and how badly Brett Kavanaugh was treated by the libs.

I mean, they're not *wrong*. They're just "boys being boys" in a culture that rewards their behavior and, I mean this in all seriousness, the men I know often don't see their own privilege.

They, too, are being pushed toward ignoring uncomfortable realities in their own, very human, struggles to survive.

The town I grew up in is isolated, incredibly white, and one of the ten poorest counties in Oregon.

A farming, logging, laboring community, Klamath Falls, Oregon, is a hardworking, God-fearing sort of place. After World War II, the US Marine Corps landed a hospital there, drawing in wounded veterans from across the continent. That's how my grandparents ended up there.

Today there is no VA hospital, but there is an Oregon National Guard base, a strong sense of patriotism, and that salt-of-the-earth Western cowboy vibe the men wear like a uniform. These men chew tobacco, drive pickup trucks, wear plaid shirts, and tend to go to church on Sundays. They love sports, fishing, hunting, their children, the great outdoors, and family barbecues.

None of my childhood friends were wealthy. There were teachers' and welders' kids. My own family and all my cousins were the children of railroaders. Some dads worked at the lumber mill and a lot of moms worked in administrative positions or for the school district. My best girlfriends in elementary school were all in line to be the third or fourth generations to farm on long-held family land.

In our community, when you work hard, till the land, come from "nothing" up through the ranks of the military, and your grandparents fought for this country, you have a lot to feel proud of.

As you follow in those well-worn footsteps, you find yourself at midlife putting in long hours to hold onto your own slice of middle-class existence. It's not so bad being solidly anchored in the same (or similar) sleepy little town, plugging away at your American Dream.

For many, the small, mostly white, middle-class suburban, exurban, rural hometown vibe offers many people a pathway to a safe and comfortable life. For others, these places represent the face of rural, white poverty.

For me the sprawling ranch houses, neatly arranged cul-de-sacs, and charming mini farms of the towns I've lived in—Klamath Falls, Oregon, Boise, Idaho, and Goldsboro, North Carolina—all felt eerie.

All of the people looked just like me, and I could visibly see them living and perpetuating a safe kind of dull circle of life, without ever leaving the comforts of their zip codes.

Regardless of how each of us saw Klamath Falls, everyone I knew was focused on getting by and moving up the socio-economic ladder. We saw the face of poverty in the mirror and in the trailer park where our best friend lived. We were urgent in our desire to work so hard we would be forever safe from the poor house.

My urgency was doubled as my eighteen-year-old cousin got pregnant by, and then married, a man who abused her. My urgency was tripled when my fifteen-year-old cousin got pregnant and turned to alcohol and crystal meth.

I had to move up, but I had to be safe, too. I was scared to death.

When I was growing up and choosing a partner, finding one of these small-town, solid values types of men to partner with was my ideal. It was what every generation of women who came before me had done, and we hadn't fallen backward on that ladder yet.

I was seeking someone who would work as hard as I would to *move up*. He would toil alongside me to build financial security so we could enjoy life. He would be steady and faithful. He would be just like my own dad, and I would be just like my own mom.

At the same time, because I was young and scared of falling *down* the ladder, I had no idea there were many versions of "having it all" out there. I only knew of one: get married, own a house, have a kid or two, be grateful.

Many of us also wanted to escape Klamath Falls physically. We knew upper-middle class, our holy grail destination, likely wasn't going to be found in town unless we were doctors or something. So, like many of my friends, we made plans to escape.

This created a conundrum.

I wanted to see and live in the big, bad world, but I didn't want to leave the safety and comfort of my childhood to do it. I didn't want to go out there and fail and be *poor*.

I found a balance in that tug of war between financial security and adventure through my husband. My ideal man had a future in the US Air Force, roots in our hometown work ethic, was a great person, and shared my values of safe, fun living. This partnership offered me a path to "having it all."

So, I signed the deal to get the picket-fence, dollhouse version of middle-class life *plus* a chance to get out and see the world.

It seemed perfect. I had gained *so much* privilege at this time. I had the bachelor's degree, the diamond engagement ring, and a passport!

As newlyweds in 2004, we bought the charming three-bed, two-bath ranch in Boise and then packed our bags a few years later to live in the UK.

But at twenty-four years old, there was no way I could see the trappings that came with this new deal might be just as toxic as sticking around in Klamath.

Turns out, when you make a deal with the patriarchy to start banking your privileges, you're just exchanging one set of problems for another.

* * *

In 2009, in that British pub when Andrea looked me dead in the eyes and said, "I am not a feminist," the growing incompatibility between my childhood worldview of "having it all" where I would just get married and be safe, and my future definition of "having it all," full of self-actualization and happiness, was in its infancy.

In 2009, I was still ten years from being able to even confidently call myself a progressive, much less articulate my beliefs and perspectives like I can today. Back then, I tried to follow the Rules so I wouldn't get kicked out of my new middle-class, married-lady life.

There are a lot of Rules about how to be a good wife as a part of the patriarchy.

The first time I was confronted with a situation where everyone seemed to be following all of *the same set of Rules* was during the extreme adventure that began in 2007 when we moved to England and I became a dependent, expat, Air Force Officer's Wife.

Imagine waking up your first week of college in a sorority house, not a dorm room. You are wearing a pink sweatshirt with three Greek letters stitched on the front. Imagine joining the waterfall of blonde and darker blond heads, all wearing the same matching sweatshirt, as you flow down the stairs to have breakfast together. You don't see anyone you know. You start to panic and whisper to the brunette sitting to your left, "Did you sign up for this?"

She gives you a blank look.

This must be a dream because *you, Holly Harper, tomboy, one of the guys for as long as you can remember, essential wingman helping single friends get laid since 1998, taker of shots, driver of pickup trucks, do-er of hard work and opposite of girly definitely would not have chosen to join a sorority.*

But I couldn't wake up.

Landing in England that dreary, rainy May of 2007 was exhilarating. I had woefully underprepared for the chilly temperatures but was instantly in love with the storybook Suffolk landscape. After we'd gone through the whirlwind weeks of moving into a tiny row house in the untouristed, historic market town of Bury St. Edmunds, I took stock of what might come next.

I planned out some trips, got a job as a substitute high school teacher at the American high school on the air force base, researched and bought my dream car (a hunter-green, vintage 1996 Rover Mini with too many quirks to count), and fell into charmed isolation.

I had no friends.

It took me a few weeks to find a woman who saw the panic in my eyes as I dared to venture to a "Spouse Welcome Event"—or maybe it was a "Squadron First Friday Potluck." I dreaded these parties, and Rebecca, my fast friend, rescued me.

Rebecca came from a military family and knew the Rules. She had a unique ability to navigate this universe, while also straining against the Rules, too, as a young professional who resented suddenly being stuck at home instead of launching her own career in medicine.

Rebecca found me, befriended me, and helped me navigate. I am forever grateful for her wicked sense of humor and grace as I bumbled through breaking the Rules.

I was so torn between wanting to follow them and "have it all," and simultaneously feeling like I was on an inauthentic, soulless path taking me away from the passion and fire I felt growing somewhere inside me. So, I tried to do a bit of both.

Coming from my dusty, rural Oregon town, being tough was drilled into me, not being "ladylike." Blue-collar, rural white female patriarchal Rules look different than white collar, college-educated lady Rules. In my world, "Stepford Wives" are useless because they couldn't drive stick and didn't own muck boots.

We bucked hay, hauled wood, camped out, rode horses, and told our peers to "fuck off" a lot. The ultimate height of popularity was the three-sport varsity athlete in the Honor Society, who also had a boyfriend on the baseball team willing to drive us around in his pickup truck while we drank cheap beer.

We weren't raised as girly girls, so most of my friends and I grew up thinking "having it all" meant fitting in with the guys.

My first few experiences out of high school, I kind of went my own way. I shunned sorority life in college and I had a hard time finding a boyfriend or fitting in anywhere. I was afraid to ask for help, so I just kind of watched how other girls were balancing life, finding success, and remaining authentic without the cringeworthy sorority vibe.

I settled into dating my high-school sweetheart as our college years wound down, mostly because our shared history and values born from an upbringing in the same physical place made me feel understood, safe, and loved.

Being married to him gave me a sense of security to start trying new things, and he was supportive of my curiosity.

By God, I thought, I was going to make it to some version of the "having it all" victory stand eventually.

But plopping a me into the Officer's Wives Club in 2007 in England was a shock I wasn't prepared for. I realized quickly I didn't want this version.

The patriarchy had gone too far.

There's a Rule about when you can call a man a douchebag, and that rule is "only when his wife is secure enough in her own belief her husband is *not,* in fact, a douchebag, to allow the faux insult to land on the comedy side of the fence."

There was a dude in the squadron my spouse and his buddies thought was a little uptight, so they teased him a bit. There was an event and this dude and I were joking around. Later I called him a douchebag in an email exchange. He laughed. He put my email up in the men's room because it was, frankly, hilarious.

His wife, however, must have not been entirely cool with (a) her spouse's reputation, or (b) a *wife* dare join in the man-banter. She replied-all, cc'ing the base commander's wife—the High Priestess and Czarina of the Officer's Wife Empire—and I learned I could be sent to the principal's office!

Well, shit!

Rule: Protect the ego of the partnership because cracks in the veneer of perfection are not allowed.

Doesn't this remind you of the stereotypical country club set where the men golf and "be boys" and the women play tennis and "be girls?"

Another time, a small group of us were invited over to play board games at someone's house I didn't know well. My spouse, myself, another couple, and three of the single guys we palled around with rolled into a dull game of Apples to Apples.

I was immediately bored, trying in vain to turn it into a primitive Cards Against Humanity.

Nobody liked my choice of "Berlin—1945" for the adjective "hot." Nobody liked my choice of "zucchini" for "sexy." Nobody appreciated my submission of "girl scouts" for "delicious." Nobody except my two guy friends, Mark and Shane.

We were giggling in the corner like twelve-year-old boys, and Mark said something silly. I punched him in the arm, and he proceeded to try and sit on me. We were like family.

The host of this party, a young lieutenant's wife, later told another wife, who told another wife, who told me she was, "shocked at my behavior with Mark." He was the *second in command* of the squadron.

Wasn't I being inappropriate and forward to be so casual? What would my husband think? I shouldn't have called Mark a dick, right? How would that affect my husband's position in the chain of command? *Holly Harper is so out of line.*

What? I was incredulous.

Rule: Officer's Wives are expected to be deeply connected to the politics of their husband's workplace and act accordingly to help advance and protect the husband's reputation and career progression.

I didn't know shit about my husband's career progression when I moved to England. In hindsight, maybe I should have paid closer attention, but he was in the United States Air Force, not me.

Doesn't this remind you of the "inviting the boss over for dinner" cliche where the wife and perfect children host the boss and *his* wife and everything *must* go as planned?

Another time, a woman told me in a crowded restaurant with a dozen other women at the table: "I pray for you." I replied something along the lines of, "What? Why? Is it because you're worried for my immortal soul due to my life of sin, or because you're assuming I'm in some miserable crisis and Jesus needs to rescue me?"

There were whispers and silence. Apparently no one had been told unsolicited prayer circles weren't universally welcome.

Rule: Do not talk about religion unless you are a good Christian.

Doesn't this remind you of how your child's school observes Christmas, but schedules mandatory testing on Yom Kippur?

When I made a casual joke about lingerie over tea with a small group of married women, in some way alluding to oral sex, I was met with Kara's wide brown eyes and her exclaims of, "Oh! I would *never* do that. That's just so gross to me." My jaw dropped to the floor, and before I could say, "What the fuck?" aloud, Rebecca shot daggers at me through her eyeballs.

"Stop!" said Rebecca's pleading stare. "You're about to crush Kara and break a Rule."

Rule: Discussion of sex is limited to the context of sex being necessary for men, and required for baby making, but otherwise a burden, chore, or source of shame and discomfort. It's sometimes titillating, but don't go overboard.

Doesn't this remind you of high school dress code and slut shaming (or pleasure shaming)?

I learned time and time again Rule Number One is "don't rock the boat."

These Rules are a legacy of the past where the patriarchy kept women at home, in line, producing babies, and cleaning laundry, while our spouses go "toil at War."

Doesn't this just remind you of *Leave it to Beaver*?

As I revisited this time in my life through writing about it, I reconnected with a number of women who were with me in England.

It's so strange because we were all part of this dynamic, perpetuating it in a way, but every woman who reached out to talk about it also felt the same way about the Rules as I did.

We all hated them, we felt left out, we felt like *we* didn't fit, and we were lonely even though we were there together.

Doesn't it sound like high school and *Mean Girls*? Or a 1990s sorority movie? Or your catty coworker drama?

What I know now that I didn't know then is there are a number of different versions of the Rules about being a white woman who is married to a white man.

The Rules change with the community you're in—progressive or conservative, evangelical or secular, rich or poor, military or civilian.

But they offer us the same deal: white women get safety, security, and access to the patriarchy's benefits in exchange for following the Rules.

These Rules just happen to simultaneously isolate us from one another and are considered unpatriotic to critique.

We've signed a contract where we get to reap the benefits of the patriarchy's security, wealth, and power, but when those benefits start to feel like *privilege,* we are ashamed of ourselves. We question our upbringing and the parents who worked so hard to provide for us, and that feels bad, too. We experience shame in our bodies first, and then our shame silences us. In our isolation, we are divided.

It's a system that perpetuates itself for its own benefit. But it actually hurts the very people it's supposed to protect.

In the case of my Officer's Wives experience, the system manifested the Rules in acute and obvious ways. The Air Force Officer Corps is extremely white, and in 2010 it was 100 percent cis and heterosexual presenting because federal law demanded it be (it wasn't until September 2011 that "Don't Ask, Don't Tell" allowed LBGTQ people to serve openly in the US Military).

The group of women and men I was stationed with were nearly all in their twenties, young and unsure about our places in the world, and now forced in community together. We hadn't done self-analysis. We hadn't been asked to take "cultural sensitivity" training or formal "Air Force wife leadership" training.

That's not the fault of the women or their spouses, it's the fault of an aging and broken system.

I remember when my spouse was appointed to a management position in the squadron where he was in charge of the HR logistics of twenty or so colleagues. When the squadron was preparing to deploy to Afghanistan for five months in 2009, I got an email from the Squadron Commander's Spouse informing me of *my new role* as a "Key Spouse" because my *husband* was in a management role at work.

"Key Spouses are commander-appointed and serve as a vital resource to command teams in an effort to support Air Force families. The strategic vision is to increase resiliency and unit cohesion amongst military members and their families throughout the military life cycle."[14]

Essentially, I was voluntold I was going to be "a vital resource" for twenty or so spouses during the deployment. I would be responsible for checking in on them, offering to

---

14   "Key Spouse Program," Air Force Personnel Center, accessed October 2, 2020.

help arrange social time, connecting them with the commander if needed, and making sure they weren't feeling isolated or having mental health issues during the deployment.

The problem isn't the existence of the Key Spouse program. The problem was I did not sign up for it, and yet I was being appointed by the commander to do it because that's how the system worked.

I wrote back to the Commander's Spouse and told her I was in no way qualified or interested in this volunteer role. I did not want to be responsible for someone in crisis. I was not trained and didn't want that responsibility. I wrote and said if she and her husband needed the Key Spouse volunteer position filled, they should probably put out a *call for volunteers*.

They did, and it worked for both the volunteer and the other women during the deployment.

I definitely didn't change the system unilaterally, but I was one of few women who gathered my courage and said, "No, your system isn't my system. This Rule isn't my rule. You are not co-opting my time for your agenda. Please do better."

And they did.

But it begs the question: how many women don't push back? How many don't even question it and happily take on a role assigned to them by the system, essentially allowing it to dominate their time and labor? How many women are stuck in isolation, feeling like misfits, feeling like others are judging them, feeling like they can't say no or else their husbands' and family's positions may be in jeopardy?

We have made this deal, so we better be good girls and do our jobs, *or else.*

I spoke to one woman who is still an active-duty Air Force Officer's Wife. Danielle was my acquaintance in England, but we never quite connected emotionally. I didn't understand her, and she didn't understand me, but we tried to like one another. She was a young mom at the time, and I had yet to have children, so there was a huge divide in how we were approaching our newlywed lives back then.

Today, Danielle and her two elementary-aged children have "followed" her Air Force Officer spouse to more than a dozen postings. She has lived and breathed different versions of the military world while maturing into her own version of our midlife crisis period.

"I want military spouses to have a fair shot at life," she said, "but the men we fell in love with are part of a system that is lagging behind in so many ways. I mean, it's changing, but so slowly because the real problems are difficult to identify. It's easy for outsiders to say it's just evangelical Christian moms who homeschool, or a bunch of white women going to brunch, but it's not that at all. It's diverse like any community, but our options are so limited. At twenty-two or twenty-four when we got married, we just had no idea what we were signing up for."

She's so right. I met teachers and TV news anchors, dentists, lawyers, stay-at-home moms, and veterinarians. These women were from all over the place, and when we connected one-on-one, we tended to have more in common than we did when we were in groups. I, for sure, had zero idea what I was really signing up for.

As Danielle and I reminisced about our divergent paths, it became even more clear the system of the military as an archetype of the patriarchy manifested is still quite toxic for dependents—mostly women and children—when it might not have to be.

I, personally, suffered from not feeling like I fit in as a liberal, secular, non-child-bearing young wife. There was no "sensitivity training" to help us integrate into this new world, just a Key Spouse and a Commander's Spouse who probably were, themselves, voluntold how to perpetuate the system and keep things running smoothly.

Danielle suffered from isolation, geographically, as she moved into some increasingly rural and underserved postings. Not only were there few job opportunities for her career field, but few employers want to hire a person who is going to move in three years or less.

Additionally, the military bases where they were stationed didn't offer quality childcare or after-school activities for her kids (priority spots go to active duty essential personnel and are limited, as they should be, so often many families have to procure "on the economy" or go without). Danielle frequently found herself at home with her kids to facilitate their individual needs, further filling her professional resume with more holes than Swiss cheese.

"I felt the pressure to have it all when we first got married. I really wanted to work," she said. "But then we went to England, and I was pregnant. I tried to make the best of it, but it was so isolating. I thought it would get better when we moved back to the States, but by and large, the system makes that impossible for the dependent spouses. They move us. They isolate us. They under-resource us. I had a great job I loved when we were in Ohio, and then they moved us to the West Coast for a single year. I couldn't find work. My kids were uprooted and plopped into a new culture in a huge city. It was painful at times, but we made the best of it."

In Danielle's voice, I hear her saying, "I know I shouldn't complain. I have it really good in so many ways. I've seen the world. We have great health care. I don't *have* to work. I am privileged and should shut up about it."

No, you shouldn't shut up about it, Danielle.

It's true you signed some deal for love and partnership, protection and mutual support, life and adventure, but that is no reason we shouldn't get to negotiate the terms. We were young, and we hadn't even begun to realize the Rules we were raised with are the problem.

In 2020, amidst the days of Zoom and mind-boggling technology at the disposal of the mightiest military on the planet, there is no reason they can't do better. There is less of a need for a person to physically relocate every 2.8 years to do their work. Yes, they may need to relocate for certain training courses or for specific specialties, but there is a lot of "moving for the sake of checking the boxes," which is hurting military families.

"The emotional toll of severing all of your social connections, preparing your kids for a new experience, of being told it would be just ten months and we would be doing it all again is exhausting. The emotional toll of explaining to our new, non-military neighbors I am a stay-at-home-mom when I am so much more than that is all so exhausting," Danielle said. "The culture is changing. I'm trying to change it from within, now that I am one of the older women and can engage with the newlyweds and young officers, but the truth is it really is impossible to have it all."

My time in the military community is an extreme example of the patriarchy's Rules in practice, but it's a good one to illustrate this point of how white women are embedded and raised in this system.

We are told we *should* put our power in the basket of the patriarchy in exchange for security and a good life. Once we sign the deal and grab the keys to the dollhouse, we are shown the fine print: if you want to change your minds, you could lose *everything*.

CHAPTER 4

LEARNING THE TRICKS OF THE TRADE

———

By 2007, I had made it "out" of my town, married, traveled some, worked a bit, and was heading off to England. I was on track to "have it all," and had started to learn some of the woman tricks of the trade that would benefit me inside the patriarchal Rule system. I could leverage white male power for my security, entertainment, and career progression.

I could use my tomboy insights and impressive sports knowledge to relate to men and boys in power and befriend them to grow my network. I leaned into my curiosity to explore the world but held safely to the arm of my adoring spouse.

By following the Rules of the patriarchy in corporate America, I flourished. By playing the part of the "good wife" when home visiting the in-laws, I felt included.

But the Officer's Wives Club was a bridge too far. I was young and righteous, judgmental and increasingly feminist. I felt left out and excluded, so I lashed out by breaking their Rules on purpose and hurting countless people on my growing progressive warpath.

I learned to break the Rules from my dad.

Dad didn't want to be cruel or be around assholes. He didn't want my brother and I to be miserable, superficial, narrow-minded adults. He grew up poor with a narcissistic, alcoholic mom and absent father in Klamath Falls. He was undereducated and unpopular.

Without articulating it, Dad wanted for us what he didn't have in his own life: unconditional love, joy, and curiosity.

He wanted us to move up and be happy.

He grew up the second son of a twice-divorced mom in the 1950s. Dad's older brother, my uncle Jim, was too book smart to slow things down to help little Jeffy catch up. Dad's mom, my grandma Ginny, was busy looking for a third husband to take care of her and the boys.

Ginny finally landed a "wealthy" (by our standards) man and moved up! She sealed the deal by promptly adopting a child with her new husband. Welcoming new baby John, Ginny and Bob pretty much ignored Jeff and Jim.

Dad didn't learn to read well until he was in his mid-twenties. He processed trauma in his body. He used and abused drugs and alcohol. He wrecked cars, got into fights, fucked, and hitchhiked. He thought of himself as "poor and dumb."

In the late 1970s, he landed a union job as a freight train conductor. In 1976, at age twenty-five, he married my nineteen-year-old mom.

Mom grew up poor and tough, too. She came from a dual-income household in the 1950s, somewhat unheard of at the time. My grandparents both worked hourly jobs their entire careers, never making much above minimum wage. They drilled hard work and frugality into their children, so when Mom married Dad, she threw the hammer down. Mom hounded Dad until he cleaned up his act, stopped the egregious boozing and partying, and kept the home in shape while he was out riding the rails earning money for our family.

Dad worked. Mom parented and worked. I didn't think much about it. But as I grew, I started to know my dad and his story more deeply. I started to become curious about people and big questions early, and he started openly talking to me about stuff well beyond the normal twelve-year-old father/ daughter conversations.

He treated me like a small human instead of a child, and I took notice.

He modeled "rule-breaking" for me, and I carried that into the world.

As a card-carrying NRA member, a card-carrying union leader, and a card-carrying Democrat who voted blue in every election of his adult life and lived on a fatty-fat railroad pension, Dad was one of the millions of middle-class, high school educated, white boomer men surrounded by other white boomers in rural America. He could have easily stuck his head in the sand, buying into all the Rules that serve white men and their privilege, claiming he had it rough as a kid and made it, so why couldn't everyone else? He was ripe for hopping on the *"reverse racism,"* and "women in the workforce *already* have it all and are ungrateful to want more" bandwagons (with most of his peers), but he didn't. I love him so much for that.

It took courage and patience for him as he carefully formulated his thoughts into wicked one-liners that called out the hypocrisy or plain ol' idiocy of his colleagues. Once at a union meeting, he was campaigning hard for Barack Obama in the 2008 election. Most of the dudes in the room were leaning "birther," and Dad was just aghast.

He told me, "I finally just said, 'You morons. Go ahead and vote against your own interests. You can spend all of your time protesting at the abortion clinic or some bullshit because you won't even *have* a union job anymore.'" (It was something like that. I wasn't there, but he relayed it thusly.)

Another time, his best friend (who happened to be my mom's older brother, David) was bitching about welfare queens and taxes and how he was so sick and tired of the lazy welfare idiots taking all of *his* blah, blah, blah. David was also a devout Christian. My dad just said, "Sounds exactly like what Jesus would say right about now?"

David was livid, according to the story Dad told.

Once when a Vietnam veteran we knew made a casual comment about how Dad's draft deferral for community college was a cop out, Dad said, "I'm a veteran...of the Drug War. But honestly, I don't remember what side I was on or whether we won or lost."

What he meant was, your journey and your values are not mine. You don't even know me, so go fuck yourself and take your judgment with you. But the man he was speaking to wasn't smart enough to even get the insult.

So, when I started returning home from the world and saying to Dad, "you're wrong," or "that's sexist," or "that's racist," he was likely unsurprised. But he put on his "be an asshole" hat and challenged me to go on offense as he played Devil's advocate.

He taught me if I was going to break Rules, I'd better be ready for the fight. This Rule-breaking road isn't easy, girl, because the people who make the Rules will defend them to *your* death.

It has always been easy for me to interrupt racism or sexism or ignorance with my dad, but learning how to speak up when surrounded by Rule followers I didn't know well was an arduous and painful journey because I was almost always outnumbered by the opposition.

During my childhood, I was a skeptical churchgoer, shamed by my grandparents and mom into silence because you just don't ask questions about *God Almighty.* In our church, God is a pissed off dude because humans are wicked creatures, and he's exhausted with our weaknesses and drained by the endless task of sending people to the land of hellfire and brimstone all the time. Escape his wrath and keep your head down.

I was insecure and curious about my body and sex, but only really Dad and Uncle Jim ever presented information about joy and intimacy and pleasure, everyone else stuck to the Rule about sex as a woman's duty (or cautioned me about the dangers of male desire and teen pregnancy).

I was confused and sad because when I cried, my cousins and aunts and mom all called me "Hollerin' Annie," I guess because I was always crying. But I never remember crying. I just remember I shouldn't ever cry. Toughen up, girl, it's the only way you're going to survive this world.

During my marriage into the conservative military officers' community, I was a closeted non-Christian, kind of an atheist. I was a closeted Democrat. I loved NPR and award-winning literature and art and "big complicated questions" like: what is the purpose of life? Is it fundamentally important or absurd? Why are human experiences so universal and well documented, and yet as individuals, we are all trapped inside of the isolation of our ego and hidden shame? Why aren't some people curious about this stuff?

I was shamed by most people for overthinking, thinking too much, being too serious, and not being able to just relax.

I didn't speak up when my father-in-law announced at a dinner party that he and the boys were late because my spouse "begged to stop at the strip club to see some real tits" on the way there—a part of a lifelong series of micro-attacks on my body and its boyishness that followed me for three decades. But then *after* I had a breast augmentation, I was shamed by the same man, asking me if I'd "gotten a two-for-one deal at Walmart" on my new B-cups. I didn't speak up then, either.

I didn't speak up when another relative said the N-word. I didn't speak up when a different relative rolled her eyes and said of my daughter's enrollment in a bilingual school, "Well, I guess she'll be able to talk in Spanish to all the Mexicans at Sherm's." (Sherm's is a step below Walmart in the grocery-buying hierarchy in our small hometown.)

I didn't speak up when my childhood friends and family questioned Obama's citizenship, lauded Rush Limbaugh, and decried the laziness and greed of "welfare moms."

Comments about how women must behave, how "minorities" (as we were taught to call BIPOC people) need to embody "better family values," and how LGBTQIA+ people were gross filtered all around me.

I knew it was limited to think this way, but I had no skill in communicating how I thought they were wrong. I had no patience for grace or empathy. I was simultaneously following one version of the Rules out of fear of falling down the socioeconomic ladder and recklessly breaking another version of the Rules out of panic and rage because nothing felt right.

But most of the time I was reminded I would be in danger, shunned, alone, poor, and outcast if I spoke up as a woman, attempting to disrupt the current power structure only if I really tried to break Rule Number One: Do not rock the boat, *no matter what.*

* * *

Growing up in my snow-white hometown, a clueless white kid who loved books, or in Idaho as a young married woman with a three-bedroom, two-bath ranch, or in England in my odd social purgatory, only a close circle of people knew the truth about me, and they put up with it as long as I followed Rule Number One.

As time passed it became increasingly hard—nearly impossible—for me to keep my mouth shut when I truly believed someone was being a privileged, entitled, prickish moron. Not to mention if they were actually being sexist, classist, or *racist.*

What this experience from 2007 to 2010 taught me was I definitely didn't want to have a traditional, snow-white, sorority version of "it all." But what other version of "it all" *did* I want?

I wasn't sure. As we moved to an even more socially isolated post in 2010, from England to North Carolina, I found myself paralyzed and hopeless. I guess it's time to just have a baby and settle into the 2,500-square-foot McMansion. After all, this is what I'd signed up for, right?

I couldn't play by the Officer's Wives Rules, like the night when Andrea said, "I'm not a feminist."

That night in the pub, I looked Andrea back in the eyes and said something like, "Well, I hope at least you appreciate the sacrifice of past feminists who risked so much fighting for women like us so we can now cast a vote and attend university and get incredible jobs—like the women in our husband's squadron who are flying fighter jets. I guess you are lucky you can just reap the benefits of their sacrifice and work, enjoying your own privilege of 'opting out' of being a feminist because you don't have anything *to fight for* now."

Oh, I was royally fucked for that one.

Andrea was pissed. The men were pissed I'd spoken in such a way. Everyone was pissed "feminism" was even something we would dare talk about, ever, in a group. My husband was pissed because I couldn't leave well enough alone.

I broke Rule Number One.

Now I'd pay the social price. Again.

These variations on Rules about what it means to be a good woman, wife, and mother have churned out generations of women who have signed the deal for the dollhouse life.

CHAPTER 5

MY RULES RULE!

———

As a middle-class, college-educated white woman married to a nice, white military officer, I definitely could have opted out of giving two shits about feminism or racism or anything more complicated than mild irritation when people brought up politics and policy, just like Andrea had.

The crazy thing about the Rules is by following them, for the most part, I was offered an open invitation to join the legions of white women before me who "don't care about politics" or "aren't feminists" or scoff at whatever the hell else annoys us about the messy world outside of our screened porches.

We are not required to care about any of this stuff, and mostly we deprioritize these bigger, complicated topics precisely because *we are overwhelmed* with how big and complicated the topics are.

We have been gifted the privilege to ignore by the patriarchy that protects us and provides us our privilege. We are offered the privilege to live in denial without negative consequences by a patriarchal culture that sees us as fragile. We can engage the privilege to make excuses about how our *personal* struggles and stressors are overwhelming and paralyzing us without being held accountable for the power we actually wield.

We rely on our menfolk and other white women to "bless our hearts," empathetically encouraging us to just take care of our fragile, ladylike, paralyzed, and overwhelmed selves.

"What can little ol' me do?" I am allowed to say, while clutching my pearls.

I began to chafe early against the passivity of my middle-class white lady acquaintances. I didn't like the default to apathy or hearing women with advanced degrees tell me it's "just too complicated."

I gently pushed back against women I knew trying to "have it all" while they were complaining to me about their stupid colleagues, charmingly inept spouses, and busy weekends.

"Hey, just stop, then." I said as I stopped.

"Yeah, but…" they replied.

My frustration with the increasing superficiality of my social group caused me to withdraw further. I wanted "it all," but didn't want a version of having it all that just resulted in a bigger cage with a faster hamster wheel.

I wanted to be immersed in an experience of America with different iterations of the American Dream. I wanted to be a *progressive* white lady.

In 2013, my husband, daughter, dog, cat, and I moved to a house sitting on the border of the inner city and the 1 percent in the Hill East neighborhood, adjacent to Capitol Hill, in Washington, DC.

We lived side-by-side with drug dealers, government paper pushers, prostitutes, political activists, and lobbyists representing industries ranging from cattle ranchers to bakery operators. I had a friend in the FBI, a friend in the Obama administration, a friend in the fire department, and a smattering of friends filling out the in-betweens. Many of them had ambitious backgrounds, advanced degrees, and hailed from Texas to Chicago to New Jersey, and beyond.

I met Black intellectuals and undocumented Latinx nannies. I avoided groups of Black men who milled about on dark street corners but waved at groups of Black neighbors hanging out on the steps of the school next door. I heard a gunshot one afternoon from my backyard, a gang assassination on my block. I heard celebrations through the walls of our house as my retiree neighbor, the family's matriarch who had lived in her home since the 1980s, hosted her large family gatherings each Christmas.

I rode the D6 and X2 buses to swanky networking events downtown to drum up new clients, riding inside grimy, mobile cross-sections of the city filled with Black, brown, old, young, white, middle class, poor, sick, addicted, happy, tragic *humans.*

Slowly, I became all "woke" and shit.

My superiority complex grew. I just can't handle hearing irrational things, like a Facebook friend posting, "I'm so not voting for any of these self-interested politicians, they're all bad." What the hell?

No, they aren't "all bad," you just happen to not have any "bad shit" going down in your day-to-day life, so you can just have the privilege of ignoring politics and policy because *they are not legislating your body, your community, and your life (taxes aside).*

I was a walking Democratic talking point.

Of course, in 2016 and 2017, I was blithely wearing my "Pussy" hat on the National Mall with half a million of my closest sisters as part of the Women's March. I donated to Planned Parenthood. I bought an "I'm With Her" button and voted Hillary.

I now found myself looking down on the rural, white, conservative "bubble" where people believe we are all equally capable of *moving up*. I was angry my hometown peers continued to deny the existence of privilege and ignore the role of white history and white laws that formed an unequal American system. I saw ignorance as a choice, and it disgusted me. I saw conservative values as cruel and inhumane.

No wonder all of those Officer's Wives are so dedicated to their Rules. Ignorance is bliss, I thought. Ignoring is access to ignorance. Tricare, security, and good government paychecks are keys to the "privilege to ignore and deny" universe.

White communities with political control over BIPOC communities are keys to the "privilege to marginalize." Male-dominated value systems that insist healthy, wide-ranging sexual preferences are sinful and seek to control womxn and Queer bodies are keys to the "privilege to erase."

By living in homogenous communities with "good school districts" where you rarely have meaningful connections with anyone who isn't just like yourself, you're offering yourself a key to "otherize" people. You have the privilege to dehumanize those who are different.

No wonder my mother-in-law whispered to her daughter while washing dishes, after a picture-perfect family Thanksgiving meal, I was "brainwashing" her dear, sweet son with all of my "liberal bullshit," and she was so ashamed because he "wasn't raised that way."

I came in with my progressive, righteous, white lady hammer swinging. I wanted to open their eyeballs to the realities I had come to know. I wanted them to see the harm privilege and conservative policies were causing to Black and brown bodies *in my neighborhood.*

What if my husband and I only had one child, not doing our duty to the world to breed better white Christian children? What if we openly supported gay marriage and eroded the sanctity of the white male's entitlement to own women that had been a part of our culture for generations? What if we told our sweet little nieces and nephews about redlining, reparations, institutional racism, and privilege, and they decided to opt *out* of ignorance? What if we advocated to raise taxes so we could invest in infrastructure, energy, education, and *civil rights?*

What if one of the grandchildren was gay, or liberal, or both?

I thought if they could see how none of those things was actually terrible, then maybe they would stop being such assholes. I thought if they could see how their actions indirectly caused harm, they would better strive to reach their Christian ideals.

I knew if I started rocking the boat, sowing doubt around the possibility even one single decision my mother-in-law ever made from her self-righteous, tsking, good Christian, family-values point-of-view might be *questioned,* the entire fucking system could come crashing down!

Hand me a paddle, honey. I want to go rock that boat.

I aggressively stepped into becoming a living, breathing existential threat to the Klamath Falls-ian way of thinking about the world.

By marrying into a family that had aligned itself with the Officer's Wives Club Rules, entrenched itself in this particular version of the American Dream, and grasped onto the idyllic, Rockwellian version of old-fashioned American values, I was directly capable of antagonizing them.

So, I did. My husband didn't know what to do, so he mostly played the role of an ostrich. He was always *just out of earshot* or would hand me a beer. He told me it was, "Only twice a year, so we could put up with it, right?"

I had been allowed inside their safe circle of tents, like a pesky raccoon tipping over coolers and keeping people up at night.

When I traveled home for family vacations, my spouse's family always tried batting me out of the campsite with a broom, but never really tried to murder me.

I was their sweet son's half-feral pet, after all. They had me outnumbered. As long as I kind of stuck to Rule Number One and didn't rock the boat, they put up with me.

In all, it was a futile, damaging relationship for both sides. They weren't actually threatened by me because they were safely entrenched in a world they reinforced with their privilege and isolation, and my provoking them aggressively wasn't going to help anything.

I was acting like an asshole, espousing my theories about poverty and crime and reparations, while shaming them for their *racism*. They were acting like assholes, telling me I was trashy and outnumbering me, beating me down with *FOX News* statistics and derision.

It was a stalemate, but I still thought, "At least I am on the side of equality, humanity, and progress. At least I'm not actually being sexist or *racist*."

* * *

In 2015, I joined forces with a few other neighborhood families to "help improve" our local public school. Next, I wanted to become an activist community member.

A small collective of upper-middle-class families living in boundary for an "underperforming" public elementary school came together to brainstorm where we would send our kids in the fall of 2015.

We were all scared as fuck of sending our little princes and princesses to a Title I, inner city, 99.9 percent Black public school. But we didn't call it "scared," we called it "supporting neighborhood schools." We didn't call it "co-opting Black spaces and trying to align them to our White values," we called it "raising test scores."

As a small collective, we set out to gentrify our neighborhood school like we'd seen our neighbors so successfully do a few blocks away.

I became another clueless white lady getting into a wacky little sitcom-level situation with a school principal, resulting in a restoration circle that included a fake candle, plastic flowers, and handholding. The district and the school leadership were spending countless hours trying to figure out how to get this pesky white lady raccoon to shut the hell up so they could run a school.

I came barging in with dreams of "helping," but couldn't see I had zero clue on what would *actually help* this school community.

I am a living, breathing episode of the *New York Times* podcast *Nice White Parents* (released in 2020). My entitlement, abuse of power, and absolute and complete blindness to how progressive white privilege works, fills me with regret and shames to this day.

I'm deeply sorry.

In the process of living in DC, exposure to true need and seeing the results of thousands of years of racist policy up close, while actually getting to know the faculty, staff, other families, and *system* making up the District of Columbia

Public Schools, I learned about how privileged I am. That was not a surprise to me.

I do not have to bus or drive forty minutes each way in rush hour traffic to find a "good school." I did not have to worry about the nutritional quality of school lunch because I could just do home lunch. I did not have to worry about finding childcare on one of the zillion teacher workdays or federal holidays.

Instead, I could *literally* run into my city council member and get an audience. I could make an appointment with a senior executive at DCPS and have an appointment set up. I could create a grassroots campaign around removing a sitting school principal and succeed.

What *was* a surprise to me was I had power. What ended up being shameful was how I abused it.

I could divert resources to what *I wanted,* and not what the children and teachers in that school *needed.*

I was a royal, Karen-esque bitch, but I did not have the cops called on me when I got into an argument with someone. Not once.

At the end of the school year, spring of 2017, I was talking with a single mom I knew from the parent-teacher association. She told me the evening prior she had a *heated* conversation with her child's teacher. I also knew this teacher. Both the teacher and the parent were Black women.

The principal, also a Black woman, intervened in this loud, expletive-filled teacher-parent argument.

This principal was new to DC and new to the school. She was principal of this school as a *direct result* of my grassroots campaign the previous school year that resulted in the old principal being removed.

I helped remove a woman from her job. I helped a new

woman get placed into this job.

The teacher had been at the school many years and had this angry mom's older children in her classroom. She had a relationship with this mother.

The teacher told the angry mom to back off. She turned to the principal and acknowledged that, yes, this was a *heated* argument, but handled. The teacher worked to deescalate.

Instead, the principal threatened to call the police on a Black single mom who was already triggered and angry.

Not surprisingly, the mom's anger at the situation was amplified, and then directed toward this new threat. She told me she called the principal names and threatened her back.

As she recounted the story, I felt physically afraid for her.

"I could have been arrested right there, and then they would have taken the kids in if I couldn't get someone to grab them in time," she said. "I don't need to be in the CPS system. I don't need that mess. This life is hard enough as it is without this fucking lady calling the cops on me at my kids' school."

All of this, just because she was yelling? When would yelling get me arrested? Never.

I became so paralyzed and ashamed for having not seen what Black families were *actually* struggling with right in front of my face.

I was blinded by my *progressive* intentions to *help* the school get a *better* principal. But what the fuck did I know about what makes a good principal in school in a neighborhood and in a city that I'd been living in for exactly two years? Nothing.

Even though I wasn't a solo actor here, I was a critical piece of an effort that resulted in violence to this single mom. I had forced someone out of their job and facilitated a new person filling the leadership role who, herself, had little experience in the DCPS system or this school's community.

It was really important to me that I had built a tenuous acquaintanceship with this single mom as a parent at this school over many PTO meetings, fundraising events, and family days. Here I had betrayed her children simply by centering my own belief the school needed a *better* leader and centered my child's *needs* through activism and abusing my power.

I felt deep shame. I contributed to this violence. I had no idea what I was doing. How could I be so arrogant and wield my power so recklessly?

I started feeling my very *existence* was "a problem." I had been so blind, and in my shame, I didn't know what to do.

No one wants to feel the powerlessness and shame that comes with knowing you are, in fact, an active participant in a system and society that is devastating to other humans.

The moment it dawns on you that you actually have done something violent—sexist, ableist, homophobic, racist—you face a choice.

You can say you're sorry. You can try better next time. You can claim you *meant well.* You can run and hide.

Shame and fear pushed me to run away from this new reality. I had done something racist. I saw the effects of my own white lady power.

This overwhelming new problem of knowing, without equivocation, I had wielded power in a selfish way that resulted in a racist act was paralyzing.

I had caused harm. I was overcome with guilt. I decided I must feel sorry for myself and heal.

It's self-care time!

My husband and I transferred our daughter to a progressive bilingual charter school, a lucky break in the school lottery system in DC, and I escaped my racist past and vowed to "do better" next time.

Maybe. If I wasn't too busy.

My privilege allowed me the opportunity to run away, licking my wounds, denying my culpability. I told my friends it was for the language immersion, but the reality was because I fucked up and had no way to articulate it, nor did I have any skills at repairing it.

So, we transferred. The shame didn't go away. It ate at me.

The relationship with my in-laws and my friends back in Oregon was eroding.

I had been such an arrogant progressive, modeling an ideal without a shred of empathy or curiosity.

I showed up in Klamath Falls like I came into that DCPS elementary school and like I came into the Officer's Wives Club: righteous and ignorant, powerful and unaware of the harm I could do.

At this point, most of the people I grew up with, including my in-laws, didn't like me much.

On family vacations, I tried to be less of an antagonist. But they were still on guard, brandishing a broom, and ready to run me out of camp when things got out of hand. They kept going on their cozy little journey, unchanged after I had gone home.

Like many progressive, middle-class, white women today who are faced with the uncomfortable paradox of being both the solution to and a major part of "the problem," I decided to just carry on, too. How could I keep hounding them for their Trump 2020 bumper stickers when I'm just as much as a racist as they are?

I swatted the pesky raccoon of my own racism out of my personal circle of tents. I turned my back on the neighborhood public school community, not because I didn't feel welcome, but because I had messed up and was full of shame and fear.

I told myself my daughter's education shouldn't have to "suffer" because of my politics. I must protect *her,* protect my marriage, be nice to my in-laws, and shove my shame back in a closet.

Meanwhile, my marriage was on the rocks and I was moving closer to personal crisis.

No time for in-depth self-critique. I must keep moving forward now that my daughter and my spouse were depending on me.

I exercised my privilege to ignore, my power to leave an uncomfortable situation for a comfortable one, and I became even more ashamed, isolated, and depressed.

CHAPTER 6

THE CRISIS IS REAL

———

In a 2017 article for Oprah.com that went viral, writer and essayist Ada Calhoun used storytelling and statistics to outline just exactly *why* middle-class women continue to follow the Rules and find themselves ignoring (or blinded to) their own power and privilege.

"The New Midlife Crisis: Why (and How) It's Hitting Gen X Women" is a thoughtful and well-researched justification for why upper-middle-class women are largely sitting on their well-manicured hands when asked to step up and actually fuck the patriarchy: it's because we are stuck under a colossal mountain of overwhelm ourselves, trapped behind our $180 balayage highlights and fretting over our child's next developmental stage.

We're in a collective death grip on the wheels of our Volvo XC90s, shuttling the princes and princesses to another lesson or practice while secretly wishing our husbands would get hit by buses so we could move to mini-farms in Vermont with all of the other newly widowed mamas and sell jams and jellies like the (Dixie) Chicks did in "Goodbye, Earl" way back when we were empowered.

Not coincidentally, the Chicks released a song in February 2020 titled "Gaslighter," an epic, post-divorce angerfest. If even the Chicks are having a midlife crisis, it just further proves we are absolutely fucked.

Calhoun leveraged her 2017 article's popularity to garner a book deal, publishing an expanded telling of the same dark story called *Why We Can't Sleep: Women's New Midlife Crisis,* released in early 2020.

From my multiple readings of the 2017 article and skimming through Calhoun's book, I clearly see this middle-class lady midlife crisis epidemic as a direct result of following the Rules.

"Why do we keep following the rules and keep ending up with the feeling of midlife crisis instead of the feeling of "having arrived at *it all*?" Because the Rules are creating the crisis!

Calhoun says her work is intersectional in that it is diverse racially; she acknowledges this is a distinctly middle-class crisis.

"The complaints of well-educated, middle-, and upper-middle class women are easy to dismiss as temporary, or not really a crisis, or #FirstWorldProblems," Calhoun said. "Although many women are trying to make it on minimum-wage, split-shift jobs (and arguably don't have so much a midlife crisis as an ongoing crisis), women overall are closing the wage gap. Men do more at home. We deal with less sexism than our mothers and grandmothers and have far more opportunities. Insert your Reason Why We Don't Deserve to Feel Lousy here."[15]

---

[15]   Ada Calhoun, "The New Midlife Crisis for Women," Oprah.com, accessed August 28, 2020.

Yes, Ada! It is shame, rearing its ugly, pervasive head yet again.

"We Don't Deserve to Feel Lousy," because we're "lucky" to have what we have so we are shamed into silence, inaction, and overwhelm.

A vicious and ugly cycle of stress returns because our lives are kinda shit, relative to not being shit, but also better than so many others, so we should shut up and stop "whining."

Calhoun demonstrates the point with loads of data:[16]

- Nearly 60 percent of Gen Xers describe themselves as stressed out.
- A 2009 analysis of General Social Survey data showed women's happiness "declined both absolutely and relative to men" from the early '70s to the mid-2000s.
- More than one in five women are on antidepressants.
- Many of us started our job hunts in the early '90s recession, which was followed by a "jobless recovery." If you were born later into Generation X, you might have entered the workforce around the 1999 stock market peak, but the tech bubble started to burst, landing us in the 2001 recession.
- The Great Recession hit Generation X hardest. According to a Pew Charitable Trust report, we lost almost half our wealth, compared with around a quarter for boomers.
- Gen X went from the most successful generation in terms of home ownership in 2004 to the least successful in 2015.
- By some estimates, we carry more debt than any other age group (about $37,000 more than the national personal consumer debt average).

---

[16]   Ibid.

- We're some of the best-educated women in history, and yet we're downwardly mobile; about two-thirds of us have less wealth than our parents did at the same age.
- Nine percent of Gen Xers "feel stalled in their careers."
- The majority of freelancers are women, and some people predict half the workforce will be freelance by 2020.
- A résumé gap is still seen as a liability, even though some 30 to 40 percent of highly qualified women take time off at some point.

The crisis is real!

Like so many other Gen X and Xennial women in my circle, I feel in my heart, soul, and bones the reality of this situation.

This was *before* the fucking pandemic!

So, how can I do much more than commit to not throwing myself out a window tomorrow morning?

I just can't. Somebody should print that phrase on a coffee mug in rose-gold calligraphy and sell it to Target.

CHAPTER 7

GASLIGHT ME NO MORE, RACHEL HOLLIS

—

I was so validated by Ada Calhoun's article providing solid proof of my midlife crisis and the societal and cultural under-pinnings that make up mine and my friends' collective misery.

Women like me—middle-aged, college-educated, moms—despite our privilege, are exhausted. We are having a hard time saving the world *and* getting dinner on the table. When we dare to complain, we are shamed, told to be grateful and that "We Don't Deserve to Feel Lousy."[17]

We end up overwhelmed and guilty, knowing how many times we've chosen manicures over marching, "our children" over "every child," and dance parties over donating. We end up paralyzed, worried we will become the next Karen if we move even an inch.

We need a savior!

Where is Oprah?

---

17 Ada Calhoun, "The New Midlife Crisis for Women," Oprah.com, accessed August 28, 2020.

In our hearts, we just know some badass, creative, empathetic woman is going to have a life-changing epiphany as she lies on the bathroom floor crying after the kids have gone to bed. Her epiphany, that *her life doesn't have to be this way,* will guide us all to the light.

Once she pulls her shit back together and KonMaris her emotional brain space, she will hence have the perspective to reflect my pain and validate me.

She will see her past self in other women who are still struggling *just like she had.* Then she'll use her new perspective and insight, a magical power, to reach me.

This is the definition of memoir-as-self-help. (It's what I'm doing here, too. Very meta.)

Her name is Elizabeth Gilbert, and she does this in her book *Big Magic.* Gilbert talks about how when she wrote *Eat, Pray, Love* it was just her processing her divorce and trauma. She didn't expect it to make her famous.

Her name is Brené Brown, giving voice to toxic shame and helping readers build shame resilience. Her name is Claire Dederer, and she's a plain-old genius memoirist. Her name is Glennon Doyle, a writer, blogger, philanthropist, and all around hilarious, amazing, wonderful mess. Her name is Yasmine, and she's my therapist. Her name is [scroll through my phone contacts and list all names].

Telling your story is you. Telling my story is me, too.

We all fail, and if we are brave and transparent, we share our truth with our own beloved communities as an offering of lessons learned, humility, and grace given to ourselves so others may find their own paths to grace.

Self-help-sharing between friends is how I came across Rachel Hollis and *Girl, Wash Your Face.* Self-help sharing is how I came across Glennon Doyle, too.

Understandably, we are vulnerable when we feel the first rush of relief when having found something that makes us feel better, stronger, healthier, seen, and worthy.

"She sees me," I thought when reading Glennon Doyle's *Carry On, Warrior.* I bought three copies to share with my close friends.

As the validation glows brighter, we want to spread the joy like missionaries after a revival. We want to help our sisters in crisis.

But with hope, enthusiasm, and discretionary income, it isn't surprising American ingenuity steps in to help out with a variety of unscrupulous and half-scrupulous companies expertly targeting our Mastercards using three very powerful marketing tools.

THE RISE OF DIGITAL TARGETED NICHE MARKETING

Marketing is my field of practice. I know how easy it is to find and communicate to a precise, niche market on Facebook through the company's powerful advertising platform. I do it all the time for my clients who are selling tree trimming services or dental care.

I'm continually impressed with how well digital marketers target me in return. I mean, how many "Coffee, Wine, Glitter, Repeat" t-shirts do I need to buy according to my Instagram feed? Roughly ten million. Also, how do they know my hair is falling out? Well done, Zuckerberg.

While digital channels have helped millions of small businesses advertise more effectively, some companies are grossly negligent and toxic. Usually, we can see it. "Miracle" products on Instagram have replaced late-night Oxy-Clean commercials. We're not usually that gullible.

The targeting tools combined with the algorithms tracking

our internet journeys put us in consumer categories. Consumer categories are siloed by race, ability, age, gender, geography, income, family structure, home ownership, political party, all the way down to whether you have a dog, cat, or bunny.

By using targeting tools to silo out the middle-class female demographic, brands like Goop and Hollis & Co. and "Keep Calm and Buy This Shitty T-Shirt" companies can test messages, audiences, and products until they get traction.

When they get traction, they make money!

All niche digital marketing is not necessarily bad. Some really cool things on the internet have found me, and I have helped my clients find their customers, too.

However, when combined with other marketing tactics, things can get toxic pretty quickly.

THE RISE OF "CURATED IMPERFECTION" AND "FEMPOWERMENT" MESSAGING

Digital marketing is helping a growing cabal of manufacturers, brands, coaches, consultants, and lifestyle influencers reach ripe-for-the-picking middle-class women in crisis.

This cabal is packaging up and selling a twisty cone of "authentic imperfection" and "fempowerment" feeding our craving *to be seen, heard, and loved in times of despair and crisis.*

In fact, self-help has transformed into a coaching, life coaching, influencer-ing, blogging, memoir writing, bullet-journaling, one-billion-dollar juggernaut.[18] A largely

---

[18]   John LaRosa, "U.S. Personal Coaching Industry Tops $1 Billion, and Growing," MarketResearch.com (blog), February 12, 2018.

unregulated juggernaut with zero legal accountability for the effectiveness of its advice, product performance, or harm (remember, "Results not typical" in the tiny print?).

Let's go back and explore how self-help plus feminism was born, shall we?

In a 2009 article for *Mother Jones,* Laura McClure extolls on a wasted weekend attending a Landmark Education "transformation" forum. Landmark is one of the original bad boys in self-actualization coaching, founded in 1971 by Werner Erhard, "a former used-car salesman who changed his name from Jack Rosenberg, moved to Northern California, dabbled in Dale Carnegie, Zen, and Scientology before seizing upon the idea that you, and only you, are responsible for your own happiness or unhappiness, success or failure."[19]

Landmark is one of many for-profit companies offering leadership and development training.

"[In 2008, Landmark] took in $89 million offering leadership and development seminars (and cruises, dating services, and courses for kids and teens). It claims more than a million seekers have sat through its basic training, which is offered in seven languages in twenty countries. Its consulting firm, the Vanto Group, has coached employees from Apple, ExxonMobil, JPMorgan Chase, and the Pentagon," McClure wrote.[20]

Now remember, this is back in 2009. Get in your time machines because 2009 was *more than a decade ago.*

Our kids might not have been born yet. We probably didn't get our first iPhone until 2009 *or later.* Instagram didn't arrive until October 2010. We did not have selfies, bae, the Twitterverse, dumpster fires, YOLO, FOMO, adorbs, emojis, binge

---

19   Laura McClure, "The Landmark Forum: 42 Hours, $500, 65 Breakdowns," Mother Jones, August 17, 2009.

20   Ibid.

watching, decent podcasts, TikTok, or hashtag anything.

Back then, Laura had her laptop or her notebook (maybe a micro-recorder, but I bet that would have violated a shit ton of rules), and she enrolled in a course where she traveled to learn from humans (sorry, no Zoom Rooms in 2009) and listened to and learned about the intoxicating, toxic self-actualization as a commodity machine.

Then she wrote about it, and maybe a few people gave a shit, but it definitely didn't "go viral."

In 2009, McClure credits the then-current iteration of Landmark for pioneering the profitable field of life coaches, time-management gurus, and productivity bloggers.

Like David Allen's *Getting Things Done* or Stephen Covey's *The 7 Habits of Highly Effective People*, Landmark is just one of dozens of quasi-philosophies promising to empty your inbox and fulfill your personal goals.[21]

Not much has changed since 2009 in practice, it seems, but now we say "Fuck" in our book titles more frequently and the printed materials feature way more floral patterns.

Brands now take the Landmark model, cast it in a lovely shade of rose gold, and sell it to exactly who they think might buy it, using powerful niche digital marketing tools.

From Rachel Hollis to Brené Brown to my own branding coach, these companies are all part of a diverse cast of characters who all fall along a spectrum of applying a business model to serve people in need of support.

Which can be *fine* if you're not an inauthentic liar pretending to be an authentic human person.

In an incredible, what I would call "takedown" on Buzzfeed News, contributor Laura Turner delivers what should

---

[21] Ibid.

be a career shattering slam dunk on Hollis & Co.'s brand of corporate feminism.

Reading "*Girl, Wash Your Face* Is a Massive Best-Seller with a Dark Message" was just a delight for sickos like me.

Thank you, Laura Turner.

I'm just going to put my favorite part of Turner's piece right here:

"The internet has given rise in the last few years to a phenomenon I've come to call 'curated imperfection,' and Hollis is one of its reigning doyens. To her Instagram following of more than 825,000, Hollis regularly posts inspirational quotes from her own writing ('You were not made to be small'), selfies in which she is not looking at the camera but is holding her book up to the camera, and photos with her husband reminding you to subscribe to her podcast or check out their marriage conference (which she calls a 'getaway weekend' and cost $1,795 per couple for two days in September, hotel not included, no refunds)."[22]

Hollis & Co. types get rich by shilling out inauthentic, often glib advice and/or varying quality household luxury goods with very little accountability for the effectiveness of the advice or the quality of their products.

Additionally, with increasingly targeted and siloed marketing tools, many brands curate the perfect audience, *for them,* avoiding critical reviews or exposés.

They fly under the radar, delivering their twisty-cone sweetness to eager buyers while intentionally or unintentionally avoiding scrutiny or criticism regarding the broader social impacts or personal, emotional, and financial im-

---

[22]   Laura Turner, "'Girl, Wash Your Face' Is a Massive Best-Seller with a Dark Message," Buzzfeed News, November 9, 2018.

pacts of the products and services they sell.

Also, brands transform over time.

It's quite possible that an authentic human—like, um, possibly Rachel Hollis—did speak her truth in her early works. Over time, as the pressure mounted for her to produce more money in her business model, it's equally possible the capitalist machine distorted her ideal, values-driven foundation into a cash printing device.

The forces of the market may have urged her to zip her trap about her marital problems or her stance on social justice issues using the justification that she was *actually helping* moderate suburban and rural white women who are turned off by strong "feminism" language.

It's hard to say what Hollis was thinking when she began faking authenticity, but it's imperative we, as consumers, are asking hard questions every time we support a brand with our money, our time, and our voices.

Brands are not our friends, and toxic feminist brands are targeting us when we're at our most vulnerable and open. With more sophisticated brands, it is difficult to sniff out the sinister actors.

Combining digital marketing tools and a Landmark-esque "fempowerment" message with the peer-to-peer nature of self-help sharing, and we get...

THE REPACKAGING OF THE ROSE-GOLD MULTI-LEVEL-MARKETING MACHINE

The Mary Kay lady in her pink Cadillac, the Avon woman at the school bake sale, and going to my first (and only) Tupperware party all hold such...memories.

We all know it, and most of us loathe it. It is called peer-to-peer, direct sales, or multi-level marketing (MLM). I remember the first time a stranger from high school friended me on Facebook to "say hi and reconnect" and then barraged me with photos of her weight loss journey trying to sell me some pill made of "juice."

Like "life coaching," MLM is also not new. From Donald Trump's 2010 support of a revolutionary "landline video phone" through the pyramid scheme ACN, to the long-running Amway company, MLM marketing has been a thing for a long time.[23]

In the digital age where "products are services," the current fempowerment movement mimics (and sometimes replicates exactly) the MLM model.

The MLM model also reinforces the siloed effect of social media targeting by creating "private groups" for members to form extensive networks of like-minded, similarly categorized prospective clients.

The current self-help MLM model is selling superficial self-help and "communities of women just like you" while asking for you to buy clothes, makeup, nail polish, diet pills, lotions, books, and workshops.

Then they ask you to "share with your own networks" and "repost."

Then they might ask you to "host a party" or "become a rep."

The MLM toxic corporate feminism cycle goes like this:
- First convince women of your *amazing self-care product OR your authentic transformation*
- Then relate to these women, holding up a mirror of your former self, literally in the case of "before and after" acne treatments or weight-loss pills, and figuratively in the

---

23   Joy de Jong, "ACN & Donald Trump," December 4, 2014, video, 2:55.

form of smiling, airbrushed faces on Instagram and glossy book covers, so these target customers can *see the potential of finding their own individual, unique, untapped joy.*

- Next, show them a Swarovski-lined, wrinkle-free, rose-gold path to the comfort and happiness found only in dreams, *Twilight* novels, and wine-club-disguised-as-book-club nights...click now, join the mailing list, come to the party, come feel loved with your sisters.
- Take all of their money.
- Ask them to be your marketing department and loop in all of their friends. Become a rep, quit your job, and be your own boss, then host a party for your friends.

This fempowerment MLM's guiding principle is as long as we stay positive, laugh at our foibles, and enjoy that glass of champagne at the end of the day, we must be doing great!

The brand-behind-the-MLM scheme asks you to turn your personal female support system into your "downline."

"Share my post," says the Jamberry rep.

"It's a great way to make extra money," says the Scentsy rep.

"Come to my $2,000 marriage conference," says the now-divorced Rachel Hollis.

We are still in the throes of a midlife crisis and seeking some relief, remember? Maybe the face cream cleared up your post-partum acne, but you really don't know how you can go back to work with this gorgeous new baby in your arms.

"Sell the face cream and be a stay-at-home mom! You can have it all!" says Becky with Arbonne.

In Hollis & Co.'s case, as an influencer business, it may not be selling a product and a downline, but it is selling a service (self-help) and asking the customer to do the work of her marketing by building a "tribe." Hollis is atop a pyramid of one.

Again, MLM and direct sales aren't necessarily bad companies with bad intentions, but just like questioning the quality of the "fempowerment" product you're buying, you should be questioning the values and system of the company behind that product, too.

But once you're in one of these bubbles, you're really not encouraged to question the upline.

Capitalism is known for squeezing labor to exact the lowest possible wage, and then turn the highest possible profit (pocketing the net). Nothing is more genius than "free labor," which is what MLM marketing amounts to.

According to one survey done by the blog Magnifying Money by the credit service Lending Tree, MLM and direct-sales reps make around seventy cents per hour. That is not a typo. It is $0.70 per hour.[24]

If you're buying or selling in an MLM business, and especially recruiting for one, tracking every single hour you spend against every single dollar you make, friend you lose, friend you gain, meaningful result you garner from the product, and failed experiment is imperative for true transparency.

Every MLM should offer a time-tracking software so their reps can calculate the value of participation in dollars and cents per hour, in addition to how they feel as humans. By ignoring or hiding the financial realities and the emotional stress of seeing someone *else* win the pink Cadillac, MLM participants are often lacking in transparency and selling hope where there are only pennies between the couch cushions.

---

24 Brittney Laryea, "Survey: Vast Majority of Multilevel Marketing Participants Earn Less Than 70 Cents an Hour," Magnify Money, September 17, 2018.

In terms of our "influencers" atop their pyramids of one, they get rich by creating a specific product to meet a very intentionally narrow and targeted demographic, isolating that demographic through sophisticated marketing tools and messages, and then encouraging "tribal" membership. They get to go from bestselling book to in-person festival to exclusive access, one-on-one events. They're your online best friends.

All the while, these brands are ignoring things like quality of product, authenticity of messaging, impact of waste, diversity of community, accessibility, and equity, all while asking their followers and customers to build the brand's wealth by spreading the gospel in your spare time.

* * *

It isn't business coaching and consulting I have a problem with. It isn't therapy or self-actualization. It isn't candles and kitchen knives or sharing stories. It's not even planning, learning, trying something different, or reaching your higher joy.

The thing I keep getting hung up on is brands are profiting by putting middle-class white women in this target group during our very difficult midlife crisis years and taking advantage of that intersection of money and pain to sell us "self-help" as a journey, "self-care" as the guiding principle, and "personal empowerment and positive thinking" as a surefire path to success, while completely ignoring powerful societal forces that are killing people all around us.

No amount of crystal therapy and meditation *alone* are going to end rape culture, battle the patriarchy, push back against unhealthy capitalist mindsets, or save Black lives.

In the case of self-help for women, *brands* are taking this MLM-style, or Erhard/EST business model, and using it under cover of female empowerment, love, and empathy, to sell wellness to a group of women who "are disproportionately well already."[25]

Journalist Lindy West, in her article "Gwyneth glows like a radioactive swan—my day at the Goop festival" writes:

"You can't honestly address 'wellness'—the things people need to be well—without addressing poverty and systemic racism, disability access and affordable healthcare, paid family leave and food insecurity, contraception and abortion, sex work and the war against drugs and mass incarceration. Unless, of course, you are only talking about the wellness of people whose lives are untouched by all of those forces. That is, the wellness of people who are disproportionately well already."[26]

West's article inspired the "WAHAM" episode of *Shrill* in 2019.

"I hear that idea repeated over and over again at the Goop conference—take care of yourself so you can take care of others. Put your mask on first. Hold space for yourself. Be entitled. Take. At a certain point, it begins to feel less like self-care and more like rationalisation (sic)," writes West.[27]

"I don't know anything about the personal lives of the women at Goop Health—who they give money to, what hardships they have endured, why they were drawn to this event— and every person I interact with is funny and smart and kind and self-aware," said West. "But it is self-evident and

---

25 Lindy West, "'Gwyneth Glows like a Radioactive Swan' – My Day at the Goop Festival," Guardian, June 14, 2017.

26 Ibid.

27 Ibid.

measurable that white people in the US, in general, are assiduous about the first part of that equation (caring for ourselves) and less than attentive to the second (caring for others)."[28]

In some ways it feels Lindy West showed up over here victim-blaming me for thoroughly enjoying the $15 French lavender Pacha Soap Co. lotion I picked up at Whole Foods as part of the relaxation, self-care, and coping process I used as I watched my dad fall apart and die in my arms in January 2020.

But West is not saying that at all.

She realizes sometimes a person just needs to feel good.

At the time I spent fifteen dollars on soap, I was just glad to have a small luxury that smelled nice and made me feel calm for a minute through a three-month episode of Holly's midlife vortex of hell.

"It is okay to love skin cream and crystals. It is normal and forgivable to be afraid of dying, afraid of cancer, afraid of losing your youth and beauty and the currency they confer. We have no other currency for women," said West. "I understand why people spend their lives searching for that one magic supplement, that one bit of lore that will turn their 'lifestyle' around and make them small and perfect and valuable forever. I also understand, especially at this moment in history, why people long to step outside of politics for a day and eat kale-flavoured ice cream (real, not satire, actually good) in a warehouse full of Galadriels."[29]

What West concludes is that it's quite possible our Galadriels—Paltrow, Hollis, et al.—may be *willfully ignoring* societal pressures and fundamental human wellness needs

---

[28]   Ibid.

[29]   Ibid.

because *they can* and because it would be really bummer-y, off-brand, and slow email list growth if their customers decided to donate to the ACLU *instead of* buying vagina jade eggs. Seriously, jade eggs are a real product. Paltrow's company, Goop, had to pay $145,000 in civil penalties to customers whose vaginas were broken due the gross negligence in touting this snake oil as self-care.[30]

It would be really off-brand if every Rodan+Fields rep *and* employee had to publish her net hourly earnings, monthly earnings, and annual earnings, collect and publish feedback on product efficacy in a peer-reviewed setting, and asked Rodan+Fields to publish its corporate policy for diversity, equity, and inclusion.

When businesses tout values around individuality, success, and community, but aren't transparent in the investment, risk, and safety net, they're square in sinister territory.

When businesses ignore privilege and claim to be apolitical, while selling us "wellness for the mind, body and spirit," it is then they cross that fuzzy boundary between the sisterly and the sinister.

When businesses exercise their privilege to ignore, they pass that privilege onto their customers.

What really happened is my friend Melanie bought Rachel Hollis' book and there was no substantial acknowledgment or discussion about how Melanie might consider her relationship to her own privilege in that very book.

Melanie was likely intentionally not made aware this mattered, but the other messages resonated, so Melanie continued to share Hollis's teachings.

---

[30]   Amy B. Wang, "Gwyneth Paltrow's Goop Touted the 'Benefits' of Putting a Jade Egg in Your Vagina. Now It Must Pay," Washington Post, September 5, 2018.

By omitting any discussion or acknowledgment of privilege, brands deliver up a sugary sweet, intoxicating narrative that feels great, while also pulling away the spotlight from other brands and causes that actually practice their stated values, are accountable to the advice and support they provide, and are radically transparent about their successes and challenges.

It is a lie of omission.

Lindy West went to the Goop Health Festival and loved the kale ice cream, but noticed there wasn't an opportunity for the attendees to even *ask* Gwyneth, "Hey, G, why do you think this auditorium is filled with white faces? Can you help us understand?"

Why? Because the panelist of white women who have millions of dollars didn't take questions.

Opening the conversation, inviting a radically transparent discussion of Gwyneth's and Goop's *choice* to target and cater to a disproportionately well audience already would have been a public relations nightmare.

So, they *avoid* that discussion, or they *tokenize* with their monthly Instagram post or "scholarship program" or appearance on a celebrity Black Lives Matter sing-along.

To protect the brand's financial interests, the brand communicators choose to ignore, avoid, tokenize, and deny they have any role in sexism, racism, ableism, ageism, and gender discrimination, among other issues.

They "remain neutral."

That is fragility. That is privilege.

And it is overwhelmingly *white.*

* * *

Since 2016, I have spent thousands of hours parsing through the wreckage of my life, piece by piece, so I could understand, grow, and learn.

I started practicing a form of radical transparency by telling everyone everything, like the memoirists Glennon Doyle, Anne Lamott, and Claire Dederer try to do, and Rachel Hollis claimed to do.

Through transparency, I felt more secure and loved.

As my friends and I all entered Calhoun's phase of midlife crisis, our lives changed in powerful, wonderful, and devastating ways.

But I had real people in real relationships to provide real, and very free, support to help me heal through all of these horrific roller-coaster events. When I did need to pay for help, I hired a licensed clinical social worker to be my therapist. I hired a certified coach who had built a reputation for *results*.

As I have found my strength through intimacy, radical transparency, small groups of female friends, and networks of people who practice honesty, empathy, and collaboration, I feel incredibly grateful and privileged.

I also feel angry.

For some reason, people are still buying Hollis's books and Gwyneth's jade eggs, giving these brands power, audience, and money. People are investing their time, attention, and resources in a curated version of a "woman" who is pretending to be their friend online, all while our actual communities drift apart and our Black and brown neighbors are murdered.

So, if we're disproportionately well off but we're super fucked up (i.e., having existential and midlife crises left and right), then aren't these sellers of hope and joy just another big group of assholes who are knowingly getting rich through predatory lending on our collective, middle-class basket of shame, despair, and vulnerability? Isn't that brazen opportunism and snake oil selling?

Hollis and Gwyneth Paltrow and Marie Kondo are more than happy to be our friends, fill our voids, clean our closets, often without any substantial, sustained acknowledgment of white female privilege and power or providing any demonstrated proof of being good humans.

They're avoiding a true immersion in the bigger picture of their role in society. They intentionally look away from seeing how truly vulnerable their target clients really are and offering us what we *really, really* need (meaningful, diverse, intersectional experiences and connections).

They will help us feel great, they will applaud us for putting our oxygen masks on first, and they will take our money and ask us to invite our friends to the party. But they are not guiding us very well along the path of how we can make real headway in healing, fucking the actual patriarchy, and rewriting the Rules so the system helps all humans.

These sinister brands tend to ignore their privilege, and their followers aren't holding them accountable, either.

We made that deal with the patriarchy so long ago for security, comfort, and the privilege of being a protected class, and we don't want to go through the discomfort of losing privilege. That's too scary.

We are offered a temporary solution to a real big problem, and we buy it. These brands get to make quarterly earnings and get some Series B funding from Arianna Huffington next year.

CHAPTER 8

SEEING SINISTER EVERYWHERE

———

The commodification of self-care and self-help using the messaging of individual fempowerment is called toxic corporate feminism. It is real. It is everywhere. It has many more shades of grey than fifty.

There are obviously sites like Goop and other out-there bullshit most women recognize as even too bougie for sane, practical people like us. But there are so many companies, brands, writers, bloggers, coaches in the cabal, and they are incredibly diverse.

The thing I want to hammer home is *how to differentiate the sinister from the sisterly, red flags to look out for, and owning your choices in the grey areas.*

We know how most brands are marketing to us now through a combination of digital targeting, feminine and womxn-specific empowerment messaging, and MLM/tell-your-friends tribe-building.

Now we have to figure out what they're actually selling and whether it's worth it to invest.

ASSESSING OUR GENDERED SOCIAL MEDIA OPTIONS

As I started to Google all of these white women transformation success stories, the digital marketing machine started targeting me for some really interesting products online.

I came across HeyMama.co, an online community that promises to deliver "the most powerful support system for working moms because having it all isn't a thing—but having a community is everything."[31]

I feel a wave of revulsion because I can hear a white, size four, post-partum, blonde Brooklyn "mama" wearing pumps and a Moby wrap saying these words with conviction.

What do I need to do to have this magical, estrogen driven, baby carrier-wearing army of supportive other "mamas" who got my back?

I click.

I apparently need to *apply* to join the matriarchy.
I can't make this shit up. This is the actual language from their sign-up page:

The Matriarchy is Here
(And We're Taking Applications)
Apply Now $35/mo
Or $350/yr [32]

According to their "Our Story" page, the matriarchy is very Manhattan, white women whose resumes read like *Wall Street Journal* porn—Apple, Intel, Unilever, Conde Nast.[33]

---

[31] "Membership," HeyMama, accessed April 15, 2020.

[32] Ibid.

[33] "Our Story," HeyMama, accessed April 15, 2020.

I would love to find out how many of them are recently divorced, over forty-five, or live in a city other than New York. From the staff page, I see one woman of color on the leadership team.

Would the matriarchy reject me if I applied? This phrasing makes my stomach turn over, especially at this price point.

Another site, Girlboss.com, promises to be my new ladies-only LinkedIn.

Yes! I like this idea.

There's a lot of pink, a lot of nice emoji use, subgroups for freelancers, side hustlers, sustainability, travel, "marketing mavens" (stab me in the eyeballs with a fork, I hate that term), and even LBGTQIA+ groups.[34]

You can get your horoscope every day on the feed. You can join an IRL group (or even lead one since they're now accepting applications for Girlboss ambassadors in most major coastal-elite markets near you!), or you can attend the Girlboss Rally in Los Angeles (starting at $375 for "Explorer" Girlbosses, and only $795 for VIP Founders, not including taxes and fees).[35]

It feels very *Shrill*-adjacent, but Girlboss gets me with their impressive crowdfunding element that claims to have truly helped real-life Girlbosses fund their endeavors with "more than $700k raised" for women-owned small businesses, to date.[36]

I tried to "join" the community and engage, but like all social media sites, the companies are really centered on scale versus meaningful connection (i.e., more members mean

---

34 Website homepage, Girlboss, accessed April 15, 2020.

35 "The Girlboss Rally," Girlboss, accessed April 15, 2020.

36 Girlboss Foundation, "Girlboss Foundation," accessed April 15, 2020.

more revenue versus few members who invest a lot).

A third model was recently brought to my attention: TheCru.com. This is a micro, virtual career coaching and networking company founded by CEO Tiffany Dufu. For $499 each year, you are placed into a "Cru" of ten women to build relationships and help one another along in your career journey.

"Through it all, I've had one goal: a world in which women's gifts and voices are fully harnessed for the benefit of us all. I work hard, but the secret to my success is my Cru. They know my good, bad and ugly. They help me create a plan. They hold my feet to the fire. They make introductions, buy my books, and retweet my ideas. They have me in stitches. They don't judge me when I leave tears on their nice clothes. We have each other's back," Tiffany Dufu writes on TheCru's website.[37]

So, we have three options here for women-centered social networks:

HeyMama offering support for "mamas" who want "it all" for $350 each year.

Girlboss, a free service like Facebook, but pink.

TheCru, a ten-person, facilitated career coaching program for women.

Which one seems legit?

Here's how you know:

1. Join an online community where the groups are intentionally small. The business model of social media commodifies community, and that is very difficult to pull off authentically. It often ends up being just another large group of strangers shouting into the abyss. *Winner:*

---

37   "Our Story," TheCru, accessed October 1, 2020.

TheCru with specific groups capped at ten people and have the potential to jumpstart trust building, accountability, and allowing everyone to feel heard.

2. Join an online community where there is a clear service offered and/or focus. The idea of "join in, jump in, be a part of something" is putting the onus of facilitation and support on the user, and not on the service provider. Girlboss is just LinkedIn in pink, from my casual engagement. HeyMama is just LinkedIn in more pink with children in tow. TheCru promises to "accelerate their personal and professional growth. You receive structure, exclusive content and a virtual guide to support your Cru with your annual membership." (ibid) *Winner:* TheCru, because you know what they're selling and what you're going to get.

3. Join an online community where there is diversity in the leadership of the company, in the participants, in the thought-leaders, and see if they have a stated policy regarding social justice issues. Again, TheCru wins! HeyMama is oozing coastal elite white privilege and Girlboss has zero byline or founder information. A plethora of generic clickbait articles and stock photos fill the blog. For all we know from the website, Girlboss could be a shell company owned by some racist orange man and his spawn. TheCru was founded by a Black woman, features a wide array of women leaders *by name* in its lengthy and in-depth blog, and is demonstrating its commitment to diversity and inclusion by its very existence where it centers BIPOC women in more than half of its posts. *Winner, with a hat-trick:* TheCru.

ASSESSING SELF-HELP, INFLUENCERS, COACHES, SPEAKERS, AND BRANDS

As we choose our mentors and our thought leaders, it is so important to do a little digging on their human credentials.

First, we have to acknowledge we are drawn to people who reflect who we are. I am a white, middle-class, college-educated mother who is cis-gendered, able-bodied, and heterosexual.

Stories by Brené Brown, Elizabeth Gilbert, Glennon Doyle, Anne Lamott, and Claire Dederer will obviously resonate with me more easily.

I want to, and have, invested my time and money in their art, stories, ideas, and brands. I have also worked to diversify my bookshelf, Netflix queue, and media consumption.

But not all artists, authors, consultants, coaches, products, and brands deserve my time and money. I try to assess them against some basic criteria before I invest.

Let's start with Jen Sincero, the best-selling author of *You Are a Badass* and *You Are a Badass at Making Money?* She says on her YouTube channel, "You are magnificent. You are flawed. You are powerful. You are loved. You are a badass."[38]

Yeah, Jen. I *am a badass.*

On her website, the sales pitch is delivered in a very guru-like way: "You have the power—through your thoughts, beliefs, and actions—to create your reality."[39]

Yeah, I sure do, Jen. I understand the power of abundance, prayer, and meditation. I get it.

But, wait, there is a dire warning, she insinuates: I am going to die.

---

[38]   Jen Sincero, "YouAreABadass," June 16, 2017, video, 0:23.

[39]   "Home," Jen Sincero, accessed April 15, 2020.

"You get one shot at being the you that is you on planet Earth, and you get to choose how you experience it. Why not choose to enjoy it?"[40]

So profound, and such a "landmark," and my first step to my new, transformed self, Jen? What is it?

It's a low, low one-time payment of just $297 for Jen Sincero's "You Are Badass® DIY" coaching program.[41]

I scroll through Jen's website, and it's *fine*. It is mostly white people and a couple of Black Lives Matter posts on Instagram back when every brand was required to post once before they forgot about Black lives again.

It's hard to say who Jen Sincero really *is*. That's fine, but so mediocre.

It's up to you as a consumer to consider: does Jen ignore her privilege? Does she gloss over social justice? Does she gloss over sexism, racism, ageism? Is she largely targeting a group of people who look exactly like me and exercising and passing on her privilege to ignore?

I dug a little deeper, and I would say the answers to those questions lean toward "yes."

Jen's universe appears to be very upper-middle class and very white.

Okay, great. Now I know. Now you know.

If I decide to buy Jen's book, it's going to be tough for me to justify the purchase considering there are other people doing the same thing while also *addressing and acknowledging their privilege.*

Jen, we need you to *do better.*

---

40 Ibid.
41 "You Are a Badass DIY Coaching Program," Jen Sincero, accessed April 15, 2020.

Readers, we need you to *do better.* The privilege to ignore means you don't ask those questions; you just buy because it's easy and popular. Quit it. Do the work.

Our resources are our privilege, and every time we make a mindless purchase, we're showing how we use our power.

You are choosing. You are not a passive actor here, even though the privilege to ignore likes to trick you into thinking these things are "innocent."

They're not.

Doing the work means applying your resources in an intentional way as much as you can. It may not be a lot, but you do have time. I know you do.

HOW TO CHOOSE VOICES OF AUTHORITY, INSPIRATION, AND SELF-HELP

1. Does the author's message resonate with you? Okay, great. Move on to the second step.
2. If the author is white and/or middle-class, does the author acknowledge her privilege as part of the journey of self-help? If yes, great! Move on to the third step. If you're not sure, then look on the website at who has given them praise. Go on their social media accounts and see who they follow, what they believe to be true and important in the world, whether they have a value system that mirrors your own and amplifies BIPOC, LBGTQIA+, and antiracist, anti-sexist, anti-abelist, and anti-"ism" values. If the author is white and/or middle-class, does the author cite and reference a diverse set of voices and other experts that brings representative perspectives to the work? If yes, great! Move on to the fourth step.

If you're not sure, flip to the appendix and read through the references. If you see diversity and effort, they're probably on the right track. If you see nothing, but you did find some validation from the social media, you might want to try someone else. But that's on you to choose.

3. Go to a BIPOC-, or Queer-owned, bookstore and buy one of the BIPOC or Queer-authored books in that last author's reference list. It's a trick! I'm telling you *do not buy this book*. Like silly Grover in *The Monster at the End of This Book,* you probably shouldn't be buying this one. I hope someone gives it to you and you read it, but you spend your cash money to find some other amazing authors to purchase from. It's time for white people like me to pass the mic. If you do buy this one, any of the profits are being donated.

THE TOXIC CIRCLE JERK AND HOGGING THE SPOTLIGHT

One of my very cool clients, a Gen X woman who runs her own business in the upper-middle-class luxury market, sent me a link to an episode of the podcast *Afford Anything* featuring Ash Ambirge, founder of the blog "The Middle Finger Project," and book of the same name released in February 2020.

Ash has a Rachel Hollis-ish, white-girl-Horatio-Alger story, too. She's plucky, hilarious, tragic, and triumphant.

Ash is an adorable woman who grew up in a trailer park in rural Pennsylvania, was orphaned by twenty years old, was completely broke due to some major financial illiteracy (a problem that plagues a lot of people who suddenly move up the socioeconomic ladder), unemployed, and then almost killed by an abusive partner before she figured it all out one dark night in her car in a K-Mart parking lot with less than $30 to her name.[42]

Ash's voice is clear. Her writing is visceral and strong, and the message she preaches on this podcast episode, on her blog, and in her book is the biggest threat to people being happy is "the advice that everyone keeps telling them over and over and over again. 'You should be grateful for what you've got.'"[43]

We know. We remember what Ada Calhoun told us.

"Right?" she continues. "Like teachers especially suffer from this. You've got summers off. You get out of work at 3 p.m. You have great benefits…Be grateful for what you've got. It is some of the world's most dangerous and worst advice because it convinces us to sell our time; it convinces us other people might be right. We get scared. It causes anxiety, and we end up staying small, and we shrink, and we live these lives that are beneath us."[44]

I agree with pretty much everything Ash says here. I love her humor and creativity. I, too believe people, humans of all stripes, should feel they are worthy of love, joy, and abundance.

Ash's brand is gritty and aggressive. She is a terrific copywriter. She comes from the same poor, white, rural sort of town I come from. She meets the first three criteria above.

I signed up for her email list but didn't buy the book. As I assessed her using my thinking-cap list above, I got to the third step and paused. What gave me pause were the scrolling reviews for *The Middle Finger Project* book that

[42]   Ash Ambirge, "#242 – The Art of Trusting Your Most Dangerous Ideas with Ash Ambirge – The Middle Finger Project," interview by Paula Pant, Afford Anything Podcast, February 17, 2020, audio, 1:12.

[43]   Ibid.

[44]   Ibid.

rotated past in the middle of Ash's home page (it has since been redesigned).

At first, it appeared to be a who's-who of empowered, educated white women who have found success in this field.

As I dug into the women listed on Ash's website, I was annoyed that a solid two-thirds of her "early praise" came from some generic white ladies who are pretty much nothing like Ash herself. They definitely did not meet the first two or three criteria I laid out, and it irritated me to no end.

This "innocent" cycle of people using their spotlight to spotlight others *just like them* in a circle jerk of insular, self-serving praise is *not passing the mic.*

Although Ash won me over with the really powerful advice in her email series, her empathy toward rural white poverty, and her outspoken support of Black Lives Matter, I have yet to fork over any of my hard-earned money to her brand.

Be more discerning, girl. Why would you want a bunch of shallow white people who don't make the grade telling you, "you done good?" They are toxic.

THE THEFT OF IDEAS

The theft of ideas of the less privileged and powerful by powerful people (historically white people) is a huge problem and has been for a *long* time.

Call it cultural appropriation or plagiarism or sexism or all-of-the-above, but the loud, privileged, and famous have a hard time acknowledging someone else came up with their idea first and giving credit where it is due.[45]

---

45   Jenni Avins and Quartz, "The Dos and Don'ts of Cultural Appropriation," Atlantic, October 20, 2015.

In this fempowerment, self-care, white lady privilege space, no one embodies this more obviously (to me) than Amber Rae, "Millennial Motivator," coach, mentor, married, no kids, rose-gold-website-owning Brooklynite "whose work invites you to live your truth, befriend your emotions, and express your gifts."[46]

She's talks about how socialization crushes the wild wonder of children, and how she has been transformed into a motivational speaker who says very obvious shit to anyone who regularly reads literature, biography, religion, has suffered loss, or has a child themselves.

Instead of wasting time on Rae's superficial, obvious bullshit, read Ada Calhoun's piece and then read Elizabeth Gilbert's *Big Magic,* and then read Alan Watts or Eckhart Tolle. Or find the Black, Latinx, or native person who is selling the exact same stuff and pay *her* instead.

One of my personal spiritual authorities is Alan Watts. This Zen-talking, counterculture lecturer of the 1960s was one of the first people to popularize Vedanta (ancient Hinduism) and Zen Buddhism in the United States, much to the dismay of the ivory-towered religious studies professors of his era.

Watts wasn't a perky white girl from the suburbs of Chicago who was "called" to New York to speak to my middle-aged ass about "wonder."

He was a British-American theology professor and scholar, speaker and writer of Chinese, and author of dozens of books and lectures that covered Zen Buddhism, Vedanta, "the new physics," cybernetics, semantics, process philosophy, natural history, and the anthropology of sexuality.

---

[46] Amber Rae, "Choose Wonder," accessed April 1, 2020.

In his 1966 book *The Book: On the Taboo Against Knowing Who You Are,* Watts speaks with depth and parable about the very nature of what it is *to be human* and why it's often really hard.

Watt's wrote some of the exact same ideas around connectedness, wonder, and play that Jen Sincero, Amber Rae, and Rachel Hollis talk about, but they're loading it with shame, catchy keywords, and rose gold, while charging you a ton to feel like shit, mildly buzzed, or kinda smug but secretly guilt-ridden because, well, you are still a privileged white lady and they won't acknowledge that.

Black women like Zora Neale Hurston, Maya Angelou, Toni Morrison, Alice Walker, Bell Hooks, Audre Lorde, and so many more have been writing about feminine community, collaboration, wonder, protection, love, matriarchal values, and fucking the patriarchy *for centuries.*

Now their white contemporaries are killing it on Twitter, Instagram, TikTok, podcasts, webinars, workshops, and as speakers, coaches, and thought leaders.

As women, as people, as advanced manifestations of energy with powers of creativity and introspection, let's just stop being patronized by people like Amber Rae who are co-opting old ideas and other people's art and research, and slapping a new coat of sparkle on it to rack up book sales and TEDx Talks gigs.

It is theft. It is wrong to steal and not cite your sources. It is wrong to hire a person who is stealing and not citing her sources.

If you just walk through the steps above, it becomes pretty clear who you might want to hire for your next corporate offsite speaker.

(Hint: It's a BIPOC, trans woman).

DESTROYING YOUR FALSE "MORE-GOOD-THAN-HARM" ARGUMENT

I was talking with Melanie and another friend, Lauren, one evening about Rachel Hollis' divorce announcement.

In early summer 2020, the beacon for relationship transparency and "raw" sharing of her personal journey announced suddenly on social media she was divorcing her spouse after three years of struggle.

When I went back to check Hollis & Co.'s Instagram Live videos covering the past three years, I didn't see any goopy mascara and existential dread, self-doubt, and gut-wrenching fear posts. I mean, that was my journey. Maybe Hollis is even winning at divorce?

There wasn't an "our relationship is in trouble, and here's what steps we're taking" podcast series, like you might imagine from someone so real.

The divorce was just dropped like a turd on her social platforms, demonstrating Hollis & Co.'s entire "transparency" gambit was all illusion.

Hypocrite defined and, I argue, that's what happens when you co-opt your humanity into a brand.

Of course, miraculously, Hollis and Co. wrote and released a book about the divorce and the ugliness released in October 2020. The new book came out mere months after the Instagram post announcement.

From personal experience, I know it takes a year for a book to be written, edited, copy edited, named, proofread, designed, printed, and distributed. I guarantee she'd been working on this "divorce memoir" for at least eighteen months, all the while raking in the dough from sponsors and readers buying her bullshit marriage advice.

Yet people will probably sop this new drivel up.

All of us "divorced" mamas can relive our separations through Rachel's. We can cry together. We can rebuild together. She wants us back. She has feelings.

But we shouldn't forget she lied to us for three fucking years.

"But some of these brands, like Hollis & Co., do broaden people's minds," Melanie said. "Hollis is more conservative and moderate, which can help some people turned off by the word feminism or patriarchy make that first step into healing and joy, like a gateway to empathy and bravery. Isn't that valuable?"

"Right," said Lauren. "Some women seem to get empowerment and empathy from people like Hollis. Wouldn't you argue learning and self-care are good things, even though the messenger can be problematic?"

"What about if Rachel Hollis reads my book and wants to write a review on my website, sharing my work to more women. Wouldn't that be an overall net win?" I mused.

No. It's a trick of capitalism. It's a straw man of the patriarchy.

It's like saying, "Trump University taught four people how to do algebra, so it helped some people, right?"

Trump University is a fraud. We need to call out frauds. Full stop.

I could see what Melanie and Lauren are saying. "Well, it's for the greater good. We've gotta start somewhere. She wants to stay in her lane and offer some help, even though she's not the end-all, be-all."

No, no, no! That would be like taking a job with Purdue Pharma to "change it from the inside." That would be the definition of Kellyanne Conway or Omarosa Maginault.

If the person is not demonstrating and living by their stated values, delivering on their promises to their customers, and being held accountable, they are a fraud. It's that simple; she's a fraud.

Hollis & Co.'s brand has been using toxic corporate feminism, in some form, to sell to, serve, and "empower" white women.

We don't need people like Hollis soaking up the spotlight and distracting poor white ladies who are "turned off" by the language of feminism, womanism, and truth to be gently guided into the conversation this way where some woman is making money off of that and not talking about the intersectionality of it all.

If there was no more noise, what would people hear?

Hopefully, they would start to hear the truth and the pain of other humans who are also sharing their heart stories and embodying the values they so loudly claim to hold.

OWNING OUR PRIVILEGE

What are you going to do now that you know how to take a critical look at these different types of feminist-aligned brands?

Now it is up to us, white lady friends.

It is up to me, my friends, and our mommies' drinking nights out on a well-lit patio near the Nationals' ballpark in the shadow of the United States Capitol dome, to do better.

I'm stripping us of our privilege to ignore. By now we should know the differences between what leans sinister and what leans sisterly.

I'm asking you to use the power of your pocketbook and your limited resource of time to be more mindful. Intentionally decide whose messages have value in our marketplace of ideas.

Do you care about women? Are you a feminist? Would you be willing to not buy another subscription to Goop until

Gwyneth addressed her brand's strategy on antiracism, social justice, and income inequality? Will you help stop a fraud before it steals the spotlight from a more worthy messenger?

You're the only one who has to sleep at night with how you spend your time and money, not me. I'm just asking.

Asking hard questions and taking more time to be more discerning in how we exercise our privilege for good or for evil is "the work." Privilege and power result in money and access. Every time we spend money or invest time in anything, it is an application of our privilege. By mindlessly cruising Target when you feel like shit and walking out with $350 worth of junk you probably didn't *need*, you've made a choice.

It's time we start owning our choices.

It's time we start spending time asking meaningful questions. How do I choose where to procure self-help? What do I do when I feel overwhelmed and need self-care? Which of brands are hurting or helping women more? Where are the women of color? Where are the single moms? Where are the women over fifty? Where are the people with access needs? Is this how I want to invest my time and money? Do I know my own values and am I living by them?

And yet, going around asking my white women friends to comment on these questions is not getting me invited to very many dinner parties.

Cue the awkward silence.

ESSENTIAL TAKEAWAYS

Now we have a basic set of guidelines for choosing what to consume in terms of self-care, social media, and self-help. We can critique motivational, inspirational influencers and their books, brands, and personalities.

The same criteria can apply to coaching or therapy, memoirists or podcasts, or any brand asking you to invest money or time in their products.

As consumers we deserve:

- A product offering that is clear and will deliver on its stated promise
- A brand behind the product that is clear about its values and operations
- A person behind the brand who is transparent, accountable, and actively engaged in conversations that advance social justice, equality, and humanism
- A reputation that supports that person via a diverse and equitable representation of critics and fans that hold them accountable to their values
- A belief system that pays respect to and cites the ancestors, thinkers, philosophers, artists, leaders, and mentors that inspired *their* work and were critical to helping them along the road to success.

As I outlined above, it's difficult to find all five all the time without doing some extra work. That's part of "the work" that is being asked of people of privilege to do, though. So just do it. Raise your hand. Ask the questions. Be critical consumers.

To compound the problem, even when you do the extra work, the answers might not be cut and dry. You'll have to make a judgment call. You need to decide and own your decisions.

CHAPTER 9

MY WHITE HUSBAND, THE VICTIM OF A TERRIBLE INJUSTICE

———

I wrote earlier about my ideal man. The one I knew growing up. The dad who raised me. The boy who became my husband.

I don't want to devote too much brain space to Gen X/ Xennial, middle-class white men, but they are pretty screwed up by the patriarchy, too.

While my friends and I are stuck in Ada Calhoun's midlife crisis, we don't want to overlook how we are probably married to a man going through his own midlife crisis.

While we go seeking self-care in the toxic corporate feminist cycle, what are these boys up to?

In her January 2020 article in *The Atlantic* titled "The Miseducation of the American Boy," journalist and author Peggy Orenstein talks about her interviews of hundreds of young men about what it "means to be a man."

"Feminism may have provided girls with a powerful alternative to conventional femininity, and a language with which to express the of myriad problems-that-have-no-name, but there have been no credible equivalents for boys. Quite the contrary: The definition of *masculinity* seems to be in some respects contracting," she writes.[47]

I could have saved Peggy a lot of time because through my very unofficial channels of anthropological research done via sleeping with a bunch of white, Gen X, often married men over the past few years, I know the deal.

They are also isolated as fuck.

I met one man who was living the American Dream. He was an immigrant, entrepreneur, father with the McMansion in the burbs, and he was miserable, lonely, and afraid. He relayed that he believed his wife was mentally ill, and he didn't know what to do. The stigma of the illness combined with the shame of her abuse was embarrassing. He was alone in this bubble and desperate for someone to show him kindness and affection.

I met at least two men who were married to box-of-wine-a-day country club wives who they explicitly understood had married them for the lifestyle. Like they had a discussion about it. Both of these men relayed to me how it had become obvious their spouses hadn't expected such a steep emotional toll in midlife after, essentially, selling yourself for a lifetime of security, the Porsche, and hair extensions.

I get that. My own cultural underpinnings *always* pushed me to lock down a rich dude, so I get they did that for security because it's something we are often encouraged to do as

---

[47] Peggy Orenstein, "The Miseducation of the American Boy," Atlantic, December 20, 2019.

women. But as I emotionally matured, the emptiness of that choice haunted me. I can imagine it also began to haunt them. In both cases, their spouses told me the women had turned to alcohol, shopping, and binge-vacationing to cope. The men had turned to alcohol, adultery, and binge-working to cope.

One of the men was incredibly sweet. He was the dad to two teenage girls. He and his ex-wife had to fight hard to start a family, and these girls were his world. But his second marriage was broken. He did the stereotypical thing and had an affair with the girl at the office.

"Don't marry your mistress or your secretary. Definitely not if she's the same woman," he told me. He was so frank about how he was an arrogant, self-interested man's-man in his thirties. His drive to compete and win at life brought in millions of dollars, so that's what he did. He got the mansion, the Jaguar, and the trophy wife, and now he is sick, stressed, isolated, and in poor health.

He told me he feels stuck, married to a woman fifteen years younger who hates him and openly fucks other men. He is permissive because he sees how much pain she's in, but they cannot heal together. In his words, they are now both lonely and full of despair.

I met quite a few men who weren't getting "enough sex" (boo hoo). But the ones in pain were the ones who I developed friendships with. Sometimes we fell into bed together. Sometimes we didn't.

The pervasive, longstanding patriarchal definitions of masculinity that involve aggression, dominance, stoicism, toughness, independence—and that sometimes veer sharply into violence, rape, mass shootings, and #MeToo moments—have churned out a bunch of half-developed, very isolated male humans.

Men often do not possess the language for, the experience with, or any healthy models for intimacy because they were raised up in the same toxic culture I was.

The same fucking culture that told me I needed to be skinny, cute, and "not rock the boat" so I could ball-and-chain one of these morons so we could "have it all" together is the underlying issue here.

It's not the men themselves, or the women in the Officer's Wives Clubs, or the woman who fucked my husband when I was on vacation, or the ones trying to sell me weight loss supplements.

The problem is the umbrella of white privilege housed under the system of patriarchal capitalism.

* * *

In short, my mommy told me women can have it all. "All" means get married, work hard, save money, don't get pregnant or raped, make love to your husband when he asks, keep yourself skinny, and play it safe most of the time.

"All" did not include enlightenment, mind-blowing orgasms, therapy sessions, or exploring my own mortality as I trim my infant daughter's tiny baby fingernails.

My mom was a product of this system, as was hers. So, she did what she thought was the best thing to protect me, which is replicate a system that took care of her decently well.

Do not rock the boat; paddle it. Then wash it, put it away, and post pictures on Instagram about your gorgeous family day on the water.

* * *

In short, my husband's mommy told him to be tough, work hard, be kind to girls, get in a little trouble, have fun, and you can have it all. "All" means get married, bring home a paycheck, save money, and play it safe most of the time.

All did not include exploring childhood attachment trauma, seeing a therapist about recurring feelings of insecurity and inadequacy, treating depression, questioning faith, or finding joy and purpose.

His mom was a product of this system, as was hers. She did what she thought was the best thing to protect her children, which is replicate a system that took care of her decently well.

Do not rock the boat; let your new wife paddle it. Then crack open a beer and wonder if you're getting laid tonight.

* * *

We all know the man-flu. We've all seen the man-babies. We all complain about our husbands and their sincere cluelessness when we lash out due to the extreme pressure of carrying the family's "mental load" as they try and score a quickie before the kids wake up on Sunday morning by pressing their morning wood into the smalls of our backs.

Often heterosexual Gen X/Xennial dads are essentially living alone without an emotional language to communicate their fear and vulnerability.

Most of the time, male friendships are nothing like female friendships in either quantity or levels of intimacy.[48]

---

[48] Ronald E. Riggio, "How Are Men's Friendships Different from Women's?" Psychology Today, October 9, 2014.

Married men often end up with exactly one person to "really talk to," which is their perimenopausal, stressed out, full-time working, full-time parenting, full-on anxious wife who is, herself, in crisis.

This is where I'd like to segue back to Claire Dederer, author of *Love and Trouble: A Midlife Reckoning.*

Dederer provides a set of words to describe the type of intimacy, sexuality, transgression, submission and *complication* that is the Gen X, middle-class, married-with-kids sex life.

Dederer talks of marriage as this strange world where two people who are committed and bound together nearly end everything because *they can't talk about carnal sexual stuff with one another.*

It's scary to rock that boat.

"What I didn't or couldn't say [to my husband] was what every stereotypical middle-aged man doesn't or can't say to his wife: I want you to be a stranger. I want you to be strange. I want you, and at the same time I want my life to change, and I want that change to happen *to me*," Dederer writes.[49]

What did this mean to me? This is Dederer's admission she still was viscerally sexual inside of her mind but craved "other things."

She wanted something fantastic and different, carnal and raw, exciting and strange in her sexual world, and had no way to tell her spouse because we're all stuck in the rigid myth marriage must equate to monogamy and romantic love. We put so much pressure on marriage to hold so much, and people are becoming increasingly isolated from their communities and from their own partners when they get hitched.[50]

---

49   Claire Dederer, Love and Trouble: A Midlife Reckoning (New York: Alfred A. Knopf, 2017), 201.

50   Mandy Len Catron, "The Case Against Marriage," Atlantic, July 2019.

In my own period of marital isolation—disconnected from my girlfriends, my family, and my morality—I was searching for others who also felt trapped, alone, and afraid, and I found them. Loads of them. They were almost always white men.

I have listened to these men, swirling a scotch, sitting beside me in a perfectly suitable bar in which to meet a future mistress. He first assesses my hotness. He compliments me. He is optimistic and knows picking up the tab, choosing this bar, and wearing that suit means he is in charge. We both went to the same school of life, so I get it.

But unlike most people looking to simply cope with my trauma, I wanted to understand his trauma, too. I wanted to *understand* why I was in this bar in the first place.

I wasn't the usual first date. I start asking questions. I don't flatter him; I interview him.

I see the surprise, relief, and some amusement wash across his face. He is suddenly in touch with a boy whose mommy told him to have fun and get into some trouble, but also made him feel safe and seen.

He leans into me and says, "Thank you for listening to me. Thank you for not judging me. I feel so comfortable with you. I don't have anyone to talk to, really. I am desperate, and I just don't understand my wife anymore. I am miserable, but I'm stuck for the kids and the house, you know? I love her, but I…"

"You're lonely," I finished his thought.

"Yes," he says, "I am, and I just want someone to share a bit of genuine intellectual, emotional, and physical intimacy with. I crave touch. I crave joy and liberation. I want to be free to be myself. Free from the pressure of this world—the patriarchy, the expectations, the definition of what is manly. All of that freedom, intimacy, and chemistry is completely missing in my marriage."

He doesn't actually say any of that last part.

He says, "Yes, and you've got beautiful eyes." Then he tries to make a move.

But at that point, I know what he's trying to say. He communicates the last part physically, leaning in to touch my hand.

Every wife out there walking around on eggshells wishes her husband could say "I'm lonely and I'm afraid," "I want to try pegging," "I'm bi-curious." "I'm tired of pretending to be 'The Man,'" or "I need help."

I would have done anything for my spouse to have been able to name the distance between us.

I am not making excuses for all of the men I met out there looking for a side girl, but I know firsthand he probably doesn't know those words yet.

He's too scared and alone to test out what might happen if he did say them to you in the pressure cooker of your relationship.

* * *

Loneliness, isolation, gaslighting, the building of resentment, stress, children, mental and physical illness, trauma—these things tend to collect like drops in a bucket until you just have no choice but to *make something happen* or open the door to let some strange thing happen *to you.*

In the case of my husband, he chose to have an affair with my hot mom friend whose son was in preschool with our daughter.

This fling was the first time he communicated his despair with his life—our life—in a way that really got my attention.

For years he acted out in subtle ways I would recognize as red flags now, but just saw as "facts of life" back then. He would withdraw or isolate himself, increase his solo drinking and hide it, act snarky and passive aggressive, and pressure me for more sex.

I confessed to a close friend once I thought he was depressed, and I was worried about him. She advised me to push him to go to therapy.

Not only did he not go to therapy, he berated me for "talking to someone outside of our marriage about me." Doors were slammed.

I wasn't allowed to talk to my closest friends or family about my marital angst and personal battle with anxiety. It was unbearable, lonely, and toxic, and I was desperate to save him, myself, and our marriage.

But before anything I could do worked, that pressure cooker sent him to another woman's bed.

Up until that point, I'd flirted with other men and gotten inappropriately close with a few others. I'd done some "experimenting" with a couple I knew well, and fully disclosed everything to my husband and he said he was surprised but supportive. I remember the time immediately after I "played with others" as being the best sex he and I ever had.

But I, alone, couldn't fix our marriage. I was trying so hard, but we had to effectively communicate with one another what was wrong in our hearts.

The end of his sentence, right before he told me the MILF had beautiful eyes and tried to make a move, may have been something like "I'm lonely … and afraid, unfulfilled, and suffering from depression."

I wish there had been a different way for him to communicate, but such is the result of our life inside of the patriarchy.

We are told men aren't supposed to cry. Men aren't supposed to talk it out. That's that.

But is it?

For the record, I am no longer a fan of being the "Other Woman" outside of a consensually non-monogamous partnership. Not only is it mildly depressing, but I'm committed to a new life of radical transparency, in general, about everything. But I don't judge "cheaters" too frequently. I recommend everyone read Dederer's book and then read *The Ethical Slut.*

Then just try and do better.

Go to therapy. Write letters to one another. Try and break down these walls between you.

Or don't. I didn't, and we all know how that turned out.

CHAPTER 10

HOP ON THE ROLLER COASTER WITH ME!

———

By January of 2016, I was starting to get the connection between my white privilege and my power in society. I had begun inserting myself in the public school system and exercising my power.

At this point, I still thought of myself as a superior "wok" feminist who rejects the sexist, racist patriarchal Rules of conservatives who pine for when "America was great (again)."

I thought I was one of the "nice white parents" who, in trying to help all of the poor Black families by making our neighborhood school *better,* was superior in using my privilege to *help.* I thought my noble intent was truly noble, while still blind to my own self-centered approach. I was overcome with feelings of guilt and shame when anyone tried to examine my actions critically.

I was anxious, suffering with high-functioning generalized anxiety I'd struggled with my entire life, and that increased dramatically after my daughter's birth in 2012. My anxiety was exacerbated by my spouse's job loss and slide into depression, our big move to Washington, DC in 2013, buying a house three times what we thought we could afford, hating a job I had formerly loved, and increasingly disconnecting from my beloved community because I had *everything I ever wanted*.

I had the progressive community, new friendships, a beautiful home, vacations, a healthy daughter, a good job, a husband who brought home a good paycheck and did the dishes and the laundry without complaint, money in the bank.... I had it all!

But my growing anxiety and his increasing depression were signs of deeper trouble. I didn't know what to do, and I didn't know who to tell. I was so ashamed that I was unhappy and afraid when everything appeared to be so picture-perfect.

I remember my mom telling me about the time my dad went out drinking with his friends for three nights straight while she cared for my colicky infant brother and little toddler me, alone.

She didn't know how to reach him. She was ashamed and afraid. She called her parents for help.

"You made your bed. Lay in it," my grandad told her. "You're an adult now, and we're not bailing you out of this."

When my dad returned, she handed over my brother and I and left.

"These are your kids, too," she said on her way out the door.

It worked. Things started to change. My parent's marriage was far from perfect, but my mom somehow stated her need, called my dad to the table, and he started to be more accountable to our family.

The lesson *I* took away from that story was, "Don't ask anyone for help. You signed the deal for the dollhouse, so you'd better not complain about it. Figure it out yourself." You can imagine that this was a terrible position to be in.

I started to turn to the self-help cycle. I went on Girls Weekends, I increased my drinking, and I read *Carry On, Warrior.* I had parties, playdates, and nights out every day of the week. I worked long hours, and when I wasn't working, I was training for a half-marathon, starting another side hustle, planning a trip, or compulsively cleaning the house.

I wanted to feel better, so I grasped at all the straws. Through this process, I started to see the superficiality of the self-help cycle but couldn't quite pinpoint its sinister nature.

When you're in a crisis, afraid, unsure, and struggling with mental health issues, these things are especially difficult to deal with.

Let's catch up on my personal midlife crisis journey and the hard lessons I learned next.

2016

SPRING LESSON: "SELF-CARE" DOESN'T TREAT ANXIETY

I took control of my persistent anxiety and found my one true love: Zoloft. I felt like the sun had risen on a new world I had never before known. High-functioning generalized anxiety disorder was its name, and Zoloft was its kryptonite.

Anxiety that represents in this way is difficult for other people to see. When you see a friend who is juggling a million things without breaking a sweat, what is inside of her is a machine stuck on high speed with no off switch. I would overschedule and overcommit and knew no other way.

I remember in May, at the lowest point, it was my spouse's birthday and somehow I had decided to deep clean the entire house the Friday of that week. I was in my rubber gloves degreasing the cabinets and scrubbing the baseboards. I had a ladder to wash the windows and dust the ceiling fan blades. I was frothing at the mouth, intent on spotlessness. I did this once a year, and why I picked his birthday weekend, I don't know.

He was livid. I didn't understand. Birthdays were no big deal, right? He was not mad about the birthday as much as he was mad about how every waking minute I am "on," channeling my superhuman strength and energy for yard sales, volunteering at the school, planning trips with friends, hosting family, creating parties for neighbors, shopping, cleaning, *doing*, and taking no time for him or for us.

I couldn't sit still without feeling existential dread. I could not relax without the day planned out from beginning to end. A weekend with nothing on the calendar made me nauseous.

When I explained the birthday fight to my dad, he said, "Girl, make a doctor's appointment right now. You are a mess. You are on the road to being bipolar or something." I don't think that's how bipolar disorder works, but if my dad thought I had it, I was worried.

Finally, by June 2016, I was feeling better than I had emotionally in my entire adult life. My parents came to visit, and my mom said, "Oh my God, can we write a thank you note to your doctor? You are *different*."

"Yeah, Mom," I said. "I'm happy. I'm relieved. I'm so grateful."

My doctor joked I should be the spokesperson for the drug, "I've never seen such immediate and dramatic results without side effects. It's really amazing, and I'm so happy for you," he said at my six-month check in.

But I felt ashamed, too, for being so miserable for so long and wasting so much time and energy. This is how healthy people feel, and I deserved to feel healthy. Why did I wait so long?

Nonetheless, I cried tears of joy multiple times a week. Thank you Zoloft and my excellent doctor.

SUMMER LESSONS: TOXIC MASCULINITY MAKES IT HARDER FOR MEN TO DEAL WITH MENTAL HEALTH ISSUES, AND ZOLOFT ISN'T A "CURE" FOR THE PAIN IN YOUR SOUL

In July, my husband told me he liked me "better the way I was before."

I was stunned. I cried and asked him, "Do you know how that feels for me? I have never felt better in my life, and you are telling me you prefer I suffer or I was more attractive to you while I was sick? I don't even know what to say except that makes me so sad."

Every year since my daughter was born, I would fly to Klamath Falls and spend a month with my parents. My spouse would come for two of the four weeks, and we would split the time with his parents, too. This particular July, we were all together the first two weeks, and then my husband flew back to DC while the kiddo and I stayed for an additional three.

Our last week of the trip, we always drove across Oregon to Idaho to see my brother and his family. The journey is ten hours and there is only cell service in the four or five small towns we pass through.

In the parking lot of McDonalds in Burns, Oregon (population: 2,783), an island of coverage between the next three cell-phone-free hours of our journey to Boise, I got a text from a friend.

"I don't know if you know, but my wife is fucking your husband."

I was stunned, again. I was stuck in the back of the car with a four-year-old trying frantically to keep my composure and reach my spouse. My mom and dad didn't understand why I was suddenly so rattled, and I didn't want to say anything until I knew more.

We got to Boise, and I locked myself in my brother's spare bedroom. I was unraveling and confused. In the hours I had to process, I recognized that my anger, grief, and surprise was mixed with this strange pride that my spouse had done something so ballsy. This was a man who told me if I *ever* cheated, it would be *over*, no questions asked. So, I never cheated.

Then he cheated on me, and Pandora's box was opened.

A couple of days later, my spouse and I had talked at length via phone, and he'd assured me it was "over" with the other woman. I told him I think I understood why he did it—getting caught up in the lust and thrill of an affair—and told him I could relate.

The next day, I called up a longtime flirtationship who happened to live in Idaho and put it on the line: "Hey, I have a unique opportunity to get drunk and screw your brains out because my husband just cheated on me. I think it would be fun, and then he and I will then be square."

It was fun.

My husband and I were not square.

I returned home from the summer trip a few days later, and we sat down to talk about "his fling."

I said, "So, now that you've done this, both broken your promise to me and had some wild and (hopefully) amazing sex with someone who isn't me, we need to start over. I feel like I understand this was a sign of something deeper going on with you and with us, and we need to figure that out, right?"

"Yes," he said.

"Also, now I want to have a pass. If an opportunity comes my way to do what you did, I want to," I said.

"That seems right," he said. "I would be a hypocrite if I said no."

"Okay, great," I said. "I already punched the card a couple of days ago, so we can just consider both of us on equal footing, a clean slate."

[Insert him imploding over the double-standard he was the owner of my body, and my sexual indiscretion was a million times worse than his because "someone fucked *his wife*."]

FALL LESSON: ISOLATION IN YOUR TRAUMA AND FEAR ARE A RECIPE FOR DISASTER

Once Pandora's box had been opened, I was seeing things through a new lens.

We got partly past our mutual flings. We started talking about marrying young, missed opportunities, and midlife crisis. There was an incredible moment when he opened up a bit and started reflecting on his own childhood, low self-worth, and insecurities.

I was optimistic we could have our cake and eat it too. I wanted more cake!

I was also embarrassed I'd been betrayed.

I was also worried he wouldn't get treatment or stop using alcohol to cope with his issues.

In October, I set down some serious conditions: he go to therapy, really dig into his intimacy and insecurity issues relating to his childhood trauma, and he had to stop drinking forty-eight cans of Bud Light every week.

He did none of those things.

In December, I sent him an email that ended, "If you don't do something to stop this cycle, you're going to ruin your life, and probably ruin our marriage."

He still did none of those things. I was so ashamed he wasn't taking me seriously after I'd come home, forgiven him, and was so naive to ever hope he would *change for me, for our daughter, for our marriage.*

I felt like he chose inaction and blaming over transformation and hard work. I felt like he didn't choose me.

I was so embarrassed I stayed with him and so afraid to leave. I didn't know who to turn to. I put on a brave face.

Things were *fine*. We would just have to find a creative solution. I could do that!

2017

2017 LESSON: YOU CAN'T "SELF-CARE" OR "IMPULSE BUY" YOUR WAY OUT OF TRAUMA

I went bonkers. I got a boob job. I wanted to buy a vacation property. I wanted to party all the time.

I was off my rocker. I was desperate to burn it all to the ground because (a) I had been cheated on, (b) I had cheated, (c) life could be different, and (d) *why wasn't my spouse actually doing anything I was begging him to do? Why wasn't he helping us move through this?*

I commenced with a series of flings with married men I met on Craigslist, eventually settling into a love affair that lasted for quite a long time.

People ask me, "Why didn't you just leave him?"

"Oh, really?" I think. "That would have been so smart! I should have just walked out on twenty years of building a life together with no job, no health insurance, no support network, and a lifetime of being told I have no reason to complain because, mostly, he's a good provider and holding up his end of the bargain."

People cheat for many, many reasons. I was coping with the codependency and isolation of my relationship.

It was unethical to cheat. I know and I acknowledge and own that. I hurt my spouse deeply, patronized him by thinking I could "save" the marriage by waiting him out, and continued to cash in on the things I needed for security while no longer tending to us as a partnership.

I know, now. I didn't know that in 2017.

I was in twice monthly, sometimes weekly therapy for nearly three years to figure it out. But way back in 2016, I only really knew I was a cheater, acting unethically, and should be deeply ashamed of myself.

It was destructive to have nowhere to go. I was burning it all down because I didn't have another set of tools at the time.

My husband hurt me, too. For those two years after he cheated, he was too caught up in his own isolation and depression to even *notice* I was splitting time between my daughter and my lover, while he was half-cocked on Bud Light listening to sports broadcasts every evening on the AM/FM radio in our garage.

He was coping with the codependency and isolation of our relationship, too. It was brutal on everyone.

2018

SPRING LESSON: WHEN THE TRUTH IS FINALLY REVEALED, THE RELEASE FROM CARRYING HEAVY LIES IS AMAZING

In February 2018, my husband picked up my phone and saw a text exchange I was having with my lover about where he should send his teenage daughter to high school. By this time, our relationship was distant, at best. He didn't bother me; I didn't bother him.

We went through the motions, but I was pretty much checked out. I spent almost every night in my daughter's bed or alone at my cottage just to keep distance. I don't know what my husband was thinking. I know he wanted sex. I know he was living in my house. But it honestly was a blur.

When he discovered the texts, he was livid. I was exhausted. Finally, it is in the open. Finally, we can start a dialogue.

I moved into the spare bedroom and slept on the floor. I asked him to move out, and he moved out in April. We were still going to therapy every week, but it was awful. I was scheduled to have a hysterectomy, and I remember him dropping me off at the hospital and I honestly wondered if he hoped I would just die during the procedure. I wouldn't have blamed him.

SUMMER LESSON: YOU ONLY LIVE ONCE, SO STOP WASTING TIME
It was so dark during the spring. I was binge drinking, still safe in the arms (and bed) of my lover when I could be, and was reeling and afraid. I started telling my parents and closest friends every sordid detail of my life, and somehow that felt better. I felt safer. I was excited to go home for my four weeks in Oregon and have my family ready to hold me close.

Then my uncle Jim died on the Fourth of July in 2018.

The sudden, unexpected, and truly devastating death of my uncle Jim was a massive wake-up call for me. After a few months of grief and time wasting, I started to study what Jim, who was my intellectual family yin, the artist and dreamer and thinker, believed about life, the universe, and everything.

I started by reading the books, understanding the Zen, doubling down on therapy, and meditation. Jim's death and the following month spent in his studio helped me start the second wave of transformation. The first was my marriage's head-on-collision with reality that got me into therapy. The second, Jim's passing, was the wake-up call I needed to explore my spirituality and life purpose *for real this time.* More on that later.

FALL LESSON: YOU CAN'T FORCE SOMEONE TO DO THEIR WORK

My husband asked me in therapy, "What do you *want?*"

I said, "I want to feel emotionally safe. Like when I ask you to choose me over Bud Light, you do it because it's important to me instead of trying to rationalize your way out of it or trying to gaslight me by telling me alcohol isn't the problem, *something else* is. Trying to convince me you'll work on that *something else* very, very soon. I want to feel like you're not holding the past against me or being passive aggressive. I want you to understand yourself so you can communicate with me clearly. I want to feel safe emotionally."

My husband said, "Emotionally safe? That's a bullshit answer."

The therapist tried to point out that my need for emotional security was legitimate, and by calling it bullshit, he was invalidating my needs. He was erasing my feelings and saying they were worthless.

He said, "She ruined my life. She made *me* feel unsafe and violated our trust by having an affair."

I said nothing.

I thought, "It's so much more complicated than your fling and my affair and your drinking. It's so much more about how we grew up and the Rules we have been following. It's so much more about the emptiness and distance growing between us for years, about anxiety and depression.

I realized he didn't understand what I meant when I said, "I want to feel emotionally safe," because he didn't get it. He thought it was bullshit.

He then said, "I want a divorce."

To me, throwing up his hands and giving up meant he didn't really *want* to get it. He didn't want to change or transform or do work.

I didn't know I really wanted a divorce until that very second, but then it was like, "Ah, ha! I've probably wanted a divorce for a very, very long time. I don't want to go back to the Rules of the patriarchy where we ignore our isolation and pain, choosing material comforts over emotional security. But didn't know that was even an option! Okay, I'm on board!"

I just wanted relief. I was so tired.

2019

2019 LESSON: UNDERSTANDING AND STATING YOUR NEEDS IS THE BEST WAY TO GET THOSE NEEDS MET AND FEEL SAFE, BUT THAT TAKES PRACTICE, SHAME RESILIENCE, AND ACCEPTING VULNERABILITY. IT'S ALL QUITE SCARY.

On Boxing Day 2019, I met a team of ragtag movers who carried my remaining worldly possessions from our lovely Capitol Hill row home into a shitty U-Haul and transported me to a new life as a "single mom" living in a fancy apartment building designed for Gen Z, with its floor-to-ceiling edgy industrial details, hallways that endlessly smell like last night's weed, and hordes of twenty-somethings carrying their cases of White Claw to the rooftop pool.

In 2019, I realized my time for being a bonkers, reckless, indulgent hedonist was over. I was lashing out at my lover. I was still drinking too much. I was going out too much. I was distracting myself with date nights and booze and networking events at open bars and anything to avoid taking the next hard step.

One night, I got drunk and picked the code of my lover's phone. I saw some emails he was sharing with other women, and my body was set ablaze. We had agreed to not being exclusive, but I was reeling because he was not being exclusive. I was still fresh off the trauma train of monogamy and thought I didn't want monogamy. But I didn't want to lose him, either.

What I realized that night and the next day was if I wanted to live a life of real intimacy, honesty, and professional and personal satisfaction, I needed to do the scariest things. I needed to do the things I was most afraid of.

I needed to think about what I *needed* and say it to the people I loved so they could decide for themselves if they could try and meet my needs.

I needed emotional security from my spouse, and when he told me "No, I think your needs are bullshit," it made it so easy to move toward divorce. Instead of hoping he would meet my needs in a vacuum and then being sad and depressed when he didn't, I identified and stated my needs and asked him to meet them.

He said no. It sucked. But I was no longer stuck in a cycle of hopelessness and pain.

With my lover, I needed monogamy, but was scared to ask him.

I wanted the stability of being in a committed relationship. I thought I was so post-monogamy, but I was not. I needed to know he would be there for me, and I promised to be there for him, too.

I asked him, after violating his privacy and acting like a child, and he said yes. It felt incredible.

Also, I needed to refocus. I needed to go back to my therapist and revisit this embarrassing, shameful violation of his privacy. I needed to revisit where jealousy comes from and reread *The Ethical Slut*. I needed to continue to heal and not stop my growth as a human just because I was in a romantic relationship. I needed to get better at stating my needs *sooner*.

So, I read *more* books, tripled down on the therapy, hired a business coach to help me take my career seriously, signed up for a seminar where I would write my own book, and slowed the fuck down.

I generally did not want to die the fiery death of a middle-aged woman who is acting like a teenage girl the first time she realizes her clit is the gateway to a magical new realm.

Yes, I've got a fairly decent body for being forty. Yes, I can pick up a multimillionaire in a fancy bar and fuck him senseless. Yes, I can sustain a long-term relationship with a man. I have very little left to prove when it comes to the power of my own pussy, so I went all-in on the "learning to state my needs and be vulnerable knowing someone might say 'Nope, you're not worth it'" department.

Okay, I feel like I've gone in this circle again and again. Fucking up. Falling down. Figuring it out.

I continued to take my life in stock like a person who has had a midlife crisis should, and realizing what a glorious, absurd, powerful, wonderful, joyful, delightful, and miraculous gift life really is.

Then my dad died.

CHAPTER 11

PANDEMIC
AT THE DISCO

At the end of August of 2019, by my calculations, I was more than halfway through ("Oh, please, God," I prayed, "let me be all the way through") my midlife reckoning, or midlife crisis, or whatever we're calling it. I knew menopause was still en route, so I was keeping my guard up. I had gone through the isolation and lashing out at the Rules of the Officer's Wives Club.

I had gone through the shame and guilt of realizing I hadn't actually changed much when I traded one set of Rules for a more nuanced set of "progressive" Rules in my lily-white, middle-class, progressive Capitol Hill bubble.

Meanwhile, I had blown up my marriage. I had felt the loss of privilege. I had learned to understand how to find meaningful help and connection through applying critical analysis to my self-care decisions. I had built a stronger beloved community.

But I still hadn't reckoned with my privilege fully just yet.

I had so much crisis and pain and transition and trauma,

and the patriarchy was telling me I didn't need to. All of that "stuff" about marriage and stress and infidelity and cancer and my uncle dying was so much—too much, fragile girl. You need more healing.

So in August 2019, I was all about the healing. I was doing the right sort of healing. Following my advice on "good guides" and rejecting toxic self-care. I was getting much better at stating my needs and being patient, empathetic, and curious.

I was in the flow of greatness and ready to write my awesome book about it.

By late November 2019, I was getting excited to welcome my family to DC to see my new apartment, my new happiness, and my new life.

It was an early Thanksgiving family trip with my mom, brother, niece, and cousin—our version of a nuclear family.

* * *

My dad, Papa, Jeffry Lee Gion, el jefe (or hefe as my mom spells it), or D as I called him (because D meant Dad, duh) was acting really fucked up on the journey, like he was drunk or something even though he was in a twelve-step program and was really committed to it.

In the Seattle airport and upon checking into the Airbnb in DC, he was loopy and complained of a headache. The entire first day they were in town, he stayed back in the Airbnb and just slept and slept. It was so unlike him.

The next morning, his symptoms hadn't changed. He was slurring his words and couldn't keep his balance. His headache had worsened, and yet his appetite was fine. We were alarmed. My cousin is an RN and was worried about sodium levels, ammonia levels, or something worse.

I volunteered to take him across town to the ER at Georgetown so my family, along with my daughter who wanted to spend time with her own cousin, could enjoy the city and their vacation. It was probably just a prescription drug interaction, one of many complications from D's many preexisting health conditions, we all thought. But it wasn't.

That afternoon, after five or six hours of waiting and chatting and reading, D was diagnosed with a brain tumor. Over the next three weeks, we waited. The tumor needed to come out, but preexisting conditions required his spleen to come out first.

They wanted to exhaust all other therapeutic options before the spleen removal. Drugs, platelet transfusions, different drugs, some spring thing in an artery somewhere. He was full of needles and holes. His brain tumor was growing and making him wacky. The ICU's endless commotion made it impossible to get good rest.

The Airbnb had long run out. My brother, niece, and cousin had to return to work, school, and work, respectively. My aunt and other cousin came to keep vigil with us as we waited and waited.

After a successful brain surgery on December 11, 2019, D was fine. The tumor was removed.

It worked. It all worked!

Just twenty-one days after diagnosis and three days after brain surgery, they sent D home with me to recover.

My mom, D, and I settled into in my one-bedroom apartment while my daughter stayed with her dad. We began our pharmacy dosing schedule, daily walks, breathing practice with that little contraption that makes your lungs strong, watching TV, complaining about politics, and scheduling follow-up appointments.

My mom had been in town for a month and needed to head back to Oregon for a couple of weeks to check in on their three dogs, two cats, two horses, and ten-acre property while D recovered.

After the first week, we were fully decorated for Christmas. D helped my daughter learn five-card draw. We watched *National Lampoon's Christmas Vacation* together.

Our morning routine included meds and D heading down to my swanky building's lobby to sit by the fire and drink coffee. In the afternoons, he would watch CNN and nap.

Every few hours or so, D would look at me and shake his head… "A brain tumor? Huh. Who has a brain tumor?"

The six-inch scar at the base of his skull right behind his right ear was pretty solid proof that he had, in fact, had brain surgery. We would chuckle. What the hell?

"I'm the luckiest guy in the world, I guess." he said. The tumor pathology report told us a week later it wasn't even cancer. It was a mass of rogue blood vessels growing in a ball. What the hell?

Things were mostly fine. There was this strange edema (swelling) in his guts from the splenectomy and the incision sites were gushing clear saline fluid all over my apartment, couch, bedding, and towels. So much laundry, but D was sleeping, walking more, thinking clearly, and recovering.

He played Clue with my seven-year-old and I on Christmas Eve. On Christmas morning, we opened presents, we ate turkey, and we did craft projects. He was eating meals, showering without help, sleeping better, leaking less, and tapering off of the steroids and pain killers.

He was going to be okay. Wow.

I went out on the eve of New Year's Eve to do some work

on a property I was preparing to sell, and called D for morning check-in.

"D, how's it going?" I asked.

"I…can't…breathe."

* * *

On January 18, 2020, my dad died.

I was so fortunate to be in bed beside him at Georgetown University Medical Center, my mom across from me, holding Dad's hand as we honored his very last breath. It was the most important moment of my life to date.

Midmorning on that winter Saturday, Papa's medical team had removed the ventilator keeping him alive as his mysterious breathing problems weren't resolving. He was on the verge of renal failure.

He had insisted, prior to intubation and sedation, that he was refusing additional intervention by machine beyond the ventilator (like the dialysis he would need soon to stay alive), if things led to that, which they had.

So, the tubes came out, most of the IVs were removed, the beeps stopped, the monitors were powered down, and the ventilator was turned off.

I climbed into bed beside him, breathing together and listening to the sounds of our heartbeats. My mom sat on the other side, holding his hand. She suggested music, so I pulled up his favorites: The Rolling Stones, Neil Young, Eric Clapton, the Beatles.

Four hours later, he exhaled for the last time during the final bars of Santana's soulful guitar instrumental in "Europa (Earth's Cry, Heaven's Smile)."

I'm not exaggerating.

Who could have known his last "vacation" would end like this?

I believe it was a miracle he was here, in DC, at Georgetown when all of it started. I believe it was an incredible gift I was given all of these minutes and hours to just be with him before that last moment.

If you believe as I do, that miracles are love in action, then this was nothing short of a true miracle.

Of course, it sounds so strange to say his coming to me to die was a miracle, but it was. I can't explain it. I am forever grateful for being able to be with him as he crossed over. The universe gave me a gift, and I am awed by it.

D was my rock, but not in the way many daughters describe their fathers. He was no hero in any grandiose sense. He was quiet, shy even. His intellect was masked by his camouflage baseball cap, bushy mustache, and big, bald dome.

I still hear him talking to me. As I write this, he says, "Thanks, H. I just did the best I could with what I had. Must've done a few things right. Not bad for a guy who didn't even graduate from Last Chance Community College."

He looked like any other Eastern Oregon dad with Wrangler jeans, a t-shirt with a screen-printed forest animal on it (he liked elk), a ball cap (always a ball cap), and that mustache. He drove one of the biggest pickup trucks Ford made—the F350 crew cab, long bed. He was a freight train conductor with a high school diploma and had lived in Klamath Falls, Oregon, all but one year of his 68.9 years on this Earth.

But people who really knew him understood the twinkling behind those ice blue eyeballs held something exceptional. D had a depth of understanding and seemingly endless patience for coping with, and allowing others to, experience what it means to be a human.

In other words, he didn't judge (much). He understood the value and sheer absurdity of life and offered grace to anyone willing to slow down long enough to hear him speak. His was a type of knowledge that didn't come from a book. He said it came from "life experience."

He sat quietly with that glint in his eye, ankle resting on his opposite knee, touching the corner of his mustache with his tongue when he was deep in thought, just listening. He listened a lot, and when he spoke the words came simply and layered in a type of dark humor and sage advice most couldn't process. So, he didn't speak to most. He spoke to few, and I can't even believe how lucky I am this man was my father.

When I was thirteen, he told me his life story on a series of road trips we made for ophthalmology visits I needed in Portland. He didn't edit it. It was about his stepdad and chain-smoking mom. His real dad opted out. He told stories about how no one ever went to his Pop Warner football games, about getting money for buying new patches for his jeans instead of getting new jeans, and about his parents not knowing (or caring) he couldn't read when he graduated high school in 1969.

He told me about parties, sex, driving fast, drunken nights, car crashes, and drugs. He told me about puppy love and being an asshole. He hitchhiked and got high. He worked and got fired. He was all the way into the 1970s stupidity and that mustache!

He didn't tell me stories to impress me. He didn't tell me in the tone of a parable or warning, like I should take away "lessons." He just offered an audiobook of what his life experience actually had been. I began to see him in context more, but he was still D.

When I was sixteen, dating my first high school boyfriend, he said, "I know you're not having any now, but you are going to love sex. It is an incredible thing people experience and is meant to be enjoyed."

"Dad! I don't want to talk about this! Ugh," I said, horrified.

"Oh, and one more thing: men are pigs."

When I was nothing, he was proud of me. When I'd barely made it off the bench of the big basketball game or couldn't figure out which college would make me happy or decided to hide from potential "success" to marry at twenty-four, he was proud of me. He cried when I went off to college. He cried more tears of joy at my wedding than I did.

"There is nothing you could ever do to make me stop loving you," he told me when I was too young to understand, too much of an angsty teenager to give a fuck, and again when I was too selfish to do anything but take him for granted. Then he said it again every single time I screwed up or was a jerk and yelled at Mom or got in an argument with my brother. His love was unconditional, and that is the truest form of love. There was nothing I could do—nothing—to make him stop loving me.

I still have a voicemail on my phone from 2018. I hope I never lose it.

His voice says, "H, this is your dad. The message is: I love you."

That's it. He left these kinds of messages all the time.

So, as life wore on and I began to do terrible things in this midlife crisis I was having, I forgot for a time that his words weren't empty.

I assumed, as so many people do, I was uniquely terrible

for having a husband who would cheat, for having a husband who wouldn't stop drinking despite how it was hurting our family, for having an affair, for being a slut, for risking "it all."

I was ashamed of who I had become and didn't think D would be all that supportive of this new fucked-up version of me.

"Of course, he said those things about love," I thought. *"Dads are required to say that shit."* I'd never called his bluff and didn't plan to.

When my spouse found the texts exposing my affair, two years after his own affair and after many years of trouble brewing, I called my dad.

I told him everything. I had so many tears. I was drowning in shame. There was so much I'd been hiding to protect the image of the perfect family made up of the perfect daughter who married the good man and had the perfect child. The perfect careers and financial success and that picket fence bullshit—it was all a lie. I was a liar, a cheater, shameful, a loser, and piece of shit.

"Well," he said, "Thank you for telling me. Before I say anything else, I want you to know two things. One, there is nothing you could ever do to make me stop loving you. Two, if [your spouse] ever lays a fucking finger on you, I will kill him."

He asked for time to think, and the next time we spoke he said, "I love you. This is an ending, and it's time to keep moving forward now. What do we need to do next?"

He was there for me every day, answering my calls after therapy, asking tough questions, offering support and time or money or love. He was there when the fights got horrible and when I got drunk and did destructive shit and when I just couldn't stop crying. He was there when I asked my spouse to leave. He was always there. He always answered when I called.

When he came to visit me, with my mom and cousin and brother and niece in tow for what should have been a lovely family gathering in DC in November 2019, our second day together we spent more than fourteen hours in the ER before they admitted him.

Finally, after rounds of tests and scans and blood draws and waiting, the doctor came in and said, "Blah, blah, blah... brain mass. Blah, blah, admitting you. Blah, blah, blah....."

"Fuck, what? Wait? Are you saying my dad has a brain tumor?" I interrupted.

"Well, yes. We need to learn more so we—" the doctor continued.

"Can I say something?" Dad interrupted.

"Of course," Dr. Emergency said, with concern.

"Does this mean you'll finally give me some pain meds? Because I have a goddamn headache over here."

* * *

The next few weeks were intense, but he was here with me, and I finally got to be there for him.

I understood things about his life and his heart. He wasn't afraid of dying, but the pain of a long, challenging life had dulled his joy. My mom called him maudlin, but he was just weary in body and soul.

In those final months, I believe he just was hanging on to see us through to some place where he knew we—my brother and mom and I—could fill his shoes. He knew it would take all three of us to do what he did alone as the hub of our family wheel, and his coming to DC was the sendoff moment. All of us together and him ready to pass the baton.

On January 18, my heart was crushed by an anvil of loss that still evokes a strong emotional reaction, even now. A part of my heart has been amputated.

When he died, I took care of my mom and she took care of me. I looked to my brother for support, and he called me to cry. I cleared my calendar. I doubled down on meditation, prioritization, self-care, and joy.

My dad and our story are critically important to fucking the patriarchy.

Men are half of the humans on this planet, and the importance of men in a woman's journey cannot be overstated. Men are our fathers, biological or otherwise. Men are our brothers. Men are humans, and we all need one another to be strong, healthy, and full of love for ourselves and our children for any of us to get through life with less trauma weighing down our backpacks.

We need good men. We need to raise good men. We can't rely on RBGs and Kamalas and Oprahs. We need men who view women as equal partners. We need men to be our allies, and we need to be theirs in return. To stop the cycle of toxic masculinity, we need to be a part of that solution, too.

We can't just be awed when one of them happens to cross our paths. D should be the rule, not the exception, and that is my point.

Fucking the patriarchy is about co-opting white male power into a matriarchal set of values which serve all of us.

Fucking the patriarchy is about owning our white men as our brothers and not saying the mass-shooter racist ones aren't "ours to begin with." They are.

Fucking the patriarchy is about owning our white women as our sisters, and not saying the Amy-Cooper Karen ones aren't "ours to being with." They are.

White men and white women need to dismantle toxic masculinity, dismantle the rules, stop hoarding our privilege, and stop being so fucking fragile about making mistakes. We're going to make mistakes. We are human.

We need to open ourselves up to love, empathy, compassion, humor, trust, and patience. We need to be brave, acknowledge our mistakes, and let our beloved community say to us, "There is nothing you could ever do to make me stop loving you...," even when you fuck up bigtime.

Through his loss, I absorbed a huge, traumatic lesson: D is no longer around to provide me unconditional love and support. I am the only person left who can do that for myself and my family. I must go all-in on loving myself so I can truly live.

I need to face the guilt head-on. I need to keep owning my mistakes. I need to be accountable and know in myself I will fuck up and the shame will not kill me, but the isolation might.

One weekend in late February, after taking his ashes home, spending a week in Oregon with family and friends, and hosting a lovely celebration of life, I was sitting in my apartment alone. My daughter was at her dad's place. I had signed up for a crazy book writing program I was weeks behind on. I grabbed my laptop and sat down and wrote seventeen thousand words in forty-eight hours.

I wrote the entire first half of this whatever-it-was book about stopping to smell the roses, finding higher purpose, reprioritizing everything, and taking true stock of what is essential and how to help. I wanted to fuck the patriarchy! I wanted to live more intentionally! I wanted to be someone I was proud of being!

D always told me I needed to write a book (quaintly, he still believed writing a book was some important and noble a way to fortune and fame). So, I did.

COVID-19 came, which delivered me the time to write it. The universe was saying, "Go, then. Practice what you preach, woman!"

To say I have now transformed into some selfless spiritual leader who has given up on the trappings of our material world would be a lie.

That's not practical and I don't have a messiah complex. I just had this journey. We are getting to the point where all of these stories start to come together, why this journey and its examination *matter,* and it does matter. Your story matters, too.

Now we'll begin the "work."

CHAPTER 12

SO, YOU WANT
A CHECKLIST?

———

My marriage ended, and I was forced through the loss of my security blanket and life partner to understand I was capable, resourceful, independent, and didn't *need* that toxic deal for security that compromises joy. I was able to rise in a new way of being ethical about my body, goals, values, vision, and heart. I could try, for real, to have intimacy and career success and financial independence.

My uncle died, and I was forced through the loss of one intellectual and spiritual guide to become my own intellectual and spiritual leader. I was able to rise in a new way of being spiritual, mindful, patient, and joyous about my time, attention, beliefs, faith, and creativity. I could try, for real, to know my soul and care for it so I could care better for others.

My dad died, and I was forced through the loss of that emotional and unconditional love so I could become my own emotional support foundation and be the provider of unconditional love in my own beloved community. I was able to strengthen in a new way of being radically transparent by sharing my truth and knowing the people who see me will help protect me. But, ultimately, it is up to me to keep being true and keep loving fearlessly.

I'm the only one who has to sleep at night with my decisions, and I am determined to make myself, my father, and my daughter proud.

The catharsis and healing of transforming these years of trauma and feelings into a form to pass on has been more about me than it has been about the book I planned to write.

As I've expanded my own learning through introspection, study, and discussion, one thing always comes to the surface: everyone needs to stop for a minute and study their ancestry, understand their own story, and find what grounds them.

The way I have been framing my own journey is based on the work of EbonyJanice Moore, an educator and founder of The Free People Project.

Moore is a womanist scholar, author, and activist. In her writing, media, and workshop series, Moore teaches the importance of taking the time as individuals to study our ancestry (i.e., the history of our people and their relationship with power) and our lived experience (i.e., your life story full of traumas, abilities, privileges, social pressures, etc.).[51]

Again, for emphasis, the very first step in transformation from something to something else is deeply understanding the thing you currently *are* before you start doing anything with it. First become an expert on your entire self.

Oh, I hear the excuses already, "I don't have time to write a memoir. Studying? I don't want to study; I want to *do something* to fight for social justice and rid our lives of sexism."

---

[51] EbonyJanice Moore, "White Urgency Is Violence." July 22, 2019. Online lecture. Produced by The Free People Project.

Don't take it from me, listen to EbonyJanice Moore. Listen to Maya Angelou, who said, "No man can know where he is going unless he knows exactly where he has been and exactly how he arrived at his present place."[52]

So, I shouldn't be jealous of Claire Dederer or Elizabeth Gilbert. I am instead grateful they, too, have been brave enough to study their history and write about their lives, so I was given an opportunity to learn from them as I write my own memoir and add to the collective story of humanity.

But putting this radical transparency, grace-giving, empathetic, spiritual theory into *practice* in daily life is an entirely different story.

EbonyJanice Moore teaches once we have built up expertise about ourselves, we know who we are, we understand the nuanced and complicated history of our ancestors, and we have dedicated time to learning about our trade or craft from texts, artists, mentors, and lived experience, we then need to develop:

- a Theory of what we believe to be true
- an Ethic of what we believe to be right, and
- then continually take action from a place where the Theory and Ethic turn into a *life being lived.*

EbonyJanice Moore calls that the Praxis.[53]

The Praxis is the answer to the questions: what do we *do* about our fucked-up marriages? What do we *do* about our secrets? What do we *do* about our privilege? What *do* we do to help save Black lives?

---

52 Maya Angelou, "'For Years, We Hated Ourselves,'" New York Times, April 16, 1972.

53 EbonyJanice Moore, "White Urgency Is Violence." July 22, 2019. Online lecture. Produced by The Free People Project.

Our Theory about sexism is it must end because men and womxn are truly equal. Our Ethic is sexism is wrong because it hurts womxn. But then our Praxis is often patronizing our spouses, not telling them the truth about our own pain, hiding things, compromising, and remaining afraid and paralyzed. We engage our privilege to ignore and evade, justifying our unwillingness to take the first, necessary step in transforming our personal lives.

We opt out of our responsibilities as equal partners to understand and state our needs so our equal partner can respond in kind.

Our Theory about racism is it must end, and humans are truly equal. Our Ethic is racism is immoral and violent. But then our Praxis is often mindlessly using our power, time, money, and access to powerful people in self-indulgent or mindless ways.

We self-care and go shopping. We read books and watch shows written and made by people who look like us about things that resonate with us. We live in places that don't challenge us and engage in communities that don't represent the world as it is.

We opt out of ending racism because we are uncomfortable. We are unwilling to build resilience to shame and are afraid to lose privilege because it sucks to lose privilege. We justify our passivity because we're so busy or *our children deserve the best we can provide.*

White women do not want to *start* with changing our ways of being in the world because that's scary and uncomfortable.

We want to start with checking items off of a checklist. We want to start with marching on the mall, donating to candidates, lecturing our friends and family. We are urgent in our desire to end sexism and racism, and that urgency is making things worse.

White urgency to *do something* to end racism is violence, according to EbonyJanice Moore. She said something along the lines of, "We are not on this two-hour webinar and going to end racism. It doesn't work that way."[54]

Moore's words were the first time an educator connected the dots for me between the self-help cycle and white female privilege.

White people are urgent. White people are indoctrinated in a patriarchal system where "producing results," being productive, succeeding at something, winning, and competition are valued.

We want to jump in and work hard and are so used to "quick fixes" that we demand them. We call the manager. We cry. When we don't get what we want, we find a different quick fix to try.

As I've delved deep into learning about intersections of classism, feminism, white privilege, and racism, every expert I've encountered says the same thing in myriad ways: deconstructing the patriarchy starts with looking inside of your heart and soul. It's the only place to start, and anything you do without starting there is at risk of being ineffective, hurtful, or violent.

I ask my friends if they take time to read. Do they go to therapy? Have they thought about journaling? Have they thought about their parents in context? Do they know where they came from? Do they have a women's discussion circle or scheduled time to reflect? Have they identified their ten-year goals or their core values? Do they know what grounds

---

54 Ibid.

them, feeds their souls, delights them, protects them, and gives them joy?

Hardly ever do I get a "yes."

I often hear my friends say, "I should…say 'no' more, stop the madness, slow down." Or they say, "I know, but…my guilt, my boss, my husband." Or they say, "Well, it's not a good time. I have too much to do." Or they claim, "I've got my life figured out, I just need to be more organized." Or they give excuses like, "I can't blame everything on my parents."

There are a thousand other deflections that avoid getting to the deepest, darkest, scariest questions of all: who am I? How did I get here? What do I want from this life? What story am I a part of that is making this world better? Am I happy? Am I hurting others?

STEP 1: SOLEMN ACKNOWLEDGMENT

The first thing I learned from all of my mentors and hours of study is the first step in breaking out of our white lady paralysis and the toxic self-help cycle that feeds it is simply solemn acknowledgment.

Stop everything.

Maybe you can't stop for months, like we did during the 2020 quarantine, but stop. Stop doing, fixing, and being busy for the sake of busy. Do a quick look back on what you *did do* and give some things up. Stop giving your time and energy to things unworthy of your time and energy. Close out the world and acknowledge you have this privilege to pause. It is a gift.

As you pause, accept that the world simply *is*, in all of its messiness. Accept you are not perfect and give yourself a huge hug. See your white guilt or your mom guilt or your wife guilt or your messy affair, half-assed career, bullshit shame. Let it go.

As you hug yourself, literally wrap your arms around your body and breathe.

For me it took forty-eight hours of reading, walking in circles, podcasts, research, note taking, and barfing out stories that did not make any sense at first to process all of the shame and guilt of my trauma and losses.

The universe gave me permission to stop in my tracks, and simultaneously the world gave me *privilege* to stop in my tracks. The time and ability to take time is a privilege, and I stopped and honored that privilege, and then began to study my history.

In that moment of solemn acknowledgment, I allowed myself to see the big problems compressing my soul, from class to race to sexism to climate change, are simply so far beyond anything I will ever be able to change alone in my individual lifetime with my individual actions and intentions.

That's okay.

No one is going to end racism in a webinar. No one is going to protect our children from heartbreak, illness, or going broke by endless viola lessons and weekend Chinese language classes. We aren't making heart friends if we're stacking pedicures and picnics back-to-back without a moment to *see* one another. We aren't able to find intimacy if we aren't radically transparent about ourselves. We need to believe in the strength and resilience of our children, and not wrap them in generational privilege.

So just take a breath, make an inappropriate joke because of the absurd miracle that this all is, and be okay with our small place in this giant, magnificent universe.

Now don't be overwhelmed by your smallness. Don't be cowed by guilt. We don't want to trigger paralysis. We will not let the patriarchal forces push us back and encourage us to hide behind our privilege. But we do need to just *be* with our smallness and get comfortable with it.

It's not until we're centered and educated in our history and lived experience that we can say to ourselves, "Now, finally, it's time to keep moving forward. What do we need to do next?"

CHAPTER 13

WHY DOES EVERYONE WANT TO MOVE TO A TROPICAL FUCKING ISLAND?

It's so easy for me to look at people like Glennon Doyle and Claire Dederer and think, "She has it all figured out. If I just do what she did—sell my business, buy an old house, set up an art gallery—I'll live happily ever after, too!"

Wrong.

It's the old-fashioned appeal of the (formerly-known-as Dixie) Chicks and their "Wide Open Spaces" dream of our youth, or the same Chicks and their "Goodbye, Earl" jams and jelly commune of our midlife crisis.

We think if we win the lottery or get the kids off to college or get through this school year or save up a little more money, then we will cast off the chains of this existence and backpack through Asia to find our highest joy.

You are wrong again.

Most of us plod along following the herd, pissing away time, resting on the laurels of our own privilege, and romanticizing a future where we will move with our best girlfriends to a compound in Vermont and raise honeybees while our children build treehouses in the woods.

Or, if we're being especially irritating, we muse about selling everything we own and running away to a palmy, balmy, island paradise. Some of us actually do just that.

Ash Ambirge did it twice.

Elizabeth Gilbert did it. In fact, she met her husband in Bali!

Tropical islands are the ultimate in escapism fantasy, but not unlike binge watching *Letterkenny* or pounding a few bottles of wine each night, those fantasies are ultimately unproductive and likely a form of coping with those big, scary questions of life: who am I? What do I want from this life? What story am I a part of that is making this world better? Am I happy? Am I hurting others?

I would know how escaping—whether geographically, emotionally, changing jobs, changing friends, diving into new hobbies, compulsive dating, binge crafting—does not work. I'm an expert escape artist.

Between 1998 and 2013, I escaped around twelve times. I went to three universities in three years. I spent 1998 at Willamette University in Salem, Oregon (too small), 1999 at the University of Massachusetts at Amherst (too expensive and big), and 2001 through 2002 at the University of Oregon in Eugene, Oregon (just right, I guess).

In 2002, I landed a competitive internship at the University of Florida Athletic Association. I drove my '91 Mercury Tracer with no A/C across the United States, Chicks blaring, and launched my career with the Florida Gators. But as my internship ended, I didn't end up launching that career.

I sputtered.

Instead of applying for jobs or grad school, I moved to the Florida panhandle to escape from the fear of failing at having my own career. I sat in the sun all day every day for three months drinking beer and reading books. My fiancé was training at Naval Air Station Pensacola and he had a beach condo! I was going to get married next year, anyway. Why did I need to do something so ridiculous as try (and probably fail) at a career, anyway? Or so my thinking went.

In 2004, I married into the military and became a dependent.

Every time I felt the walls closing in on the anxiety I had about life, whether it was my crazy boss at my job in Boise, Idaho, or my fears about my spouse's drinking, or my feelings of inadequacy and anxiety because our sex life was dwindling, I practically ran toward the next change of station—Idaho, a stop in Texas, England, North Carolina, and finally, Washington, DC.

I was pushed to escape through consumption. I had the privilege to escape and start fresh. Go West, young woman! Get Lasik, take off your braces, cut your hair, and the high school quarterback will take you to prom! It's the American way, right?

Rachel Hollis's website reads like a table of contents for a hopelessly sexist 1950s issue of *Seventeen Magazine*: fashion, style, recipes, self, career, beauty. It's the same old scam Slim Fast and Summer's Eve douche where companies try to profit from our shame, insecurity, and despair by selling us quick fixes and easy escapes.

By harnessing my own escape talents, I was continually distracted through my list of hopelessly futile consumable attempts to satisfy my needs. Instead of "style" and "career," I was addicted to being caught up in the whirlwind of change, the details of choosing and furnishing a new home, traveling to exotic places, and getting away from people who might uncover my secret emptiness.

I was addicted to being busy, escaping in home renovation or compulsive gardening or travel planning. Some of it made me very satisfied. I am a creator of things and stories, so being "busy" is my most relaxed state.

But like alcoholism or porn addiction, the levels of "busy" distraction needed to be more intense and dramatic to keep me moving.

Eventually it was baby-making time, the ultimate reason to not put myself first. It is then I truly became a servant to the family unit. The idea I should—or even could—stop and decide whether I was living a life I truly loved was locked away in a little pressure cooker inside my soul because now we have to "think about the children first."

We have developed chemical and habitual addictions to escapism and quick fixes. Shopping or planning a vacation can literally infuse us with dopamine; it feels great. Or we drink or smoke weed to numb the fear.

The desert island utopia is our brains telling us we crave the slow breeze of the palms, the lapping of the waves, the warm sand under our feet, nowhere to be, and a cool coconut drink. Our brain is screaming at us, "slow down, relax, I need this, I am in pain, I am maxed out, *help me*," which freaks us the fuck out, so we ignore the warning. We put real "self-care" on the fantasy shelf off and go do something superficial and toxic instead.

What I learned, obviously, is there is no physical escape and there is very little emotional escape without stopping everything. Solemn acknowledgment requires a good, long look at what we're running from.

What Ash and Elizabeth Gilbert did was geographically "escape," it's true. But they also appeared to do the hard part, too. The proof is their "escapes" just become backdrops for the art they've created with their lives as they transformed that work into *The Middle Finger Project* and *Eat, Pray, Love.*

The really hard part isn't quitting your job and getting a new one to refresh. It isn't filling your calendar to the max so you can stay busy. It isn't putting $100,000 into your home renovation as you keep telling yourself after you have a perfect living room it will become the setting for amazing, intimate dinner parties to connect.

No. The really hard part is drilling down into your own mortality and seeking pathways leading directly to your highest joy while also helping others, too, every day for the rest of your life.

If you just escape by having another baby or moving to a penthouse in Chicago, you'll soon realize your new nursery or skyscraper utopia is still furnished with all the shit-filled baggage from the storage unit of your past. You can take it will you. In fact, you can't leave it behind until you do the work to burn it up and start again.

The problem is capitalism doesn't want us to do that kind of work. They entice us and tease us with quick fixes and superficial, feel-good moments.

Rachel Hollis' and the sinister crew offer a form of "self-actualization" based on a commodified shame-driven "tropical island escape" message that does more to reinforce your own misery than help you get to the bottom of it.

The entire point of Hollis and the rest and their toxic corporate feminism is to never truly help you leave the sales pipeline, but to send you on mini-escapes through makeup, weight loss, a patio project, a bit of moxie, and better orgasms (with a few dollops of "very serious topics" like politics or faith).

The tricky part is when you find yourself among legions of other women, alongside Lindy West at the Goop Health conference or spending a weekend in Charleston boozing over a seafood tower, you do actually feel good in this community (often temporarily, like halfway through that bottle of pinot grigio or when I was able to photograph my perfectly decorated North Carolina McMansion and share it on Facebook).

People like Rachel Hollis are really fucking good at selling escapism and healthy "escapes" are a real part of self-care, but that doesn't mean what they're selling or what you're buying is actually is good for you.

What is actually really good for you is a transformational shift in how you see yourself, how you heal yourself, how you honor yourself with appropriate indulgences, and how you help others, too.

How?

You need to define and create your own happiness. A balanced recipe of introspection, study, learning, creating, connecting, conversation, and then "doing."

Maybe you truly, deeply want to grow vegetables in Vermont. Good for you! But this isn't because you want Rachel Hollis's life, it's because you love the soil in your hands and need that awful backache you get from pulling weeds to help you feel alive.

You need to define and create your own happiness, and the only way to do that is figure out what really makes you happy in a deliberate and patient way.

The first step was solemn acknowledgment, right? We have to ponder it, mull it over, and sit with discomfort awhile. Process it through writing or reading.

The good news is we don't have to ponder it alone.

There are so many people offering to help you figure it out! Like Gretchen Rubin's *The Happiness Project* or this book right here! Lucky you! Remember back in the eighth chapter where we parsed through all the different sorts of women-brands standing at the ready to whisk you away into your magical, new, actualized future?

Now it's time to use that checklist to help you choose the right guides.

STEP 2: COMMIT TO CRITICALLY EVALUATING YOUR GUIDES

ASSESSMENT OF WHERE WE INVEST OUR MONEY

In this fucked up world of womxn selling "empowerment and happiness" to other, more desperate women, we have to be able to decipher the sinister from the sisterly. My checklist about how to choose "a brand" to purchase from, back in the ninth chapter, gives us a good starting place.

A brand is defined by being a company or entity that is not a single human being. It has been incorporated, likely, and may have employees, surrogates, contractors, marketing support teams, products, and multiple people making decisions.

Brands may be for profit or nonprofit. When you're purchasing from a for-profit brand, you are giving them money in exchange for goods and services. They really want your money. Some brands will do anything to get it, like lie to you.

We know this, right? But then why don't we look at a brand like Landmark or Rachel Hollis or Brené Brown more critically?

Do they deserve our money?

Just so you don't have to flip back in the book, here are the elements we should look for when choosing brands to purchase from:

1. A product offering that is clear and will deliver on its stated promise
2. A brand behind the product that is clear about its values and operations
3. A person behind the brand who is transparent, accountable, and actively engaged in conversations that advance social justice, equality, and humanism
4. A reputation that supports that person via a diverse and equitable representation of critics and fans who hold them accountable to their values
5. A belief system that pays respect to and cites the ancestors, thinkers, philosophers, artists, leaders, and mentors that inspired *their* work and were critical to helping them along the road to success.

Humans learn through storytelling and making emotional and physical connections with ideas that help rewire our brains. Marketing teams know this and they leverage this to trigger our emotions so we believe their brands care about *us*. Sometimes they do, sometimes they don't. But it's up to us to be critical and keep our guards up. Don't get lazy. Don't fall back on your privilege.

But not everyone is "a brand." Sometimes we are looking for a friend or a therapist. Sometimes we are looking for a book to read or a movie to watch. Sometimes we want to buy a painting or go to a museum. Sometimes we need $15 lavender soap because we are sad. Sometimes we want to simply be inspired.

ASSESSMENT OF WHERE WE FIND OUR INSPIRATION

Guides are all around us. Sometimes they are brands. Sometimes they are friends. Sometimes they are artists, doctors, legislators, historical figures, deities.

Good guides inspire ideas that bring out our "inner child," spark creativity, engage wonder, tap into our joy, and connect us with our own humanity. Good guides challenge us, startle us, surprise us, or bring perspectives we haven't even considered before.

Bad guides are pointing us toward toxic shame, fear, and isolation.

We cannot only be critical about what "brands" we follow for recipes and silk pajamas; we also need to be critical of the sources and context of the ideas and beliefs we are weaving into our Theory, Ethic, and Praxis.

Sometimes we learn from people who are deep in despair or pain, as they can mirror for us what that looks like for them. Inspiration often comes without offering a solution or a lesson.

I would argue Rachel Hollis has been a guide for me throughout this process. As I built my criteria for consumers and what we deserve, she missed the mark. As I built my criteria for the guides I would choose and how I would choose them, she shows me what misses the mark.

But people who miss the mark are often just as important as those who hit it.

Often, we just get a picture or a perspective from our guides. Often that picture or perspective is complicated or ugly. Was Picasso a rapist? Was Hemingway a depressed, bipolar alcoholic? Was Dr. Martin Luther King, Jr. an adulterer? Was Jefferson a slaveowner? Was Rachel Hollis a big, fat liar?

Those questions need to be debated. We need to juggle the contribution of the art with the reality of the artist. We need to hold these two things at the same time and decide *for ourselves,* based on our values.

As we seek our inspiration, we deserve:

1. A message that resonates with us, delivering on its stated promise to connect with our hearts.
2. A messenger behind the message who is vulnerable and brave.
3. A messenger behind the message who is accountable to her critics, who has dedicated time to learning from other experts, and is actively engaged in conversations advancing social justice, equality, and humanism.
4. A messenger behind the message who is behaving in the world in a way that demonstrates she is practicing her values, not just espousing them. She conducts herself in a way that allows her audience to hear values in practice. She is accountable to what she creates and puts out into the world and to the violence it may have caused.
5. A belief system behind the messenger that respects and cites her ancestors and the thinkers, philosophers, artists, leaders, mentors, and critics who inspire her work and have been integral to helping her along her journey.

When we get to the third item on that list above, it often falls apart. It doesn't mean it invalidates the creator or the inspiration, but it does ask for further critique, analysis, and a decision on how to move forward. Do you still watch

Roman Polanski movies? Do you still listen to Michael Jackson albums? Do you still visit Monticello?

I don't know. Do you?

You are the only person who has to live with your decisions on what you buy and who you follow. I'm just asking you to make thoughtful, critical choices.

GIVING YOURSELF PERMISSION TO PARTY IT UP!

Sometimes we want to indulge.

That is totally fine, too. It's encouraged, even.

We can both be critical about where our self-care, our consumable goods, our inspiration, and our ideas come from and also be indulgent, decadent, and be a bit of a selfish prick now and again.

It's not that a tropical escape is wrong. It's just not *enough*.

I mean, right now in October 2020, I've finally fulfilled my own dreams of living in a little urban commune with my best friends on Main Street, picking out dazzling quartz countertops and planning my big backyard garden. I am happy. I feel healed. I spend 1,000 percent more time and energy on meaningful issues I care deeply about because I have the time and heart to lean into "the work" with joy.

The point I'm trying to hammer home here is toxic feminism sells us solutions that are too small, too escapist, too untethered to reality. Privilege allows us to spend, spend, spend and discourages us from critical analysis, hard questions, and holding ourselves accountable.

When I stopped my toxic cycle of self-care and started to explore ideas instead of consuming experiences and objects, I found what really brings me joy and meaning.

Sometimes that joy and meaning is spending a week in Cancun at an all-inclusive resort with a best friend as part of our now annual "Our Lives are Awesome and So Deeply Fucking Raw" conference.

Seeking guidance and taking time to know yourself, defining your happiness, and opening up your heart to loving the gifts you've been given is work.

We've been too fucking lazy to do the work. We've been too safe and healthy to really own and give thanks for how lucky we are. We've been too fragile to name our privilege and ask for help. We've been too dazzled and manipulated by toxic capitalist bullshit and cheap thrills on sale at Walmart.

That is our privilege as middle-class white people. That is part of why everyone around us who has less privilege is so fucking pissed off at us. We wander around guilty and trigger our tears or excuses when called out for being "bad."

When we get a little bit "woke," we can be righteous and angry, suddenly wanting to *fix everything right now* so we can absolve ourselves of the guilt and move out of paralysis.

I certainly was pissed off at all of my married white friends after my class. It seemed like all the married couples got everything—the opportunities to be entrepreneurs, the security, the family vacations. People stopped inviting me over for dinner parties or for weekends at the shore because I didn't have a plus-one, and I was having a tantrum.

When I stopped the tantrum and went back to solemn acknowledgment of my privilege and my life, starting to explore new and different guides to teach me, I started to see my tantrum wasn't helping. But I also started to see the bigger picture.

I realized being a woman was a gateway to understanding the centuries-old pain and frustration of being BIPOC, Queer, an older person, a person with disabilities, or a person in crisis in a world built and designed based on Euro-centric, patriarchal values from the fucking Middle Ages.

The American ideal *is* white culture. Even if we say it's not about skin color, we code it. People who buy into hard work, production, competition, and capitalism are true Americans.

People who go to our good schools and get high scores on our standardized tests and jump through our impossible hoops are successful. People who act, dress, speak, dine, and dance "properly" are cultured and sophisticated.

Just look at how we treated Ebonics as a nuanced linguistic manifestation of Black urban culture. It's considered "less than" for no other reason but white people said so.

By just accepting labels like white, middle-class, heterosexual, cis, and academic (to name a few) are not necessarily anything special, you're getting somewhere.

It's just a legacy of our past, and it's deeply fucked up in some spots. If we deny it is fucked up, or we don't even see it's a construct of history and not any sort of special divine creation bestowed on us by European colonialism, then we can finally critically assess that, too, and we can finally change it.

It's not personal when I say you've been sexist or racist or able-ist or privileged. It just is the truth.

Stop being such a snowflake about it and start studying the truth. They say it will set you free.

When you finally feel liberation, you gain capacity for more empathy and love. When you have that, you want to wake up and fight to make life better for you and for the world.

Yes, have your trip to Bali if you have the privilege and monet to take a trip to Bali. Yes, decorate your home with new throw pillows.

There is nothing wrong with the happiness that brings. But don't stop there.

When you're sitting in the hammock on the beach, listen to an EbonyJanice Moore lecture as she teaches us accepting and thanking our privilege is necessary, loving others is liberation, love has a purpose, action should be deeply personal, and the work to end racism as grounded in joy.

What could be more joyful than ending racism on Earth? Nothing. That feels great, especially with the sand between your toes and a cold drink in your hand.

The list is forever long of those who have shown me life in the form of art or art in the form of true living. They all share the same values: introspection, curiosity, empathy, tenderness, and humanity.

Those values are the matriarchy, and you don't need to apply to join. You just need to join.

I am a words person, obviously, so I took myself on this journey through books, writing, and talking. But the feelings of wonder and joy and intense emotion and empathy can be found from so many guides. Find them, stay there as long as possible, and take notes.

Then we can move closer to taking action.

CHAPTER 14

ASPIRE TO BE AN ELEPHANT

———

One of my favorite guides, Brené Brown, is a writer, speaker, podcaster, with a PhD and multiple bestselling books and two jobs in higher education (UT-Houston, UT-Austin).

She has pretty much one drum she beats over and we must dig down into the feelings of shame and vulnerability and sit there, stay there, to become grounded in empathy for ourselves. It is here we find our courage to act with empathy and grace in our lives, where we are able to follow our highest joy and be a helper of others on their own journeys.

Brown is not selling a DIY avocado hair mask, but she is a brand.

The fundamental difference between the sinister and the sisterly when brands and personalities approach the attainment of individual happiness is centered on empathy, grace, patience, and persistence. Those steps we identified in our last chapter are our tools for investigating whether this brand is worth our time and attention.

Empathy and grace are not calligraphy infographics on their website, but a deep exploration of the *feeling and practice* of empathy. It's not just grace in the abstract or the Bible definition I don't really understand, but *grace* as goodwill and forgiveness for yourself and for others as we fuck up.

STEP 3: DIG YOUR HEELS IN ON THE MATRIARCHAL VALUES

What the checklists from the thirteenth chapter do is help us identify the stated values of a brand and see if their actions mirror those values.

Brené Brown offers a paid training course called Dare to Lead. It meets the criteria of the checklist in that she offers a clear service with defined results, she has stated values, she has expertise, and she is transparent about how she engages with and chooses sponsors.

The next step in our journey to make this process run quickly is to really define our own values so we can recognize them in the brands and guides (and friends, employers, etc.) we choose to include in our beloved community and our community of practice.

When speaking of "matriarchal values," I'm not harkening back to a modern-day application of a likely mythical, whitewashed "ancient civilizations" with female-led tribes. In my reading, matriarchal values are not gendered, and they are not necessarily tied to anything that has existed perfectly in human society before.

They are abstract ideals. The matriarchal values are not exactly opposite of patriarchal ones, either.

Patriarchal values have been dominant in our society since its inception. While we shouldn't seek to eliminate them, we do need to put them in the back seat. These patriarchal values of strength, power, survival of the fittest, competitiveness, stockpiling wealth, extreme individuality, and exceptionalism need to be turned down to level one intensity.

Matriarchal values need to be amplified to the maximum power.

My favorite definition of "the matriarchy" is from a 2018 article in *The Independent* that summed it up thusly:

Patriarchy: power over others.
Matriarchy: power from within.[55]

Power from within is the acceptance and continual practice of the eternal hard truth that each one of us is brave and worthy of love and belonging. This is one of Brené Brown's go-to phrases. Brave is taking a risk. Worthy of love is, when it all falls apart, not letting the failure and the shame define you.

When we believe we are worthy of love, we say "I failed" instead of "I'm a failure."

Worthy of belonging is bravely taking the risk of loving yourself, loving others, and accepting that everyone deserves love.

In *The Independent* article, the ultimate example of matriarchy is elephants, a species that chooses their (female) leaders because of their accumulation of wise, instinctive, and collaborative decisions over time.

"Through the years, older females become repositories: of social and ecological knowledge. So, natural leadership qualities and long experience combined are the makings of a wise matriarch."[56]

---

55 Harriet Marsden, "International Women's Day: What Are Matriarchies, and Where Are They Now?" Independent, March 8, 2018.
56 Ibid.

Now where can we find a group of older females with lots of life experience in different environments?

Oh, wait, it is us.

We are experienced, stressed out, middle-aged moms.

We are reevaluating our life path, the meaning of it, and whether what we were raised to believe, do, and feel is actually what we want.

We have found some guides, friends, and teachers.

We have chosen to learn about ourselves.

We learned we are awesome. We are brave. We are worthy.

We may not feel like we're going to be the next Brené Brown, but we are going to be better mothers, friends, spouses, partners, workers, artists, thinkers, and lovers.

Once we start to feel amazing, we feel powerful, we look outside of ourselves, and suddenly, we can serve others with joy.

Welcome wise, collaborative matriarchs ready to shake some shit up.

HOW DO WE DEFINE OUR MATRIARCHY SUPERPOWERS?

There are so many guides for this; go back to the second step in chapter thirteen.

Then start writing down your values.

As I look to build my own business and my own brand of marketing consultancy, one of the most concise examples of the matriarchal values I came across for entrepreneurs and business owners was at Sister.is, a consulting firm focused on helping people "birth" businesses based on matriarchal values.

To be perfectly honest, I was writing on a stupid deadline (imposed by the Gods of writing seminars that helped me plow through this crazy project), so it was late in the game when I came upon Sister.is.

The founder and lead consultant, Jennifer Armbrust, is promoting her feminist business school and related principles to entrepreneurs and executives who genuinely give a crap about people, and value empathy and humanity. She is a brand offering a clear service with stated values she appears to live by.

I didn't get a chance to talk to Jennifer, but I did buy her book Proposals for the Feminine Economy and was dazzled with its simplicity.

Thank you, universe! I don't have to invent Proposals for the Feminine Economy! Thank you, Jennifer Armbrust.

If you are living in the capitalist economy under a patriarchal set of cultural values and it's hard for you to figure out how to navigate, buy her book right now. In it, she outlines the "12 Steps" for applying the matriarchal values to your capitalist context. It's the Twelve Commandments of my life at the moment.

Armbrust's "12 Proposals for the Feminine Economy" are the cliff's notes to my own book. From her to Brené Brown to EbonyJanice Moore, we are getting beaten over the head with the same things in different ways. [57]

To feel healed, you need to stop and tend to it in a meaningful way. To understand something outside of us, we must understand ourselves really well, first. To change the world, you must be able to act in actions guided by a healed heart and grounded in matriarchal values, so you're not causing more harm to yourself or others because you didn't do those first two parts right.

So, sit down and write out your own personal values.

---

[57]   Jennifer Armbrust, Proposals for the Feminine Economy (Topanga: Fourth Wave, 2018), 55.

HOW DOES LISTING OUT A SET OF VALUE WORDS HELP AT ALL IN THE REAL WORLD?

Good question! The value of Armbrust's list of values combined with EbonyJanice Moore's very, very practical Theory, Ethic, Praxis Model can be applied in almost every sticky wicket situation I've come across.

For example, I was in a seminar in September for white progressive women for active discussion on being a better ally.

One of the women, a consultant, asked, "What do I do when I am on a contract with a company, and I am in a situation where I witness a micro-aggression or a sexist statement? I am not an employee there, but just the hired help. I don't know how to interrupt racism or sexism when I am not technically sitting at the table. I could lose my contract, too."

"It's Armbrust's Proposal #5: 'Embody Your Values,'" I thought.[58]

"If this woman is saying yes to working for racist clients, she's not embodying her values of being antiracist. Don't take the work. Figure out a different way. Walk the walk, woman!" my inner monologue lectured.

The moderator was a little more empathetic. Bless her. This is why I am not a coach.

She said something along the lines of, "If you are an ally, if you have defined your own values and are living those values every day, it's going to be something your future employers, or in this case clients, already know about you, expect from you, and understand as one of the assets you bring to your role as an employee or consultant. What it sounds like is you aren't quite in a place where you are able to define what you believe and communicate it confidently to attract the people

---

[58]   Ibid.

you truly want to work with. That is your personal journey and you need to hold yourself accountable to what you want to be and how you want to show up."

In other words, this woman's Theory is she wants to run an antiracist consultancy practice, and her Ethic is racism, sexism, and other -isms are wrong and should be not tolerated in corporate cultures. But her Praxis has been to "stay neutral" to get the contract and pay the bills and then be a bystander when racist or sexist aggressions take place.

The moderator of this group impressed me so much with her response. Embody your values and the answer will be shown to you in due time. What do you value? How strongly do you value it? How firmly will you commit to your values over your fears or your privilege because of those fears? How can you move forward in this journey without being paralyzed, but also be critical and accountable to who you really are deep down in that soul of yours?

My own Theory, Ethic, and Praxis was challenged in how I responded in my mind, too.

My Theory is white urgency is violence, as white people we want to act and we want people to do stuff, but that often causes harm. My Ethic is I believe we need to take things slow and be measured and empathetic because we need to protect our beloved community and those around us. But the "voice inside my head" was like, "White lady, burn it down! Don't work with racist, sexist pricks! Call them out! Quit your contract!"

But that is not right. The moderator was right.

She said, "Look inside yourself and get more confident and grounded in your values. The right path will be revealed to you through your own conviction and how you show up as a consultant who embodies antiracist values every day. It becomes who you are, and then there will be no more confusion on the part of your clients."

That took me all of ten minutes to process. At the time, I was at a seminar led by a trans-BIPOC woman whose job is to help white women navigate.

The consultant woman's question was valid. I *could have* offered my own opinion since we all can speak up. But I did not. I am not an expert in that forum. I instead wrote my opinion down and set it aside to see if I was on the right track.

Our moderator answered and I realized, "Fuck! I'm so close, but still fucking it up."

That is two steps forward one step back. I am *in the seminar.* I *paid for the seminar.* I am *learning from BIPOC leaders.* I didn't *say shit…I was silent.* I also was wrong, but not ashamed. Just got what I paid for right there: a learning moment.

Now, for each sticky wicket situation I come across, I give myself time for solemn acknowledgment. Am I ashamed? Am I embarrassed? Am I on the right track? Am I just not sure?

Then I go back to my guides, a lot of the time it is Ebony-Janice Moore and her very practical Theory, Ethic, and Praxis. I take out my values list and apply them to the logic I'm engaging in and see what's fucked up.

This is practical stuff now! Aren't you excited?

The hardest part about this is I feel like I'm failing more than I'm succeeding. But that is probably just persistent pressure to give up and engage my privilege to ignore and run away.

I have been *busy* this fall pandemic season. It's late September and I have moved all of my belongings into a 10x10 storage unit. I'm living in the studio apartment on the top floor of my new four-unit commune.

I'm renovating my unit, managing the contractor, and choosing all the appliances and door pulls and fancy tiles.

Every weekday, our five-kid homeschool pod shows up and eats Kix in my bed while listening to Zoom. We've hired a chaperone so the moms in the pod can work, but they're *in my bedroom and living room and dining room and kitchen at the same time all day every day.*

It's still a pandemic, and my work has largely dried up. I am lonely and want to go out into the world and date and fall in love. I crave a vacation (or just a good pedicure). I am still negotiating the terms of my divorce. I am running out of money.

I am in crisis, right? I should self-care so hard right now.

My Theory is we can and should do *both.* We can self-care appropriately to conserve and build our strength, but we must not lose sight of how we can care for others and do good in the world with our privilege.

My Ethic is we are brave and worthy of love and belonging (and self-care) and we must be compassionate and accountable to our brothers and sisters of humanity through our words and deeds.

My Praxis right now is a little like this:

- I am going to invest in a gorgeous emerald green bathroom with glossy white subway tile and a historic apartment with original wood windows and refinished heart pine floors because I just am. It fills my soul and is now my home.
- I am brave for taking a risk to buy a home with a friend, and our bond and our place has become a refuge for our beloved community in transition. We are the destination for the homeschool pod. Our pod is supporting our children and the children who join us and the parents who depend on us to help support them in this difficult time. Our home is centered on providing a safe space to the people who need us, and it is already doing that.

- I am tired at night and like to drink Belgian IPA and watch a good episode of *Trailer Park Boys* before swiping through Bumble and falling asleep so I can recharge and tackle the next day.
- I am compassionate and working on approaching any new relationship by leading with my values and offering patience and empathy as others struggle to understand me or themselves. I have met and spoken with quite a few new suitors, and have had some ups and downs, but I am getting better at putting my needs and values first.
- I am rested when I wake up, so I listen to the news and engage with information and ideas that are intentionally designed to desegregate my media consumption. I have a list of books, podcasts, movies, news outlets, Twitter voices, and so on who are from BIPOC, Queer, women, and from other marginalized identities to try and ensure at least 50 percent of my media consumption is diverse and not white-centered.
- I am accountable to my brothers and sisters of humanity and have voted already, will serve as an election judge in my state, have donated to my local and national campaigns, have spoken with people about my values and beliefs, have paid people to teach me about womanism, humanism, antiracism, and more through books, lectures, podcasts, and other outlets. I have begun to purchase less, and purchase mindfully.
- I am not perfect by any means, but I am applying this. I am building shame resilience. I am asking for help.

This is all practical. It's something we can *do*.
I can see my progress.
I have done *better already*.

CHAPTER 15

THE PROBLEM OF PRIORITIZATION

———

One of the best-selling authors I saw on Ash Ambirge's scrolling list of accolades on *The Middle Finger Project* website was Sarah Knight, author of the *No F*cks Given* series. The brand includes journals, calendars, books, and other expletive-filled motivational tools focused on prioritization and spending time on what matters.

Sarah's work is worth a mention for two reasons:

1. Prioritizing is critically important so you're spending your precious time on the most valuable activities.
2. Not giving a fuck can be another privilege or entitlement only our select rose-gold universe citizens get to enjoy to its fullest and can be dangerously close to erasure of empathy.

STEP 4: LEARN TO PRIORITIZE WHAT MATTERS

Prioritizing, especially for the Gen-X-midlife-crises-ladyboss community we are walking with on this journey, is core to being able to honestly opt out of societal pressures and protect your time and soul.

We've all read (or read about because who has time to read?) books like *Overwhelmed, Work, Love and Play When No One Has the Time* (2014) by Brigid Schulte, a former *Washington Post* journalist and mom, wife, writer, and superhero, *Drop the Ball: Achieving More by Doing Less* (2017) by Tiffany Dufu, *All The Rage: Mothers, Fathers, and the Myth of Equal Partnership* (2019) by Darcy Lockman, and *The Second Shift: Working Families and the Revolution at Home* (1989) by Arlie Hochschild.

We know a mom carries the "mental load" for the family and is pressured to dutifully conform to the norms of "having it all" and not dropping the ball in the process, and we're working more hours than ever, too.

In her prioritization series, Knight uses clever ways to present the idea of letting shit go and prioritizing more effectively, and after selling "Over 2 Million Copies" according to her home page, it appears to be working.[59]

I agree with her basic theory about prioritization.

What got me to prioritize wasn't Sarah Knight's books. It was my uncle, Jim Gion, dying from a cardiac incident at his local Portland, Oregon, pancake house at age seventy-one.

It was July 4, 2018, six months after my spouse discovered my affair, four months after my spouse had moved out, and two months after having a hysterectomy due to early signs of cervical cancer.

In June I had sent Jim a long, long email I had earlier written to my spouse called "Our Story."

It was my way of unpacking and processing how I felt throughout my marriage so my spouse could have insight into my development, mistakes, and feelings. I sent it to Jim, too, and he called me right away.

---

59 "Home," No Fucks Given Guides, accessed April 20, 2020.

"What a year, Hot Dog. I've read your story. We can talk about it when you're in Portland in August," he said over the phone one afternoon in June 2018.

Jim was my dad's older brother. Jim was my guru and guide. He was the only family member I had who wanted to talk about ideas all day, every day, over coffee (and in between studio sessions with naked models because he was a sculptor).

He was one of the guys who made Portland weird, and by 2010, was kind of annoyed Portland had morphed his brand of weirdness in some ugly, capitalistic, half-assed ways. He was the guy who dragged me to his damp basement filled with dusty, unsold bronze figures of women, dogs, abstracts, and the smell of Portland rain and made me listen to hours of Alan Watts lectures he'd found on YouTube.

Jim was the guy who explained his definition of intimacy to me when I was eighteen and scared the crap out of me. He always seemed to know what my worldview was going to be before I did. When I was still convinced I was going to win life by being Perfect Mrs. Air Force Officer, he was the guy who already knew I would probably fall flat on my face in a decade or so.

He lived a life of Praxis and examination and being present. He knew what Sarah Knight was talking about before Sarah Knight was even born.

Then he died.

Jim was an artist, writer, thinker, Alan-Watts-style-secular Buddhist, reader, idea generating, committed-to-the-life, fuck-The-Game, fuck-the-patriarchy, unemployed, coffee-drinking, intellectual eclectic. He spoke Japanese and Vietnamese and traveled extensively. He had hundreds of friends and acquaintances who loved him dearly.

I am exceptionally lucky to have had him as my uncle.

He was comfortable with people from any walk of life, went from homeless to a billionaire, and approached everything with curiosity, grace, and good humor.

I'm not sure of his innermost struggles. I'm certain, as we are so similar, his own were also centered around intimacy, connection, and pleasure.

His biggest contribution to my life was his gentle questioning of the Rules and offering me lessons in prioritization.

Coming from my cowpoke village, even with an all-access pass to the library, everything Jim did and said was threatening to me in the way my former Mormon best friend felt when he started using Google. It was threatening like I ended up being to my husband and his family's world view.

When my ideas of what is true, normal, and right were blown up at regular intervals, my instinct said, "run for cover!" I was often very, very confused.

My parents were able to provide the platform for me—an all-access pass to the library, encouragement, open-mindedness—to prepare for escape. When they sent me to stay with Jim and his family in Portland, they knew Jim could help launch me in ways they couldn't.

Jim was the one who planted a seed of doubt in me about the Rules. I can still imagine his thoughts: "You don't know anything at all because your parents don't either, and you kind of knew for a while, but the taboo of someone else bringing it up is a little too much for your twelve-year-old mind to absorb. It's okay. Nobody really knows anything. Everyone is just scared. Be brave. It will be okay."

My curiosity won over my fear of challenging the Rules. He felt like a safe space.

I spent weeks and summers with him between the ages of twelve and twenty-two. We would talk about Alan Watts,

Henry Miller, and William Blake. Those were his wise men. We would talk about art and creativity and relationships. He had naked women in his studio at all hours for coffee, creating art, and connection, beautiful humans creating and conversing.

I became less afraid to ask Jim things like, *why am I afraid to die? Why does no one in our family communicate about feelings? Have you read the Bible? Does the Christian narrative seem really strange to you, too (hint: it did)? What is wrong with Grandma (unrelated side note, she was diagnosed as a narcissistic sociopath by her psychiatrist, so that's cool)?*

While my dad was my unconditional supporter and cheerleader and my mom is one of the hardest working people I've ever met, Jim was always standing at my crossroads like a docent, gently nudging me to a path I hadn't considered.

He was there when I was twelve, reminding me to phrase a question with a curious insinuation instead of a small-minded tone that would close hearts, doors, and ideas to me.

"'What is that?' can sound very different, depending on what you truly want to communicate," he said. "If you ask me in that snarky, small-town, judgy voice, I don't even want to tell you what I'm doing. What I'm doing is really interesting, so come check it out."

When I was eighteen, he introduced the concept of intimacy to me. We talked about how it is so different from marriage or jealousy or love or duty or respect. How it is thrilling and tenuous and fleeting and probably the only thing in the world worth a damn.

When I was nineteen, we talked about sex and taboos, about how his experience in different cultures contrasted with our American prudishness and how sex can be enjoyed and casual. Kink is fine. Lust is fine. Masturbation is encouraged. Sex is great but know it. Understand it. Don't let sex get confused with intimacy and love. They're not necessarily related, but they often come delivered in the same box. He told me of his past loves and heartbreaks. He read some of his journal entries to me.

When I was twenty, he encouraged me to flee. Become a turn-of-the-century beatnik before the internet destroyed everything. Hop on a sailboat his friend had invited me onto and skip school for a term. Grab a backpack and walk. Get on a plane, go to a foreign place, buy a bike and ride it.

"Just go," he encouraged. "Why wouldn't you? The only thing you're working for now is a future that isn't guaranteed."

But I was too afraid to go.

What he said made logical sense. It was a Theory I could believe in logically. The Theory of "follow your heart."

But my Theory at twenty was good, smart girls go to college, prove how good and smart they are by accruing degrees, build security through hard work and a good marriage so they feel safe, loved, and successful.

Jim was encouraging and probing, welcoming, and his own authentic self. He never told me in words I shouldn't get married and be a good girl, but there was something unsaid between us about my decision.

"How are you?" was the question he asked as I prepared to marry a military officer at twenty-three, jump into a world of Rules that would constrict me, graduate university with honors (and without a passport stamp), and follow the well-worn path.

"Fine," I answered with smile because I believed it. "I am really, really fine!"

* * *

Jim's death was a wake-up call. The gift that allowed me to be prepared for what came next: the sudden death of my own dad just eighteen months later. How come I had to lose both of my very best friends in the world during my midlife crisis and divorce? It isn't *fair*.

Yet I was able to joyfully and openly navigate these losses precisely because of Jim's lessons in prioritization and D's grounding in joyful acceptance.

I know I am lucky to not give fucks about things that aren't going to feed my soul, bring me love, and take me closer to intimate relationships with other humans on this journey.

Alan Watts writes in *The Book*, "The individual is taught to live and work for some future in which the impossible will at last happen, if not for him then at least for his children. We are thus breeding a type of human being incapable of living in the present—that is, of really living,"[60]

We are working so hard for our *retirement,* as stated by my uncle David who died of kidney cancer just months after his retirement.

We are working so hard for our *children,* said my friend whose daughter ran away to Europe with her girlfriend, opting out of using that college fund.

We're working so hard because we need *the money to make us feel safe,* said my mom who is a widow with everything she's ever needed and enough money for two more lifetimes, but all that hard work destroyed D's body and he didn't make it to his sixty-ninth birthday. She's living alone.

---

[60] Alan Watts. The Book: On the Taboo Against Knowing Who You Are (United Kingdom: Knopf Doubleday Publishing Group, 2011), 80.

Sarah Knight, Ash Ambirge, and Alan Watts are telling us to slow the fuck down. Be more present.

Live like Jim Gion did—following your dreams, finding joy *in the work,* connecting, studying, and when you are done it will feel like it is exactly as it should have happened.

A WARNING: NOT GIVING A FUCK CAN BE WIELDED LIKE A PRIVILEGE

Not giving a fuck is one way of taking time from your guilty feelings of obligation to others and letting yourself have time to play, right now, right here, and right in this present moment with the people and ideas that matter most.

Maybe go buy Sarah Knight's book and embrace the art of saying, "No, but thanks anyway."

Or better yet, go find EbonyJanice Moore on Instagram and sign up for everything she's teaching right now about joy. Moore has positioned herself as a pleasure advocate.

In Moore's teaching, she continually touches on the human need for joy and liberation. Her spiritual grounding and passion are so evident.

Back in the last chapter, we defined our matriarchal values. What we stand for and live by. Defining our values is only partly helpful until we can embody them, too. Believe in them.

EbonyJanice Moore is also a faith leader, teaching us to believe in a higher calling to better embody our Ethic.

I need faith. I need to hold truth in my heart and soul. I need to know how to love humans. I need to shut up and feel, listen, and stop being urgent and self-centered about any topic I know little about, including racism.

Finally, I can enter Praxis successfully.

Part of our Praxis needs to be a continual, gentle acknowledgment of our privileges. We are able bodied. We are healthy.

We are loved. We are white. We are educated. Thank you, universe, for these gifts.

Acknowledgment and naming help prevent feelings of shame and overwhelm that paralyze us or push us frantically into the sinister, competitive, selfish self-help cycle because we're coming undone.

Holding space for our imperfections, finding ways to give ourselves grace helps us build resilience and practice empathy—which is real self-care. Then we are better able to lift ourselves and our brothers and sisters of humanity up, shattering that rose-gold glass ceiling.

Alan Watts does the acknowledging. Lindy West does the acknowledging. EbonyJanice Moore does the acknowledging. Brené Brown does the acknowledging.

Then they do the joy and *celebration of privilege*. They encourage relaxation, creativity, and curiosity. They all extend grace.

By directly tying the idea of a playful spirit, living in the present, and acknowledgment that it's all miraculously absurd and amazing, we find the energy *to give a fuck*.

We care deeply, and yet can be calm and grounded as outside forces push us toward paralysis, overwhelm, urgency, and privilege.

Watts goes on to say the only way to solve the most important problems society faces—civil rights, international peace, and the restraint of nuclear weapons—is to be flexible, respectful, and conduct your life like you're playing a game that can never truly be won with a strong opponent you respect in her ferocity, to avoid hard lines, sworn enemies, and the rigidity that breeds xenophobia, divisiveness, and hate.

In other words, empathy, curiosity, collaboration, and joy for *all humans* are our paths to salvation and liberation.

These values put into practice is the matriarchy ascendant.

It's not super complicated, but we're choosing to ignore it and go on about our busy, consumption-driven American lives.

Is that who you are? Is that the story you're creating for yourself? Is that your joy?

If not, what is?

CHAPTER 16

DRINK FROM THE FIREHOSE OF MY FRAGILE WHITE FEELINGS

———

In an appearance on Brené Brown's podcast *Unlocking Us* in March 2020, memoirist Glennon Doyle talks about her newly-released book *Untamed* and articulates almost exactly all of the feelings I was having in my marriage back in the early 2010s.

"I had a good enough marriage. I had a life women are trained to be grateful for. Yet, I was angry all the time. I was just this low-level river of rage, and I felt this constant ache, this longing for a truer, deeper, realer love," said Glennon to Brené. "We are part of this universal gaslighting that tells women over and over again, 'No, no, no, no, that's not real. That longing inside of you, that imagination you have that it was all supposed to be more beautiful than this is not real. Stay in your place; be grateful.'"[61]

Untamed, the title of Glennon Doyle's 2020 book, is a great way to describe how I experienced the deal white women make with the patriarchy where they set the Rules to control my body, my labor, and my soul in exchange for comfort and security.

But I was so isolated by the same patriarchy, the one that told me not to complain or not to "hurt the children" by putting my own needs first. I thought I was uniquely alone in this dark place. I was miserable and failing at everything, including getting my own husband to do anything to help himself and our marriage, and the isolation, frustration, and shame drove me into a frenetic, impulsive place.

Through pain I self-medicated with my affairs and alcohol and work. I started going to the gym obsessively. I started meeting men and flirting with them shamelessly. I encouraged my husband to go fuck someone in a bar, just to get out of the house. In late fall of 2017, I posted an anonymous ad on the personals section of Craigslist.

Holy shit, not only was I not alone, but there were hundreds of lonely people out there looking for someone exactly like me. By January of 2018, I had settled into a wicked love affair with a married man who commuted to DC during the week because his wife and children had relocated to another city.

He had his own place.

By the spring of 2017, I was drowning in personal crisis. Living two lives, I was in the throes of a wicked love affair,

[61] Glennon Doyle, "Glennon Doyle and Brené Brown on Untamed," interview by Brené Brown, Unlocking Us Podcast, March 24, 2020, audio, 1:05.

one that consumed every minute of my weekday, waking hours.

I was consumed with thinking about *him*. When could I get away? Up late at night secretly texting, making excuses for escape to be in his oasis and escape my own real life.

The constant knot in my stomach pushed me awake at 5:47 a.m. three days a week to go to the 6:00 a.m. CrossFit class. The constant knot in my stomach pushed me out past midnight, drunk at a bar with him, coming home late with the husband snoring on the couch, drunk from too many Bud Lights after tucking our kid into her bed.

Rarely would my husband get in bed before 2:00 a.m. I often found him in a deep sleep in front of a TV that had turned itself off long before, a half-finished beer dangling from his hand. I mastered the "coming home late, letting the dog out, getting to bed" routine without waking him.

The next morning, I would be up at 5:47 a.m. and home by 7:15 a.m. and in the shower, barely saying a word to him as he rushed out the door to work each morning. Each evening, I went out or fell asleep with our daughter during story time, crashing in her bed as a way to avoid going to mine, lest he come find me.

The ball of toxic energy, confusion, anxiety, and frustration I carried was splicing through me out into the real world in the form of an affair or a bottle of wine opened and finished in one sitting or lashing out at people I loved.

I was sick with a disease, a tumor of self-loathing and terrible choices, and I thought it was just something I must carry alone. So, I carried it, alone, leaving a wake of misery and destruction in my path.

My spouse finding out about my affair exposed the truth.

Exposing my truth was the first act of liberation. I no longer had anywhere to run, so I came clean.

Then I started on the long journey of understanding who I was and how I got to this horrible crossroads. I used therapy, long phone calls with D, crying, and long conversations with my lover. I had my books, too.

Although my spouse had given up on therapy, I was all in. I was obsessed with drilling down into who I am and what I want. I saw this as a huge opportunity to not make the same mistakes again.

My education, healing, learning, and vulnerability became my first path to joy.

Following that, it became a constant, painful, beautiful struggle to hold on to the edge of healed and stay present and *do more* with my joy, my power, and my privilege, especially as the traumas of death, illness, pandemics, financial turmoil, and loss never seem to cut me any slack.

I could have gone full-throttle with my privilege to ignore everything and turn to toxic self-care, like I did after my ex had his affair and I wanted fancy vacations and breast implants.

I could have gone full privilege to escape, claiming my personal trauma somehow rendered me powerless, so I could just throw my hands up in futility, like I had when the school principal pointed out my white privilege and the violence it caused.

I could have gone full privilege to blame someone else, giving myself a pass of exception, where I tell myself white *men* have all of the power, and I am a victim here, too. It's the mental health *system* causing *those white men* to become mass shooters. It's the Karens who are the problem, not *me*.

Or I could have hunted around and found a moderately well-adjusted, gainfully employed partner and written a new deal for a new dollhouse with a new picket fence.

Instead, I just kept pushing the boundaries of this conversation we are having.

I wanted to stop doing the cheating, self-indulgent, toxic feminist, hypocritical, superficial colluding with the patriarchy for my comfort and security. Especially since it always came with terms including white guilt, mom shame, isolation, fear of failure, fear of isolation, and fear of *losing it all*. I wanted out of the labyrinth of dead ends.

I wanted to figure this shit out so I could find peace, relief, respite.

I finally found peace by making this commitment to holding myself to a Praxis. I liberated myself from always having to intellectualize or "prove" everything. I'm just trying to *practice*.

WHITE WOMEN'S PRIVILEGE TO PRACTICE JOY

The difference between EbonyJanice Moore and Glennon Doyle is the levity and lived experience of enduring racism a powerful, educated Black woman can bring to this conversation that a cis, white, female woman largely cannot.

The unacknowledged privilege to practice self-care and actually find *liberation* is why we have to be so critical of our guides. I love Glennon Doyle's spirit, energy, and writing. Her words are true to her values and she is a vocal philanthropist.

But with all of this learning, trauma, healing, and pain, the final piece to this puzzle is that—through it all—I still had a lot of white lady privilege to help me through it. That's not something I need to feel guilty about. It is just the truth and I need to note that here.

I was able to cry in public or yell at the pharmacist who couldn't figure out my dad's medication. I was able to walk around with my hood up, menacing and wearing sunglasses, and no one thought I might mug them. I was able to write this book because I have a substantial safety net built from generational wealth.

I finally understood *the missing* in the toxic self-care conversation:

White women we are privileged to have the freedom to practice joy and self-actualization. That privilege is not inherently bad, but it is deeply violent when we don't name it, acknowledge it, own it, and acknowledge the negative consequences and pain we cause when we actively ignore it.

"Many [of Glennon Doyle's *Untamed*] stories end too neatly, with heavy-handed messages of inner power and freedom. Freedom is an important concept in this memoir, but the language of freedom and liberation has larger connotations outside of white women's experience of patriarchy," writes book critic Sarah Neilson in the *Seattle Times*.[62]

"Agency is essential in *Untamed*—the ability to trust oneself is, according to Doyle, the key to so-called freedom. But there are things individuals can do and things they can't, often based on outside constraints. Doyle swings between recognizing this and insisting that women have everything they need inside them. Often overusing the words 'power,' 'freedom,' 'knowing' and 'self.'

---

[62]   Sarah Neilson, "Is Glennon Doyle's New Memoir 'Untamed' Inspirational or Heavy-Handed?" Seattle Times, May 6, 2020.

"*Untamed* reads like a self-help book for wealthy white women. When it treads lightly into the complex territories of race, privilege, misogyny and capitalism, it boomerangs back to the tired language of every affirmation book ever written: 'I am fireproof,' 'Life is brutiful,' 'To be brave is to forsake all others to be true to yourself.'"[63]

I want my own stories to read like a self-help book for wealthy white women, too. I want these stories to be affirming and reflective and double-down on middle-class, progressive white women who are also unlearning the patriarchy, owning our power, demanding our freedom, boldly exposing our vulnerabilities, and finding joy.

But I am listening to what everyone keeps saying about white women. We need to rise up, healed and strong, and pick up that big, fat, angry hammer and use it to smash the glass house of white fragility surrounding us and *do better.*

We must Praxis what we preach, EbonyJanice Moore tells us.

The conversation can't stop at "To be brave is to forsake all others to be true to yourself."

No, that is where the conversation *starts.*

Once you're true to yourself, it takes a load of energy to stay here. There are fears and doubts and sick kids and death and pandemics. There are money issues and job woes. There are bouts of loneliness and sadness. But we are still the second most powerful group of people on earth, and we can grab one of our other privileges as a life preserver and get back out there, hammer swinging.

To maintain a consistent, patient, powerful, joyful Praxis— the daily lived embodiment of your truth guided by your moral compass— is never, ever over.

---

[63]   Ibid.

Yes, we must do the Glennon Doyle thing to break ourselves free, but we must at the same time be comfortable with the fact that our individual work to end the -isms will never be well-and-truly over. (Which kind of is the beauty of Glennon Doyle as a writer and human. I'm going out on a limb here and guessing her next book will be about privilege, just like Brené Brown's 2020 podcast lineup has been all about antiracism.)

Let's get our priorities straight and not withdraw into privilege disguised as toxic self-care when we get stressed out. Let's stop leaning into the privilege to ignore when it suits our short-term comforts.

Living in Praxis takes reading and mindfulness, grace for pettiness and anger, building resilience to shame and failures, and determination. It means indulging in joyful pleasures because you know yourself well.

It gets easier and easier over time to find our own true north. Finally, it becomes second nature to pick up that book, call that heart-friend, say something to interrupt that is framed with empathy and not loaded with shame, or just press the "donate" button.

I learned through Brené Brown how to pass through personal shame and come out the other side. I learned through Glennon Doyle how to be radically transparent. I learned through EbonyJanice Moore I have *just started* learning and need to stop talking soon.

I learned through experience the people who continue to show up for me are my beloved community, and so I am loved and protected through their collective support.

Yes, it does take a fuckload of energy and faith to stay right where I am, on a tightrope of joy and fear and love and life and pain and optimism and deep, soul crushing sadness because I miss my dad and my innocence and my young and my healthy body.

But I am working on the Praxis of staying here, patient and strong. Every minute I work at holding that space of being true to myself, I get better at it. A second is given back to me next time I face crisis. I have built resilience where I collect those seconds, and I find a whole minute where I am healed, rested, centered and joyous.

I lean into that minute and feel full, powerful, "fireproof."

Then I open my laptop and read the tagline, "Video shows Minneapolis cop with knee on neck of George Floyd, who later died."

According to sociologist Robin DiAngelo, I have so many ways out of this headline. I can close my laptop. I can Tweet some thoughts and prayers. I can do the thing where I condemn the rioting following this murder because "violence doesn't end violence."

In fact, DiAngelo "sets aside a whole chapter for the self-indulgent tears of white women, so distraught at the country's legacy of racist terrorism that they force people of color to drink from the firehose of their feelings about it," writes Katy Waldman in her review of *White Fragility* in *The New Yorker*.[64]

Yes, either that or we don't say anything at all. We exercise our privilege to ignore.

So, maybe my stories are part of the self-indulgent group of distraught white women. I have no doubt they are distraught, but this work isn't for BIPOC people.

---

[64] Katy Waldman, "A Sociologist Examines the 'White Fragility' That Prevents White Americans from Confronting Racism," New Yorker, July 23, 2018.

This is for my white female friends. This isn't even about my feelings about racism, this is about my building of Praxis— *doing something to end all the -isms created by the patriarchy through the power of embodying matriarchal values.*

White women have unprecedented access to the power of the patriarchy. We have unprecedented access to money, education, and privilege. Yes, we are all in a midlife crisis and we all are struggling with what we do when we are leaning into that minute of power, fullness, joy, and fearlessness. What we *actually do* in those minutes of Praxis is what I want to talk about.

First, it starts with calling out the bullshit of other privileged white women who are profiting off of our pain. Bye bye, Hollis & Co.!

Let's find them and punch that toxic corporate feminism, self-help cycle bullshit in their collective tacos. They need to *do better,* and we need to stop partaking in the nonsense.

Next, we need to work through the shame of what we *have already done* in co-conspiracy with the patriarchy that has hurt other humans.

Get out your feelings, cry your tears on the shoulder of your white sister, and then step into your Praxis and power with us. We cannot do this without you.

CHAPTER 17

GETTING ALL
"WOKE" AND SHIT

———

"I think it's really hard to talk about race as a white person and not come off as a total jerk," said a white woman whose career is centered around issues of racial justice.

So, if a white woman whose *job* is working to achieve racial justice, equity, and build antiracist values in her community of practice thinks it's hard to talk about race, then how the hell am I supposed to talk about race? If the organizers of the Women's March failed at being antiracist, how am I expected to take action that won't co-opt or drown out Black and brown voices, too?

But think about sexism. What if a man said to you, "I don't want to talk about sexism because I'll come off as a jerk?"

I'd tell him to put on his big girl panties and deal with it. From the #MeToo movement and the gender wage gap to toxic masculinity and mansplaining, progressive white women are generally eager to call out men for their sexism. We are fierce, remember?

But when it comes to being called *racist,* we often feel so triggered we feel like we might die of shame. So, we don't say anything, or we do the white fragility things like close the book, turn off the TV, argue it's just *one bad actor,* or refer to our token POC friend as our reference for our allyship.

Not talking about our racism is a privilege. Just like for men, not talking about their sexism is a privilege. I have the privilege of not writing these words and still being perfectly happy in my rose-gold life.

So, what I'm doing right now is really scary for me. Robin DiAngelo, the author of the book *White Fragility,* would qualify this as my "white entitlement to racial comfort."[65]

I'm not used to being scared. I'm not used to being called out as part of any problem.

I grew up in a place where there were three Black students in my high school. I blissfully live in a socioeconomic bubble of college-educated, middle class, mostly white people who have lived near me since I turned eighteen. I am part of the wealthy-white-woman cohort who *feels* distraught about systemic racism and wants to *talk about it all the fucking time.* I have *feelings.*

But do you know what I'm risking here? Nothing. Maybe my ex will be mad because I talked about our former sex life. Maybe my kid will count all the swear words in this collection and charge me a quarter for each one. Maybe I'll get someone on Twitter to tell me I'm a stupid, racist, opposite-of-woke person.

Maybe someone will Instagram me about being a virtue signaler, a term I learned recently means I'm superficially trying to get followers or money by trying to position myself

---

65   Robin DiAngelo, White Fragility (Boston: Beacon Press, 2018), 104.

as a thought-leader on a trendy, popular issue. I might have already been told that.

But how do they know anything about me and my Praxis? I'm the only one who has to go to sleep at night knowing how I showed up today. I am accountable to me, and I am fierce and committed to fucking the patriarchy. I am committed to my matriarchal values of antiracism and ending sexism, ageism, gender bias, and all of the other gross anti-human -isms.

All of the "risks" I've taken writing this are nothing compared to what it means to be a BIPOC person in this country, and so fuck anyone who is bored enough to call me out for what I'm *not* doing.

What I *am* doing is tireless and joyful, deeply personal and patient, mindful of my real-life constraints, but not overwhelmed by them. I am in study of my ancestry. I have written about my lived experience. I am building a Theory, grounding myself in an Ethic, and engaging in a Praxis every single minute of every single day.

I'm also writing about it. I am more often *not writing about it.* After editing this memoir, I am just trying to live in Praxis and show up in a life I am proud of more days than not. I am the score keeper of my wins, losses, failures, mistakes, shame, and do-overs.

I believe stories matter and connections matter. If just one white person reads this and donates just one minute or one dollar to the organizations listed in the resources section, it will have been worth it.

If maybe one white neighbor who reads this doesn't call the cops on a Black family trying to check into their Airbnb, it will have been worth it. If one white friend speaks up and tells *their* white friend "choosing" to celebrate Women's

History Month and not Black History Month because "there are just so many months" is a privilege, then I will be thrilled.

If one person goes and follows EbonyJanice Moore on Instagram, I will be happy for both of you.

Critics can call me whatever they want. It has already been worth it.

Facts are, I could have chosen a different topic for my very first attempt at book writing. I could just write a memoir about good white men I've had in my life and how lucky I was to have had them so I could end up here.

I could have ended back with "choose good self-care and don't critique beloved memoirists like Glennon Doyle," but I'm writing about what comes *after* self-care, about what will make Glennon Doyle's work better.

What comes after self-care is going beyond the self and putting the mask on the person next to you.

People are literally dying in 2020 America at the hands of the patriarchy, and it has been going on for an embarrassingly long time. Like, they've been dying the entire time we've been here.

This centuries-old deadly power we refuse to acknowledge, much less overthrow, is killing, maiming, and incarcerating Black and brown lives. It is controlling and raping and murdering female and Queer bodies.

This same power is ignoring wage gaps, underfunding childcare and education, and trying to strip people of their rights to control what they do with their bodies. This same power is killing poor white people by convincing them they're part of the patriarchy and should die to protect it as their jobs disappear, their wages stagnate, and they continue to die of suicide, overdose, alcoholism, and despair.

It has to stop. White women need to figure out how to use our power to join with the less privileged and help stop it.

* * *

In our world of 230 characters, "woke" is shorthand for this destination of finally realizing you live in a society currently systemically unjust and built on a long tradition of oppression, segregation, and theft of land, body, and life.

Woke sounds like a destination, like the lights come on! You see it! Wow, holy fuck, this is terrible!

But that moment of "woke," of which I'm certain anyone who has somehow found themselves reading these words has had, is only a pinpoint in time.

Just like we wake up every single morning, and we don't just "wake up" one time the day we are born, "woke" isn't a place we end up, it's only a place we begin.

Getting "woke" is just like getting to that place where you are centered, grounded, and powerful. It takes massive amounts of energy to get there, and even more to hold on to the ever-fleeting foothold of staying there amidst the moving waters of life.

It's so easy to say, "It's just too hard. I have too much on my own plate to work on being a good friend, mom, and wife, *and* being a brave, powerful patriarchy-fucking ladyboss, *and* fighting the war against racism in America."

Well, too bad badass friends. We have to do hard things.

You can fragility-argue your way out of this with your privilege, but you shouldn't.

By now, you know I'm not going to let you off with your overwhelm and paralysis. We know you've got extra time and energy if you just stand up and claim it for yourself, prioritizing based on your values.

I can totally see why Black and brown people are enraged by our inaction, silence, and the privilege to ignore we've been happily leaning on for generations.

After just a few months of delving into antiracism, I also see my white friends and family members tuning out completely.

By the time I was completely done with the first draft, only a few have stuck with me (shout out to Amy, again, and the dedicated group of two dozen people who read each and every chapter and made insightful, compelling comments that helped me rewrite and rewrite again). Right now, Amy continues to push me to stay in Praxis on antiracism as well as finish this writing.

Amy sees the value in my story, but also the trap of self-indulgence and centering I could be confronting every minute because of our shared experiences of privilege. As we both sit by our community swimming pools talking about privilege and antiracism, we laugh because it is incredibly joyous, important, and absurd. Then we donate. We sign up. We do things.

So, don't give up and pretend we never had this conversation. Email me. Give me a shout out. Let's ask tough questions about how to develop and commit to a Praxis of self-care *and* care for others.

Please, you should stay here and know it's hard. Know you can do it and know when you do, you'll feel worse than ever before about racism and privilege and helplessness.

Sorry I don't have better news.

The good news is you will have done the hard work of being a strong, powerful, wholehearted, fearless warrior to fall back on once you clear that first hurdle. The good news is you're strong, brave, and not alone. You are worthy of love and belonging. So, go out there and keep your compass pointed toward personal joy plus "woke," and then simply do what feels *right*.

BEWARE THE WHITE LADY CENTERING

So, you're on board, I hope. You see your privilege and are going to critique it. Go back and write down all of the times in the last year you were a Karen. Go listen to *Nice White Parents*. Read *White Fragility*.

This work is our collective and individual responsibility to humanity, and this is our opportunity to *serve*.

Notice, I didn't say *end racism*. I said *serve*.

As middle-aged, middle-class, college-educated white women, we are so used to being the second most powerful group of people in the room. We're the default "woman" while everyone else is "Black woman" or "young woman" or "poor woman."

We are not used to following anyone other than white men, and that shows up all the time.

My own third or fourth attempt at "woke" ended with an act of privilege. I withdrew my daughter from our neighborhood public school and shipped her to a bilingual charter school nearby.

"I want her to have the two languages," I said. But what I meant was, "my marriage is falling apart, I'm borderline manic, I'm having an affair, I have pre-cancer cervical lesions, and I just can't put any more energy into racial justice issues in the fucked-up system we call DC Public Schools."

I was using Robin DiAngelo's "individualism" argument to avoid facing my privileged act.

Like, "Well, my *individual* circumstances mean what I'm doing—adding to the segregation problems of my neighborhood public schools—isn't *actually racist* because my *personal* health and marital problems are so unique that I need less stress."

Nope. It was 100 percent privilege. I know it, and I've felt it in my bones since the day I entered her into the DC school lottery the spring between preschool and kindergarten.

There, I said it. No excuses. I was scared of sending my kid to a majority-Black school if I couldn't be central to the shaping of how the school would engage with my child. I am the DC version of the white dad in the *New York Times* podcast *Nice White Parents*, released in July of 2020.

Nice White Parents is about groups of upper-middle class, urban gentrifying families in places like Washington, DC, Brooklyn, New York, and any other diverse neighborhood where single family home prices have shot up 50 percent in the past two decades, and realize we have the power and the numbers to change the school demographics and school curriculum to suit our children's needs.

We often couch it in a "we're so excited to help your failing school as we lift all of the children up together" message.

This is so fucked up, but we do it anyway. Why?

Well, as DiAngelo would say, I've been sent a "constant message that we (white people) are more valuable," so how possibly could this school improve without *my* valuable help?[66]

In the patriarchy, *the experts* are mostly white people. The academics in their ivory towers are who we rely on for "scientific research," and that system is full of white faces, too.

---

[66] Ibid.

We are used to gathering data and evidence, making a case, instituting logic, intellectualizing, litigating, and *winning*. The data and evidence have been compromised, though. It's part of the patriarchal cultural history.

The logic case-making works in bureaucracies built by the patriarchy, so we can step in and navigate that through our fluency in white culture.

We're in this cycle where white leadership and white thinking is constantly validated by structures of "authority"—government, academics, culture—which are all filled with experts and geniuses who are also products of the patriarchy and are, largely, very white.

We cite experts and argue with data. We assume the leadership positions because we are the ones who defined what "appropriate professional behavior" *even is.*

When I think back to that time I showed up at that school, the shame that fills my soul is so deep. I acted with arrogance. I centered myself and what I *thought* would be a *path to success* for a school in a system I knew less than nothing about in a community I was new to.

I have remained close to the preschool moms of that shameful time, and one of my friend's kids still attend the school I took my own daughter out of.

Graciously, Rosie didn't hate me. She didn't call me out for my racist, segregationist privilege. Somehow she just did her own thing, guided by her own compass, and continues to be generous with her love and support.

Instead, when I told her about writing on this topic, she encouraged me to reach out to Laura Wilson Phelan, the executive director and founder of Kindred.

Kindred is a nonprofit organization in Washington, DC that "builds trusting relationships between parents of diverse backgrounds and supports them to work with school leadership to drive equity and diversity in their schools and communities."[67]

Phelan created a model where she puts together groups of human people from the same school community and has them *get to know one another.*

Then once they build trust, they actually start to address diversity, racism, inclusion, and equity issues inside of their own real communities.

It's not solely Theory. It's not a one-day conference. It's not a lightbulb moment of "woke."

It's not solely Ethic. It's not a meditation on the virtue of antiracism and diversity. It's not a rally, protest, or feel-good experience.

It is the combination of Theory and Ethic into a Praxis where humans embark on a journey together to explore their shared humanity and their own lived experience in community, together, all housed inside the framework of their children's experience in a shared public school.

It centers the conversation around the humans in the community and is intentional about putting BIPOC and other marginalized voices *first.*

The Kindred framework is designed so white parents are in the backseat, learning, listening, changing. Then they can be more useful in their service once they understand and become a meaningful part of this community of shared values.

So, stop leading and start following.

I spoke to Laura Wilson Phelan on the phone during the pandemic about Kindred and how she came to this place in her life and career.

---

[67] "Our Vision & Approach," Kindred Communities, accessed March 31, 2020.

She's well-known in DC education circles for her work and for the positive response to Kindred's programming models, so I assumed she was some sort of racial justice academic warrior in a past life.

But instead, I learned she was a college-educated white woman in a segregated school district who began her own racial awakening through what she described as ignorant efforts to help improve her own neighborhood school.

"Hmm…. that sounds familiar. Go, on Laura…," I said.

"I felt like I was not really welcomed by my neighborhood school when I approached them as an engaged parent back before enrollment," she said about enrolling her children in a neighborhood public school back in the late 2000s. "In terms of the assets I thought I could bring, I was a certified teacher, and I saw myself as someone who did really good community work all my life. I went to the school and was like, 'Let me help. Let me help.'"

I remember, I told her over the phone, doing the same thing at our school. I was begging to help with communications or event planning or fundraising or *anything*.

I was centering and just had no understanding that *my kind of help* at that moment was superficial, selfish, and taking up so much of the principal's energy and time that she probably wanted to drown me.

These schools didn't need e-mail newsletters or language immersion programs, they needed functioning leadership, instructional coaching, and more hands on deck to help the kids and their families.

I had no idea; nor did I ask.

"There is so much about trying to do what we think is going to protect our own children, and then there's the ego part—like I've done this before—and then there's a lens through which I saw the world," Phelan said.

That lens? That's privilege. I couldn't fathom a universe where *my kind of help* wasn't needed. But it wasn't needed.

Phelan leads an organization with the purpose of helping individuals from diverse backgrounds to examine their own identities and racism in a shared space and to co-construct how they'd like to show up for each other, their children, and their school in a way that advances racial justice and educational equity.

Before she started Kindred, she made the same sort of privilege stumble I did.

Her journey began when she showed up at a school that served mostly Latinx and Black students in a district that is still under the heel hundreds of years of racist policy, and she thought her unique education background could help improve outcomes.

Maybe she felt the same shame I felt. So, I asked her.

"How did that feel? To be pushed out of that school community because they didn't see you as adding value?" I asked.

"At first I was a little incensed, like 'What a missed opportunity. I had so much to offer,'" she said. "At first I focused on finding some ways I *could* get involved and help. Slowly I made connections, but it was much different than when I first started.

"Meanwhile, I saw the people who *were* showing up to help were not representative of the school population. I wanted to find ways to facilitate the hearing of the silent voices in our neighborhood schools. I ran and won a seat on the State Board of Education, thinking I would work on the systemic side of things to help. But what happened was I ended up in a racial equity training workshop, after winning my seat in the election, but before I actually took the seat on the board. That training was truly life changing."

THE NEUROLOGICAL POWER OF HUMAN CONNECTION

Kindred uses the ancient art of storytelling to build shared narrative, connection, meaning, and new ways of "grouping" people.

Over and over again, the white antiracist people I've talked to and learned from on issues of the -isms, including about race and equity, tell me *it's the showing up, hearing stories, connecting with other humans, doing the self-assessment, making emotional connections to this topic* that changed it for them.

"Before that training, I think I would have counted myself among the 'woke' white women of the world, but then you just awake to a new level of knowledge and understanding," she said. "I had to be in a place where I was ready to see and feel how I have been contributing to the white supremacy culture, and how I have been perpetuating micro-aggressive acts. I had to learn the vocabulary and learn to see things differently."

So being "woke" is not the destination in this journey, friends, it's just the starting point.

Notice how Phelan went from "woke" parent looking to "help" her disadvantaged neighborhood school to "woke" elected official looking to help people in her neighborhood have a more equitable voice, to being a "woke" person staring down the barrel of her own fragility and privilege.

At that junction, Phelan, instead of using her privilege to move to the suburbs and send her kids to a "good" school, she used her privilege to put herself in the line of fire.

She is now a middle-class, college-educated white lady who is *leading* an organization that directly and productively addresses equity and antiracist values in DC's public schools.

Her Theory is interpersonal relationships between adult decision-makers will result in more empathy, stronger communities, and more equitable outcomes for children and families. Her Ethic is systemic racism in education is wrong, and ending it means those of us with power and privilege have a responsibility to do the heavy lifting via organizing, showing up, donating, and then sitting down and listening. Her Praxis is Kindred.

"It became really clear through my being a parent and volunteering with the school and sitting on the board of education and talking to people in my ward and my school community that there were wonderful intentions everywhere," Laura said. "Parents, grandparents, caregivers, and teachers all have similar intentions—to be helpful, to support healthy children, and to protect children.

"Yet there were these incredible blind spots as individuals tried to 'help' inside of the school system. I kept seeing this missed opportunity because people's *intentions* were to be helpful and useful, and those intentions weren't being captured and used for helping," Phelan said. "I started to study and collaborate and work with some of the leaders in this space to help figure out how an organization could help guide individuals to first understand themselves, then each other, then racism to work together, across lines of racial and class difference, to advance equity. By taking an individual, then small group, then small community building-block approach, we can build an army of aligned forces which could actually change the way these schools engage as communities with children and families."

Phelan's dream of changing schools by building community had me hooked. I remember the best part of being at the school where my daughter went to preschool was when I could say hello and have a conversation with a parent who didn't look like me, but knew me and *wanted* to talk to me. The feeling of community and shared experience was incredible.

THE PATRIARCHY IS USING YOUR CHILDREN TO MAKE YOU FEAR THE WORST

What about the "fear of the failing school" and my "precious child?" I asked Laura.

She laughed. "Yeah, there is that white supremacy undertone in our culture telling white parents to hoard resources, like 'I have to get into the best elementary or my kid won't get into Harvard.' But that is part of that systemic pressure for white people to segregate to help reinforce the inequity in the system. We are working at this micro-level that says it doesn't matter whether you go to Harvard if you have a foundational value in things that matter, communities that are strong, people who care for you. But to break down that system, we need to be *influenced by each other, and each other's stories and experiences.*"

Whoa, so she's saying by getting to personally know and care about other humans, your deeply entrenched biases may start to erode and your mindset might change?

Then maybe you'll realize your human child might not be happy at Harvard or experience "success" if they haven't first spent time in community with others different from them, exploring many aspects of their own identity and purpose? Really?

"Exactly. Stories and experiences are what moves us, as human beings, to shift mindset and then behavior. As part of my work, I started to do a lot of reading on neurology, behavior change and group dynamics and how that overlays with race and racism and how *that* overlays with schools and how *that* overlays with ages of kids and social capital, and all of these factors that play a role and how we live and internalize our own life experiences. The outcome of all of those conversations of all of that reading was Kindred."

My mind was blown.

So the true value of all that is good and great in the whole wide universe is sharing stories and experiences to build empathy, connection and curiosity, then turn around and change mindsets and empower people to help *dismantle the fucking white supremacist patriarchy*?

Okay. Got it. Let's do this shit!

Wait a minute. Now, I'm not saying we put on the white savior complex and march out into the world. I'm saying we start with "woke," and keep going with "woke," but we need to find a way to do it that *still isn't racist.* That's going to be hard, but we can do it. I know we can.

CHAPTER 18

BEING ANTIRACIST AFTER (WHILE) BEING RACIST

———

When my daughter started kindergarten at her perfect bilingual public charter school in the fall of 2017, a school centered on equity, inclusion, sustainability, and all the warm-fuzzy values I wanted to *live*, and perfectly packaged up in a way I didn't have to do the *work* (yay, privilege), I was relieved.

I was relieved because I could focus more time on my affair, my hedonism, and the untethering I was deep in the trenches of. I was relieved I could escape the shame of my racist behavior at my neighborhood public school.

No more PTO meetings! No more volunteering! No more work helping others!

I could be wholly and truly wrapped up in my self-care.

At the end of the first week of school, my daughter had told me she now, officially had a best friend.

The next Monday, I asked her to introduce me to this new best friend.

Kindergarten drop-off is a loud, messy whirlwind of backpacks and spilled Cheerios and "one more hug" with parents rushing off to work. As I trudged through the throng of sticky-fingered five-year-olds to help Madeline put her *mochilla* on the hook, she let go of my fingers, turned to her right, and tackled a little girl nearby to the ground.

"Madeline! What are you doing?" I tried to pull her out of the bear hug but couldn't because now this other little girl was equally wrapped up in an M-ball of kindergarten love on the floor strewn with lost sweatshirts and runaway crayons.

"Mommy, this is my best friend, Maya," Madeline said after they'd both somehow untangled and stood up.

"I'm Black," Maya said as she and Madeline stood arm-in-arm.

"Hi, Maya," I said, "It's nice to meet you." I was trying not to simultaneously laugh, cry, and scoop these two gorgeous beings up in a bear hug of my own.

Something about Maya's very first words to me, "I'm Black," made my heart stop.

"Yes, kiddo. You are Black," I thought. "You are incredible, amazing, a friend to my daughter, funny, kind, and all the things in the world."

But my mind didn't know what to say to her other than "Hi." I had no idea why these would be her first words to me, but I knew they were important.

Reeling a little, I side-hugged both kids and said goodbye to Madeline.

"Maya," I heard behind me, a woman's voice, "You forgot your water bottle."

I turned and saw Maya's mom standing in the doorway. Maya came to retrieve the bottle and before the woman could turn to leave, I said, "Hi, I'm Holly, Madeline's mom. Apparently our daughters are inseparable."

"Michelle," Maya's mom said. "Yeah, I keep hearing about Madeline."

Then she turned and left.

A few weeks into each new school year, there is an event called Back-to-School Night where parents come and learn about curriculum, school events, testing, and other such boring things I no longer had to care about since I was at the perfect school. But I went anyway.

Seated in the row of folding chairs in front of me was Maya's mom, Michelle.

Sitting behind her at Back-to-School Night, ignoring the drone of boring lectures on math curriculum and brushing aside the uncomfortable warmth in the crowded auditorium, I wondered what Michelle thought of her daughter having probably *the whitest of white girls* in the entire class as her new best friend.

I wondered what she thought about me, part of the privilege-laden, gentrifying class of white people swarming DC. I wondered about whether or not I was going to somehow mess something up, say the wrong thing, offend her, do one of the micro-aggressions, or be good enough she would trust her daughter in my care by the time the girls would want to do sleepovers.

I didn't talk to Michelle at Back-to-School Night. I didn't really talk to her until a few weeks later when we found ourselves on a school bus, trekking to a fall harvest field trip in the farmlands of Maryland. On our brutal ninety-minute journey with a pile of hungry children, rush-hour traffic, and all of the loud, bumpy, crowded discomforts you can recall from the school buses of your youth, we shared some small talk.

I don't even remember the exact conversation. It was casual and friendly. I tell myself I felt a change in her energy toward me, like maybe she thought she got a little lucky this white lady wasn't as clueless as I could have been. At least that's what I hope she thought.

We briefly discussed school, the kids, and the awfulness of field trips. We didn't delve into friendships or families. We briefly discussed work. Michelle is a director, drama professor, actress, and lecturer on antiracist practice in theater and media.

My internal dialogue at the time was: "*Oh Fuck*! What does antiracist mean?"

This was 2017. Then, I was still so worried I was *actually racist*, in that culpable fragile white-people way (segregation, avoidance, individualism, argumentative, etc.). I had just left public school for charter school and was dealing with that shame.

I now I had to figure out what antiracist meant and try to be that, too? Or should I be that instead?

I was scared of fucking this up with Michelle and hurting Maya and Madeline's chance of being best friends.

* * *

Dr. Ibram X. Kendi, a leading scholar on racism and discriminatory policy in America, the man who launched "antiracism" into the mainstream dialogue around race, both as concept and value, and the founding director of the Anti-Racist Research and Policy Center at American University in Washington, DC, writes in his memoir *How to Be an Antiracist*:

"To be antiracist is to think nothing is behaviorally wrong or right—inferior or superior—with any of the racial groups. Whenever the antiracist sees individuals behaving positively or negatively, the antiracist sees exactly that: individuals behaving positively or negatively, not representatives of whole races. To be antiracist is to deracialize behavior, to remove the tattooed stereotype from every racialized body. Behavior is something humans do, not races do."[68]

To be antiracist, each individual human must focus on assessing their immediate surroundings and behavior of the other individual humans in that environment.

Antiracism is choosing every day to think and act based on a deeply held value/belief (as Kendi puts forth) or Theory/Ethic (as EbonyJanice Moore would say) that an individual person's behavior is in no way tied to their race.

Racism is a construct, and to be antiracist is to reject the construct *actively*.

Dr. Kendi argues racism is a construct created by the innate human drive to survive and compete for resources. It was invented in Europe a few centuries ago so white men could categorize Black and brown people as property quickly and easily. It was a label for filing their assets.

I would guess Kendi's Theory is people invented racism to build wealth, have status, and feel secure and comfortable. Just like people invented serfdom or religious dogma or decided woman couldn't own property. I would describe Kendi's Ethic as people are equally perfect and flawed, regardless of their skin color. Kendi's Praxis is helping people actively fight societal and sociological structures that allow racism to persist through both public policy and helping people identify and reject racist social behaviors.

---

[68] Ibram X. Kendi, How to Be an Antiracist (New York: One World, 2019), 105.

Circling back to what Laura Wilson Phelan was saying about Kindred, when we put people together to know one another as individuals, neurological pathways will shift, and mindsets will begin to transform.

Kindred is about facilitating individuals seeing one another as individuals, outside of the racial construct. Kindred was founded with antiracist values and practices based in part on Kendi's work, so this should come as no surprise. Kindred is an example of how one organization has tried to apply Kendi's work in a real setting.

But Kendi goes further in his "how to" guidance. Becoming truly antiracist is choosing every day to think and act and advocate for changes in the systems and policies contributing to racism in our current sociopolitical systems, too.

We have to get involved in policy change. We must learn to interrupt racist ways of thinking or deciding.

In other words, it's common knowledge that newborn babies are not racist. So, where does racism come from? According to Kendi, racist policies, rules, systems, and societal norms are built into the fabric of every part of American society. It's just the way things were built.

Most of us now know about slavery, segregation, immigration, redlining, stop-and-frisk, the War on Drugs, and so on through our "woke" understanding of history. We see the structures continuing to perpetuate racism at the macro-level. We read the travel bans, see the Black and brown incarceration, murder, and police violence data, and hear the "Build the Wall" chants.

We tend to think of "racism" as bigotry, neo-Nazis, and high-school-educated, rural, white poor people.

A PRIMER ON WHITE FEMALE RACISM

It's time to dig into our legacy of white lady racism, learning about how white women are a core part of the racist, patriarchal system, too. We can't blame it on the white men. We can't say racist white women aren't our sisters. We own them, now, remember.

So, let's learn some history:

"In 1980, conservative white women convinced the Republican Party to abandon its previous support for the [Equal Rights Amendment], adopt an anti-abortion stance, and become the party of 'family values.' They campaigned successfully for Reagan's nomination and election. In 2016, they campaigned for Trump. Yet white married women who vote Republican are largely invisible in the media, which often speaks of the Republican base as a body of 'angry white men.'"[69]

Going back further, it's the angry, screaming faces of white women protesting six-year-old Ruby Bridges as she became the first Black child to desegregate a New Orleans school in 1960.

Going back even further, white women have been instrumental in fighting for legal segregation. White women hired and abused Black and brown domestic servants. White women joined and marched with the KKK. White women have been throwing our hats in the ring with the white men in the patriarchy for as long as it has been around.

We've learned to code it by claiming "poor test scores" are why we're transferring schools, "weak family values" are to blame for Black poverty, or "limited government" is why we hate all of these pesky laws.[70]

---

[69]   Marjorie J. Spruell, "Women Can Be Racist, Too," Democracy Journal, (Winter 2018): 47.

[70]   Ibid.

We need to know upper-class white women sexually assaulted and committed sexual violence against Black enslaved men, using "sex as an instrument of power, simultaneously perpetuating both white supremacy and patriarchy."[71]

No, white women do not get a pass. No, white women are not just taking orders from our white men. Because white women have benefitted from, live inside, and have actively bought into *Leaning In* instead of opting out, we have to face that and own it.

We have signed a deal with the patriarchy and have been willingly and actively upholding the terms of this deal for centuries.

It's at this point most white women curl up into that protective cocoon of white fragility, convincing themselves these systemic problems are the problems of the evil, conservative white men in charge. They are the rural and suburban white women who helped elect Donald Trump in 2016, not *us*.

Wrong.

Unless you're actively trying to live by matriarchal values—in Praxis—including learning about and *practicing* antiracism in your daily life, you're still buying in.

Learning about antiracism begins a domino effect of understanding how "the powerful et al" are stealing labor, co-opting resources, concentrating power, harming people, and destroying the planet, while simultaneously actively creating messages for moderately powerful groups to feel helpless, isolated, overwhelmed, and ultimately inert.

White women are *the best* at avoiding this and hiding behind the neatly-pleated slacks of our angry white men.

---

[71] J. M. Allain, "Sexual Relations Between Elite White Women and Enslaved Men in the Antebellum South: A Socio-Historical Analysis." Inquiries Journal/Student Pulse (2013): 08.

Here we go, ladies: *We are the powerful. We are the patriarchy.*

The patriarchy, just like the matriarchy, is not gendered. It's power. It happens to be majority white, but it's not always. It's tricky and it's everywhere.

Until we accept that, own that, and start digging into it, we're going to get nowhere. We're going to continue to hurt other humans with our actions and inactions.

People are *dying* at the hands of *our* patriarchy. Our patriarchy loves privilege. If our patriarchy can contribute to our feelings of helplessness, paralysis, fear of losing all we've worked so hard to gain, for the futures of our children, or for our identity and connection to community, then we are right where it wants us.

As white, progressive, middle-aged women, we have been conditioned our whole lives to live in a mild state of anxiety or fear so we would continue to sign these deals with the patriarchy's system for our protection and comfort. For *the children.*

We continue to second-guess our instincts, instincts screaming at us that something is wrong and people shouldn't be dying. We *choose* fragility and paralysis.

When we do muster the courage to speak up or do something, we are often socially punished, often by other white women.

Our playing by the Rules of a culture grounded in the patriarchy built by a European, white male-and-female dominated history and built on the backs of chattel slavery required us to "invent" race. This invention of race continues to ensure our mostly-white politicians, CEOs, cultural conversations, wealth, and social norms are protected and enshrined as the ideal, the normal, and set up at the "Great

America" the white minority faction is always trying to get back to "again."

Power stays in the hands of the powerful. White women *are relatively powerful.*

We break the Rules, we are punished back toward conformity. Often by other *white women.*

We speak up or stand up and are told to sit down because our voices don't need to be heard. Often by other *white women.*

It's all a part of the labyrinth of the patriarchy.

White women have convinced ourselves we are *not of the patriarchy* because we're women.

So we are in this crazy place of false logic where we have so much privilege and we have committed so many historical acts of violence, but the only people who are calling us out *legitimately* are people who have less power than we do, like BIPOC, Queer, people with disabilities, poor people, and so on.

A lot of the time their legitimate criticism is we jump in and center ourselves. When we get called out immediately for our patriarchal approach to whatever the fuck situation was, we're hurt. We're not used to *that sort of hurtful treatment.*

So, we usually just ignore those voices or run to a place of comfort where our patriarchal pass for "good intentions" is always waiting on our dollhouse doorsteps.

At the same time, our dear friends, the toxic brands, jump in and "rescue" us from our shame and guilt, offering mostly superficial self-help cures, taking our money, bandaging our infected wounds, and not doing anything to connect us with *how to use our power for good.*

The privilege to ignore actively encourages us to deny, avoid, and escape the truth about the nature of and *our position in* this violent and horrible patriarchal system.

That is the problem.

We need *white women all over the place engaging with other white women, owning our history, owning our stories, connecting in sisterhood, and learning from the less privileged.*

We are all viewing the world from our position atop the patriarchy, like those little plastic figures on a wedding cake. We mean well. We have it good. We don't want to rock the boat. We see how bad it is *down there.*

We are told the gift of empathy will expose us to harm. Others will take advantage of us.

We aren't encouraged to collaborate, but to compete. We withhold ideas and force nondisclosure agreements. We want to know our cut before we care about our impact. There aren't enough spots at Harvard to go around.

We are told the gift of sharing will dilute the finite amount of resources in the world, and we'll end up with pittance. Others won't share with us.

We are shamed by one another for trying new things and failing, especially if we make the "mistake" of choosing the wrong partner, divorcing, quitting our "good jobs" to take entrepreneurial leaps of faith, unless we're "doing it right" by the definition of the patriarchy.

We are discouraged from trying to escape the grind through policies like lack of quality health care being lorded over us as something only "worthy" for a person in the capitalist machine. Others can do it, but we can't. We will fail and lose everything. We must play it safe for the children.

The patriarchy, as I've defined it, is the white-dominated historical system that originated in Europe around the middle ages. It is the model for the crusades, colonization, serfdom, chattel slavery, capitalism as manifested during the Industrial Revolution, sharecropping, Jim Crow, redlining, the pro-life movement, and pretty much every law, history textbook, and "Norman Rockwell" myth white men tote around in their backpacks.

It is not gendered, as so many people of many races, abilities, and ages have bought into.

The patriarchy is critical to critiquing the identity of the white woman.

We need to own it, ladies. Only then can we figure out how to stop centering ourselves, stop being so goddamn fragile, stop being cringeworthy, and *start* having hard, loving conversations with our sisters during wine-and-book club.

STEP 5: COMMIT TO EMBODIED PRACTICE

I believe the universe places things in my path I need, and I needed Michelle. She gave me this incredible word: antiracist. She also gave me, over time, her trust.

Madeline and Maya have had many sleepovers and birthday parties and day trips and phone calls together over the course of their three-year-long friendship.

Michelle knows about my divorce, my affair, and my work. I know some things about her life, too. I wouldn't say we are besties. No, that's not it. But she opened up just enough of her heart to me that I feel blessed with those gifts.

I spoke to her about my writing project, specifically because I had been reading about antiracist practices, values, and workshops and wanted her professional take.

"Will you put on your Professor Michelle hat and educate me on your practice, your expertise in antiracism?" I asked her.

This was a huge ask for me.

No, I did not call up my only BIPOC friend and ask her to solve racism for me. I asked Michelle, faculty at an Ivy

League theater program, to give me an hour of her time to teach me about her approach to teaching antiracism in the workshop setting for theater and media professionals. She travels the country and the world teaching antiracist theater.

That's Michelle's work, her job, her expertise, field of study, advanced-degree-holding j-o-b.

I asked her about a typical workshop. I pictured a theater space, maybe a rehearsal room with black walls, black ceilings, and black floors. There would be lovely, bright lighting over a whiteboard and chairs in a circle. Cups of coffee. White faces and white hearts aflutter, anticipating what they might expect from this expert in antiracist practice and how much it might hurt or trigger them.

At least this is what I would be feeling and expecting.

The best part about this is participants are showing up. They pay Michelle to teach them how to *be antiracist.* They are investing their time and money in the action of doing work to dismantle racism. This would be a great place for any progressive person to start; find a workshop or a training and *go.*

In Kendi's view, the individual person invests time and money (an action) in a workshop where they learn and reflect on their broader actions in their professional sphere *so they can implement change in the spheres of influence in which they operate.*

In her workshops and classes, Michelle shows participants, pointedly, how the structure of the theater industry is racist and then guides them through a collaborative approach, centered on storytelling and empathy, to creating actionable solutions that might erode or eliminate racist structures in their individual context as theater professionals—owners, operators, actors, producers, production companies, directors, operations managers, and so on.

Antiracist practice is about working to break the cycle of where a policy or system *leads to* a group inequity that *leads to* a biased, sexist, misogynist, and/or racist belief.

Guess where antiracist workshops begin? Right back where I began and right back where EbonyJanice Moore tells us to begin. We begin at the very, very beginning.

"When I create a workshop anywhere, I always center it on history. I center it on my own ethos around stolen land and stolen people," Michelle said. "So, no matter what I do, I always acknowledge the indigenous people of that land. Always."

"*Whoa,*" I thought immediately. I realized I had already incorrectly assumed Michelle's foundational teaching on antiracism would start within the lens of Black history, but she's going way back to native peoples.

"By acknowledging the first peoples on the land where we are physically standing, I help participants create longer memories," Michelle said. "Longer memories help us remember what we have today is part of a long story of humanity learning and changing together, not because of our own individual effort. We acknowledge we hold a position based on an accumulation of ancestral effort."

That's just it. She's not asking you to apologize that your great-great-great grandparents were slave owners or your great-great grandparents were Nazis, or more likely, just regular old racist people from Texas.

She's not asking you to cry about the fact white women are just as culpable in creating and perpetuating our system of the patriarchy for our own material gains.

She's just saying by solemn acknowledgment of our ancestral effort, we can see that whole of the progress of the society and identify our unique position within it.

She echoes EbonyJanice Moore's language about ancestry and lived experience merging with study and expertise.

"From there we move into doing some type of embodied exercise," Michelle goes on. "Intellect is a white privilege we don't often talk about. Literacy is a newer tradition for many people, and white people often have an advantage with wit or clever comebacks or quippy responses. So, I work on having participants do an exercise that puts us on a universal ground, into our bodies first. From there we can talk about our first layer of individual, human differences, our abilities and ableism."

It's worth repeating: "Literacy is a newer tradition for many people."

Holy shit, I'd never thought about that. How many times have I caught myself saying, "Well, I *think*...."? A million times? More? But when I reflect back on literacy and intellectualism, I could safely guess I am only four or five generations removed from illiterate on my maternal grandfather's side.

Literacy and the ability to think, talk it out, logically puzzle, plan, make laws, and keep account ledgers is a *newer tradition* for some people. The patriarchy failed to mention this to me in history class, but now that I know it, I can even more clearly see how much that view of "normal" and "right" is skewed by the patriarchy itself.

If you plan to counter-argue what I've written here, I will first ask you: where do you get your information? Where did you go to learn the counterargument to my position? Because through *the way we learn,* the way we define authority, and the way we litigate everything, you might be able to come back at me with some "good, logical points." But unless those arguments are not centered in whiteness as the ideal, normal, and authority, I'm going to have to push back.

Go to images.google.com and search "the most beautiful women in the world." The standard for beauty: 99 percent white women. Google "the smartest people of all time," and you'll find dozens of articles and listicles that don't feature *even one Black or Latinx person.*[72]

Check out Google's AI "solution" for why Black people were being identified as animals in its advanced facial recognition software.[73]

Why is that? Because in Europe in the Middle Ages, white men started consolidating power and creating structures that allowed other white men to achieve their highest potential and document it in drawings, words, and books.

Take Leonardo da Vinci and Michaelangelo, for example. Who knows if there was an equally gifted thinker and artist in Machu Picchu or Botswana? The ancestral traditions in those places, in that century, weren't centered on literacy. It doesn't make those forgotten geniuses better or worse, it just means our collective knowledge of them is lost.

The European literary tradition turned to the Enlightenment, which turned to colonization, which turned to the Industrial Revolution, which spread capitalism and Eurocentrism around the world like a disease.

The result is our American history is incomplete. An incomplete history gets perpetuated when we tell our children Einstein was the smartest man who ever lived. But we actually don't know that for sure. We just know Einstein, Goethe, Galileo, Newton, Darwin, and Marie Curie were *remembered* because they were in a particular context of an ancestral

---

[72] Natasha Bertrand, "The 40 Smartest People of All Time," Business Insider, February 27, 2015.

[73] James Vincent, "Google 'Fixed' Its Racist Algorithm by Removing Gorillas from Its Image-Labeling Tech," Verge, January 12, 2018.

tradition of literacy and science that allowed them literacy so they could start building knowledge from other knowledge.

If Einstein had been illiterate, what would have happened to his genius? If he had been indigenous to Australia, would we even know his name?

The patriarchy has ancestral effort that has resulted in astonishing advances in knowledge, science, technology, and art. That is true. But our literary tradition and our technology for domination means we venerate and elevate ourselves and our history at the expense of others.

Yes, it's normal to want to remember and honor our history. Let's celebrate our advances, sure. But the negative and violent elements of the patriarchy are also served and perpetuated by this history being held up as the ideal and standard.

When that history starts picking and choosing the feel-good stories, often completely eliminating the contributions of others, that history is passed to our children in an increasingly sugar-coated way that results in erasure of violence, diminishing of others' pain, ignoring stolen wealth, and reinforcing the status quo.

According to *NBC News*, "In Alabama, up until the 1970s, fourth graders learned in a textbook called 'Know Alabama' that slave life on a plantation was 'one of the happiest ways of life.'"[74]

If you were a child in Alabama in the 1960s and saw poor, angry Black families all around you protesting and sitting in, causing your parents to be angry, had a legacy of racism and slave ownership in your white ancestry, lived in a segregated place where you were not in community with your Black

---

74 Danielle Silva, "From Juneteenth to the Tulsa Massacre: What Isn't Taught in Classrooms Has a Profound Impact," NBC News, June 18, 2020.

neighbors, and were taught in your *schools* this all could have been prevented if those Black people just appreciated their "happy" lives as slaves a little more and didn't make so much trouble, it would be really easy to see how you could develop a racist view, advocate for racist policies, and put the antebellum South on a pedestal.

That's *exactly* how this works.

By venerating and institutionalizing these sugar-coated or patently false narratives, the generations who are learning history and not experiencing it will buy in and take it at face value. We believe our teachers and textbooks. We invest in the American Dream, aim to go university, fight to get a job in a mega-insurance company, and grind away.

We live by the Rules, then we start consuming life, Netflix, and all-inclusive vacations until we breed, fear for our children, and double-down on the buy-in so our offspring don't starve. Then we teach our kids how to survive just like we have. The powerful structure of patriarchy remains well-fed and unchallenged.

This is also not new.

As white people, when we think of the police, we think of Mayberry or *Law & Order.* Do you know the history of the United States police force? Do you know when police were first hired by the state and what their purpose was? I certainly didn't.

As I started this journey learning about antiracism, I kept hearing about criminal justice, community policing, and police violence toward Black and brown people. Defunding the police became a rallying cry for many.

For many white people, that seemed shocking. Police are here to help us, right?

Did you know that in the American South, beginning in

1704, the police *were* created to help white people?

They were "centered not on the protection of shipping interests but on the preservation of the slavery system. Some of the primary policing institutions there were the slave patrols tasked with chasing down runaways and preventing slave revolts... During the Civil War, the military became the primary form of law enforcement in the South, but during Reconstruction, many local sheriffs functioned in a way analogous to the earlier slave patrols, enforcing segregation and the disenfranchisement of freed slaves."[75]

So, by the 1860s, the local sheriffs were essentially tasked with keeping Black people in line. Before that, they were designed to recover stolen *human* property for wealthy slaveowners. Think about it. It makes sense, right?

We know the Reconstruction Era led to Jim Crow, which led to the civil rights movement. What we didn't really think about was how involved the institution of law enforcement was in maintaining the racist status quo even after the 1960s.

We'll tokenize a super racist "bad actor" like Jim Clark, the sheriff in Selma on Bloody Sunday, but never examine the fact that *it was his job.* Or then go further and say, "What *is* the job of the police and how is it helping or hurting?"

We've taken the position that the job descriptions, mission, vision, and values of the police as an institution are above critique.

So, it is not surprising to BIPOC people who know their own history very well and understand police are dangerous *to them.* It's equally unsurprising the white patriarchy feels very safe, supported, and protected by that same institution.

It was designed to be that way.

---

75   Olivia B. Waxman, "How the U.S. Got Its Police Force," Time, May 18, 2017.

THE ULTIMATE IN PROGRESSIVE PRIVILEGE: THE INTELLECTUALIZER

The problem of white people not truly and deeply understanding our own history, mostly because we consume history written by and for ourselves to reinforce our dominance. We only know our sugar-coated versions of it.

When we're confronted with the fact that our own history, venerated on that pedestal, is *problematic,* we tend to be triggered and fragile about it.

"It's not *me,*" says the individualist.

"It's so terrible and awful," says the white lady in tears.

"I'm so glad that was in the past," says the post-racialist.

"Now we face such a huge, systemic problem. I'm only *one person.* What can I be expected to do?" says the overwhelmed and fragile.

"It's not all of the police. I mean, it's just a few bad apples," says the intellectualizer. "Each case is different."

The person who *has* read the books, does know the data, follows the news cycle closely, and really does think they're an ally is one of the most difficult white people to critique.

Same with the person who *has* done the research, works in the nonprofit, follows the new data closely, and really does think they're an ally.

The problem of the intellectualizer came to a head for me when Jacob Blake was shot and paralyzed by police in Kenosha, Wisconsin, in August 2020.

The shooting was on video, and it became another Twitter "outrage" moment, just like the recorded murder of George Floyd and the recorded execution of Ahmaud Arbery. These people are part of an ever-growing list of Black and brown bodies destroyed by our system of criminal justice built by our patriarchy.

My Theory, based on learning about this, is there are huge, systemic problems entrenched by decades of systemic racist history that formed our police forces. My Ethic is humans deserve to be treated with humanity, even in their darkest hour, and the police need reform. My Praxis is to support mental health organizations, listen to BIPOC leaders who are experts on this matter, and donate to candidates who are working for criminal justice reform.

That's the same Theory, Ethic, and Praxis of one of my friends, too, I thought.

But he also said something like, "I really would like to see the video before I decide on the Jacob Blake situation. Each one of these cases is unique, you know?"

"No, I don't know," I said.

A few weeks before, I had heard a powerful message from someone I respect and admire, Akilah Hughes, a writer, actor and comedian who hosts my go-to morning news podcast *What A Day* produced by Crooked Media.

Listening to Akilah Hughes, a Black woman, read the news every morning is part of my Praxis. Her informed and personal take helps me understand what is happening in the world from a Black, female-centered perspective.

Hughes' words changed my Ethic, which changed my Praxis.

The intellectualizer's Theory is the police force is fundamentally problematic. The Ethic is the police need reform. But his Praxis was to "seek more data and get first-hand proof" that this new bit of evidence was valid to his body of knowledge on the topic.

Listening to what Akilah said about white people's *need for individual intellectual validation* was so valuable in changing my views on this issue.

Akilah's monologue:

The video of George Floyd's murder was haphazardly retweeted into the feeds of Black people everywhere to say, "look at this horrible thing a police officer did to a Black person." But the voyeuristic nature of sharing Black human beings murdered like it's just a normal thing on a Tuesday didn't bring that guy back. It didn't stop racism.

In fact, racism didn't end when we all saw Mike Brown laying in the street, or when the Ahmaud Arbery video went viral, or when Eric Garner was choked to death over a few cigarettes, or Walter Scott getting shot to death. Did racism end when Danny Ray Thomas was shot on video by police? Did Stephon Clark's viral murder change the way white people react to Black people just living their lives? When Keith Scott was shot to death, did white people even have a conversation about a culture that produces this kind of incessant bias and violence? Did Philando Castile's murder video end racism? Did the photo of Emmett Till in a casket stop racism? Did it stop murder? How about Alton Sterling? Did it force all police departments to rebuild from scratch, weeding out the "bad apples" that have spoiled the whole goddamn bunch? Did it make white people evaluate themselves for even half a second?"

Are there people on earth who are unaware Black people fear the police because the police disproportionately kill Black people? Do we need videos to prove it? Do the videos ever result in justice?

I mean, we've had smartphones that shoot video since, what, 2005? We know this happens. Awareness isn't the point. We don't share white death like this. When Steve Irwin died, we didn't share the video of the stingray millions of times online to "raise awareness." They took down the ISIS beheading of a white man on YouTube. How many white men have you watched die in HD video? Can you name five? I bet you can't name ten.

The video footage is shorthand for desensitization. Ask yourself why you're even comfortable looking at a video of someone being murdered. Then ask why you'd share it with everyone you know. If it was a dog, you wouldn't. So, what is the reasoning? For what reason should we share footage of a person being murdered?

I'm traumatized. Black people are traumatized. Four police officers got fired. They didn't get murdered. They will hopefully be charged with murder, but they probably won't. But that isn't justice and it doesn't address a system that puts a gun and a badge in the hands of a person who could hear someone pleading for their life and not move.

When I say "don't look away" I don't mean consume Black death like it's a meme on TikTok. I mean look in the mirror. Look at your family. Look at the community you live in. Look at your friend group. Look at the wealthy white woman with the rescue dog in the goddamn park. And don't look away. Because we know what the problem is. No one is unclear on what the problem is.

So where is the justice? [76]

* * *

Akilah's words changed my Ethic. I believed her in my body. I empathized with her pain and understood what she was saying. Don't look away from your culpability in this cycle

---

[76] Akilah Hughes and Gideon Resnick, "Racism Cont'd," May 27, 2020, in Apple Podcasts, produced by Katie Long, 25:43.

of "watching the video" to "prove" police need reform. *Just listen to Black people.*

Now, friends, tell me whether you need to watch that video —or any video—to know we need police reform.

What the intellectualizer was doing there is using his patriarchal value of individual intellectualism, which made his Praxis, or his *action*, become "go watch a Twitter video of a violence against a Black body."

Somehow he has internalized he *needs to know the facts* in this particular case to make a decision on how he can decide about *this particular case.* Learning the facts was the action he chose, not *listening to Black people.*

"Every minute you spend watching that video could be spent doing something in Praxis that is more powerful and effective." I said. "What Black leaders in policy, media, activism, or education are advising white men to weigh on the Jacob Blake shooting by watching the video? Can you name one? Who are you listening to and learning from when it comes to applying your Praxis in this situation?"

"How does *your individual opinion on any one single act of police violence* do anything but reinforce the patriarchal need for you to center yourself, center your needs for intellectualism, and divide your energy into things which dilute your eventual impact in changing policy?"

If you truly are embodying antiracism, then you *know* the police are in need of reform, so you listen to what antiracist leaders are saying in regard to what to *do about it.*

My Praxis is to donate and say their names. My Praxis is knowing that and listening to BIPOC leaders. My Praxis *does not include and should not ever include needing proof for something I already believe in my soul and body.*

CONNECTING WITH OUR HUMAN BODIES

Now our minds should be right, but what is missing in white, progressive antiracism is our Ethic.

That fucks up our Praxis and causes ineffective action, urgency, centering, and violence.

Our Ethic is our faith, our beliefs, and our souls, embodied.

As Michelle walked me through an antiracist workshop, I felt it in my bones when she said, "Put it in your body first."

Learning to engage your Ethic through embodiment helps us feel first, pause, and then choose *better ways of acting*.

In the meditative exercise of "grounding," you imagine your body as a tree rooted to the Earth and the roots connected deeply into the loam, clay, and stone. You visualize your roots, steadfast, pulling up the water sustaining you. You feel the Earth as your body and your body as the Earth and the universe. You notice the physical sensations that result via a practice. You let these physical and emotional feelings pass through you, noticed.

Every time I go back far enough in meditation or Zen or religious studies or astrology, the core belief is always the individual person is an embodiment in flesh and energy of "God." God, the Earth, the universe, the "energy," whatever you want to name it, is in us, of us, and we are of God.

We are connected to everything through our bodies. Each living thing holds in it a spark of the divine universe, too.

This is why it is of the utmost importance to *say their names*. Saying the names of the humans who have been murdered at the hands of the white body patriarchy is embodiment. You must speak aloud and form the words on your tongue. It is physical, and it is powerful.

By starting antiracist practice with an acknowledgment of "the land" as "of the energy of God, of you, of humanity" and then working through all of the various individual societies that have touched or "owned" that land, it's pretty easy for me to see why this technique can help our minds. Our minds are opened to our shared human ancestry.

But embodiment is what helps our souls.

Michelle said, "By asking participants in the workshop to first acknowledge the ancestral effort and then to acknowledge the majority part of this world is built for a certain body that can climb steps and read signs and hear warnings, we all have found a common understanding of the generous gift of privilege.

"Like your hearing," she said, referring to the total hearing loss I experienced in my left ear in 2017. "In a workshop, I have to honor the fact I'm privileged to be an able-bodied person at times. I can hear in both ears. You can't. But even that is not the same experience as someone whose body is physically manipulated in a different way, without a limb or sight or other access needs."

"Then we can start talking about needs. We're all just on a spectrum of having different mental, physical and emotional needs which need to be met. I think it helps to uncover some of those invisible access needs before we explore the more visible ones, like racism and sexism," she said.

Michelle, at this point in our conversation, has me near tears. She is so talented, clear, and clearly a gift to the practitioners, students, and faculty in her care. She knows how to talk to me about my fragility and antiracist yearnings without shame. Just like Laura Phelan described in setting up Kindred communities.

Of course, this is Michelle's life's work. It is her profession.

I am lucky she is in my life and willing to talk to me about antiracism.

My conversation with Michelle helped guide me to the works of Resmaa Menakem, a trauma therapist and licensed clinical social worker, and Lama Rod Owens, a writer and Buddhist teacher.

Menakem's book *My Grandmother's Hands* is a "how to" guide for embodiment. Literally, exercises and practices. It is breath and touch. It is feelings and soul. His psychology-based framework is about recognizing your ancestral and lived experience and the trauma, such as macro and micro aggressions, you've experienced just by being inside of this patriarchal society, and then learning how to heal that trauma in your body.

Owens book, *Love and Rage,* is another "how to guide" for embodiment. Literally, exercises and practices. It is breath and touch. It is feelings and soul. His Buddhism-based framework is about recognizing your ancestral and lived experience and the visceral anger (or guilt or isolation) we feel from existing inside the patriarchy. He also teaches us how to welcome our love and our rage and heal the trauma in our bodies through acceptance and embodied practice.

We have relied on our intellectualism and our patriarchal values for too long, and now it is violent. As Ta-Nehisi Coats writes in his memoir *Between the World and Me,* "All our phrasing- race relations, racial chasm, racial justice, racial profiling, white privilege, even white supremacy-serves to obscure that racism is a visceral experience, that it dislodges brains, blocks airways, rips muscle, extracts organs, cracks bones, breaks teeth."[77]

---

[77] Ta-Nehisi Coates, Between the World and Me (United States: Random House Publishing Group, 2015), 11.

Every time we "need to know" in our minds or "need to do something" to help, we should stop.

Give a minute to *first* feel in our bodies before we act. Our urgency and our knee-jerk pivot to intellectual action or "better understanding" is violent in that it supports the intellectual and individualism values of the patriarchy.

Accept we don't need to know anything about Jacob Blake except his body was destroyed by racism. Say his name. Feel empathy for his family. Then turn to our Black and brown mentors and guides and ask them, "What do I need to do to help end racism?"

Akilah told me back in May I should, "look in the mirror. Look at your family. Look at the community you live in. Look at your friend group,"[78] so I was easily prepared in August to challenge my white intellectualizer friend's *need,* and I was able to be gentle about it. I was able to send him to a resource I trust to unlearn about his own patriarchal violence in that instance. So, I have, and that is antiracism.

By now most of my progressive white friends have picked up Dr. Kendi's *How to Be Antiracist* or read Dr. DiAngelo's *White Fragility.*

But that's just the prequel to the basics of antiracism. Now it's time for you to put down the research novel and start building your Ethic. Start to feel things. Start to cry powerful white tears.

Stop making excuses because the truth is you cannot be an ally, you cannot have an effective individual Praxis, if you don't get right with your soul, your body, your whiteness, and your Ethic.

---

[78] Akilah Hughes and Gideon Resnick, "Racism Cont'd," May 27, 2020, in Apple Podcasts, produced by Katie Long, 25:43.

Sign up for a workshop in *community*, practice embodiment in a new way, begin to feel your Ethic, tap into it more often, and *begin to live better.*

We've got a new universe to explore. For a lifetime.

CHAPTER 19

WALKING THE WALK THROUGH A BROKEN HEART

—

In June 2020, I was wrapping up the first draft of this memoir. We were still in a pandemic. Racial injustice wasn't solved by protestors. Income inequality still persists. Sexism is as pervasive as ever.

Shit is still flying at the fan at the speed of light. But my writing journey must come to an end. There is a deadline. Revisions and editing still to be done.

My biggest concern, aside from utter irrelevance, is in six months or in twelve months we will have gone back to "normal."

Maybe Biden will be elected in November and we'll flip the Senate and hold tight to the House, but that doesn't mean the work is over. Maybe police reforms will sail through Congress, but that doesn't mean the work is over. Maybe the Equal Rights Amendment will finally pass, but that doesn't mean the work is over.

The work, like meditation or learning a second language or the first time you had the sensation of "woke," is ongoing.

This work is a lifetime commitment to continually refresh, refine, and engage our Theory, Ethic, and Praxis, and I've decided to commit.

* * *

My friend Amy asked me the other day, "What words do you use to interrupt racism or sexism or whatever?"

"Well, I usually say, 'I'm not sure of your intent there, but that statement is racist or sexist,'" I said. "It's tricky to figure out when to say it or whether the person on the other end is capable of hearing it. Are you satisfied with holding that space or are you begging for an argument or opportunity to lecture? It's nuanced."

In *White Fragility,* DiAngelo explores the concept of white solidarity, "the unspoken agreement among whites to...not cause another white person to feel racial discomfort by confronting them when they say or do something racially problematic."[79]

In some cases, I've been the young college liberal coming home to face a cadre of beer-drinking boomer uncles and their twenty-something-year-old white sons sitting around the cooler in the driveway. I *know* what to say, but I'll be pummeled, humiliated, and shamed if I *dare* say a word.

In one case, I was the sassy white college co-ed crashing for the summer with a bunch of male Air Force aviator trainees in a beach house in Florida. My fiancé being a resident of the beach condo, I was happy to shack up to enjoy the

---

[79] Robin DiAngelo, White Fragility (Boston: Beacon Press, 2018), 57.

ideal summer of escaping to a tropical paradise. Then one night a man started to goad me over my discomfort with *Playboy,* something I was very uncomfortable with then as an insecure young woman.

I lashed out across the crowded poker table, the only woman in the room, "Dude, I've asked you three times to put the fucking porn mag away, not because I give a fuck about you looking at porn, but because this is my fucking house, and I've asked you to stop doing something. So, stop, or get the fuck out."

Queue the awkward silence. Not only did these boys not know what to say, I was their shrill older sister who stopped shaving her legs and could be dismissed. My fiancé said nothing. The temperature in the room came down, and a few people congratulated me on ruining a fun night. The party fizzled and moved out to the bars.

Calling out sexism isn't popular.

Triggering someone's defense mechanism because they don't believe they are sexist isn't effective.

Just recently, I was sitting around the patio on a lovely summer evening with a group of white progressive women who I adore, and one of them says, "It feels awkward that my child is a minority" in her public school.

Well, this mom's *feelings* are real. But how do you interrupt that statement without preaching or launching into a history of segregation? "Why can't your child be a numerical minority? We expect BIPOC children to bear that discomfort every day, and yet we have the privilege to remove our own children from the discomfort confronting them? Do you know how that is grounded in anti-Black sentiment?"

Who the fuck am I to say any of that after withdrawing

my own daughter from a majority Black school just a few years prior for the same reasons?

On social media, a high school classmate posted a meme about Michele Obama having a penis and Kamala Harris having to suck it to get the nomination for vice president.

"Disgusting," I posted.

Tapbacks of the laugh emoji ensued, egging me on.

My friend, Jessie, called me out for provoking this man. Jessie is still living in our segregated home town and works in education, health, and human services.

Her Theory is white-supremacy culture has pushed poor white people into a position of fear and self-protection. By living in rural communities in segregation to protect their own scant resources, they are fed cultural messages that reinforce "othering."

The patriarchy's messaging around Black and brown people's "laziness and dependency" on "the system" are why they don't have jobs and opportunities and why *our* taxes are so high. Poor Latinx immigrants competing for *our* jobs are why we can't make a living wage. Welfare recipients are such a burden on *our* society that if we had universal health care, we'd have it worse off than we do now because resources would be spread too thin.

The overt messages of the patriarchy, especially in politics these days, are that *those people* and their progressive policymakers are coming after your jobs, wages, savings, land, and security. Protect yourself.

These are powerful messages, reinforced by FOX News, small town gossip, and the lack of immediate, humanizing personal connections required to transform neural pathways and build empathy toward the things we are afraid of.

Jessie's Ethic is all people are brave and worthy of love

and belonging. She has a lot of empathy for the people in her community and a lot of patience for herself.

Her Praxis is continual learning, openness to being challenged, and working in roles to help.

When she told me I wouldn't help if I posted on social media about my classmate's blatant sexist and body shaming (and racist) meme, I was triggered.

When she told me I would probably just be making things worse by proving liberal snowflakes can't take a joke and he should entrench further into his viewpoint, I knew she was right.

I was pissed. But wrong.

I went back to the post and suggested the person share the meme with his female friends and his Black and brown friends, and then see if it weighs in as "innocent joke at the expense of politicians" or "hurtful sexism causing violence."

He replied, and I reminded him of our shared childhood experience and invited him to join me in conversation sometime. He didn't reply, and that's okay.

I tried to repair and realized I need to focus my energies on how I can help in spheres of influence I hold. Like talking to my white male friend about not needing to watch the Jacob Blake video. Or talking with Amy about interrupting racism.

I told Jessie since this man and I do share a space—a shared social media space—I intend to try and gently interrupt racism or sexism as long as that space is shared. I don't want to leave the space. If this man will keep me as his Facebook friend and not leave the space, maybe someday we will find common ground. I have faith because it has happened before.

A few years ago, the same man posted a meme about #MeToo and how awful, nasty women are ruining good white men's lives over harmless behaviors of childhood. I respectfully replied this man's mother, Renee, was the one who believed me and protected me from sexual assault when I was fourteen.

It was minor sexual assault where two boys were known to slap my breasts with a ruler or a spare spiral notebook and tease and shame me relentlessly. Renee was our school bus driver for a decade, and her not allowing toxic masculinity, sexism, and bullying rescued me.

I don't know if he changed his mind much about #MeToo, but he did reply and tell me he was sorry for what happened to me and for his post. That was more than I could have hoped for. He is human, and we connected.

* * *

In so many cases, interrupting is subtle. I might miss, or I might be ashamed, or it flies by and I connect the dots after too much time passes. It is hard.

I've decided to start saying, "That feels like a nuanced way of addressing complicated issues. I'm curious as to what is under that statement." Then say nothing. I am usually talking with intellectually dominated white progressives, so this works for me. Sometimes I'll say, "Can you please rephrase that?" or "Be clearer, please."

But essentially, be gentle. Feel you are triggered and want to fight racism or sexism, but also feel the empathy and humanity in the person in community with you. Hold the space. Hold tight with the yin in one hand and the yang in the other. It will take all of your grip and your fear and your strength. Hold on, girl. You can do this.

I love this person. ←→ They said something problematic.

I respect this person. ←→ They deserve an opportunity to see things differently.

I am scared of the retaliation. ←→ I am strong and unafraid.

I could be wrong and be ashamed of my behavior. ←→ I am brave and know how to recover from shame and be humbled by my mistakes. I am unafraid to learn.

Every single time I interrupt racism, sexism, another -ism, or personal goading and cruelty, later I will remind myself it would have been easier to say nothing. I'll second-guess the risk-reward.

I will take a shame bath for daring to *ruin the mood for the sake of my own selfish comfort.*

When I do speak up, I nearly always bumble and stumble. The shame and fear and self-consciousness of deciding "to stand up for" something—an abstract concept, a real feeling, a mix of both—coupled with a heightened emotional state is a recipe for disaster.

My voice pitch rises. I am shrill, emotional, and feeling "crazy." Sometimes I'll cry. Or yell. I might scream. I might lash out with needlessly cruel attacks or post something snarky on Facebook.

In these moments of overflowing emotion, I feel out of control. I am not in Praxis of my Ethic around empathy, curiosity, and not being violent. I am out of control.

Then something falls out of my mouth and lands with a big splat.

Later, I will wonder if it was worth it. Did they hear me? Did I just make it worse? *Was I* overreacting? Did I attack with too much emotion of my own and do more damage than was warranted?

What have I done?

Here's what I've done: risked my ego, challenged my

privilege, dared white supremacy culture to a duel, pissed off some white people, taken a risk that may have made me look like a crazed hippy witch woman with devil eyes, or said something truly hurtful I may regret later.

I also possibly made things worse.

None of these risks and actions are going to kill me, like these same risks and actions kill women at the hands of their abusive partners, like kill trans and Queer people, Black and brown people, disabled and mentally ill people every day in white America.

But many of my personal risks and actions *are* working to fuck the patriarchy. To be effective, we must always hold and see the humanity in our opponents and enter the space embodied and grounded in our Ethic.

I can do this, apologize for losing my shit, learn from any mistakes, and then get the fuck up and do it better.

When BIPOC people say white people need to "do more," more than protest or carry a sign or donate, they're partly talking about ending white solidarity, interrupting racism in its darkest progressive corners, and stepping into an anti-racist, humanist *way of being.*

Embodiment helps us practice antiracism more effectively. Some days, I'll feel like a racism-interrupting yellow belt. I can give *advice.* I can see it, interrupt it, and walk away knowing I did right by the person and the higher calling.

But just like being "woke," you'll be tested when you least expect it. You'll be reminded by the universe you, child, are at square one. Humility is continually required for growth.

So, if you resolve to follow this new way of life, if you *mean it* and truly mean to commit to the practice and life of anti-racism, then you fight the urge to give in, give up, and return to the comfort of whiteness. When that test comes, you will know whether you made the right choice.

You will own your decision, whether you acted racist and colluded, whether you did a mix of both out of inexperience or frustration, or whether you spoke up, consequences-be-damned.

Sometimes you will fail. Sometimes you will end up confused. Sometimes you will walk away broken and yet completely and totally in awe of your power.

In June of the dumpster fire that is 2020, I was wrapping up this collection and trying to figure out how to end the book. Should I write a how-to guide? Doesn't feel right. Should I give some more examples from experts? Those are flooding the world right now (and good! I'm so excited by my media and learning lists).

As I was gathering up people to help me with editing the first draft, starting to "announce" I've written more than a mediocre, too-long Medium post, beginning to tweet and post to (gag) self-promote my work, to donate and march, buy, consume, and support BIPOC businesses, I was starting to feel exposed.

I'm not just sharing a journey of the last few months of enlightenment. I am not just doing that thing—virtue signaling—where I want the accolades for being this new-level white, progressive, middle-aged, single-mom, multi-"woke" blog superstar.

I am not the Rachel Hollis of anti-racism here to say I should be your leader. In fact, that is a very dangerous position to take, based on Rachel Hollis herself. Hanging her hat on *being an expert* in perfect white wifehood, framed by values of "honesty and transparency," Rachel's brand took a major hit when she suddenly announced she and Mr. Hollis were divorcing after "three years" of struggle.

Hollis's professed Theory is centered on the values of radical transparency, self-care, and community. Her professed Ethic is centered on women being worthy of love and redemption from toxic cultural Rules. But her Praxis? She was *hiding* her ugly and real marital struggles from the very audience relying on her to be transparent about "hard things."

She failed in practice to live up to the brand image that supported her ever-increasing position of wealth, comfort, and power. The ivory tower crumbled, and she is very publicly being shamed.

I want to stake my own ground in a version of radical transparency and community, so I can continue to grow and fail without the stakes being so incredibly high. I would argue it would have been better for Hollis to share the ugly arguments and therapy sessions as they occurred, weathering the smaller storms of brand disruption, instead of listening to her marketing director's dire warnings about her business collapsing.

She fully bought into the rose-gold, superficial, toxic corporate self-help industry. I'm sorry it may be falling apart, Rachel, but you now have a chance to get better. Channel some Glennon Doyle and start again.

Solemnly acknowledge how things went so wrong, give yourself grace, create a new Theory, embody a new Ethic, and *practice* this time.

You've got all the time in the world.

* * *

Before writing this final story in May of 2020, I drew a tarot card: "The Magician." I use the tarot to help me trigger embodiment. The interpretations are meant to surprise your mind and trigger sensory feelings based on the "surprise" of the card's meaning. Some people believe there is divine energy involved, but I don't believe it matters either way.

If you're not familiar with tarot, "The Magician" card generally means your powers are coalesced and now is the time. I have everything I need from the spiritual fire and the embodied grounding to the financial resources and the intellectual knowledge to manifest my truth in a powerful way.

Soaring in the flow of "The Magician," surfing on the energy of the universe as I stop fighting it, empathizing with Rachel Hollis (of all people) and stepping into the, sometimes brief, moment of peace is the most incredible and thrilling experience.

It's like an orgasm for the soul.

But for every action there is an equal and opposite reaction.

I have mentioned my marriage ended in a fiery love affair. My lover was going through a dramatic divorce at the time, too. There was an immediate chemistry. The undertow that pulled us deeper and deeper into a trauma-bonded relationship was irresistible. I didn't plan to resist, and I have never been so immediately awash in lust and attention and pleasure in my entire life.

I could write an entire novel about my affair, how our relationship blossomed, how we moved through conflict, the way it feels to finally have someone say all the things you needed to hear about yourself over and over and over again, and how we lived happily ever after.

But we didn't.

It ended three years later, as suddenly and passionately as it began.

One Saturday in June 2020, he and his daughter invited me over to watch a film they had started the night prior.

I'd been introduced to his teenage daughter months before and was confident she actually liked me as a person. She sometimes even hung out with us!

Earlier that day, she had told him she'd like to finish watching the film that night and asked if I was okay catching up so we could all watch the ending together.

"Of course!" I said.

I would quote him here, but this isn't the time or the place for me to get sued for misquoting a person. I don't want to libel him. I am only telling this unbelievable story because I still can't believe it myself.

Instead, I'll write a bulleted list that I will swear under oath is the truth:

- The movie was called *Mudbound* and is about two families, one Black, one white, in the Jim Crow South—a sharecropper and landlord in Mississippi during WWII.
- Between the three of us, there was silly commentary on the dire situation of these families (How does anyone live in Mississippi without A/C? Can you imagine showering only once a week? Whose dream is to be a farmer in the 1940s?). He and I were drinking wine.
- The white characters used the N-word liberally, and "appropriately" considering the context of the film.
- The director and screenplay writer Dee Rees, a Black woman in Hollywood, is exactly the type of film I wanted to be watching at this point in my life. Rees clearly understands how to use the power of film to convey how ugly, overt, and accepted violence to Black bodies was then. How the Black body is physically harmed over and over in our culture, reinforced by the collective shoulder shrugging of white people. She was able to help the audience achieve levels of embodiment through her art.

- For anyone who has brains, *Mudbound* is also a not-so-subtle commentary on today's America, and Rees' ability to make me feel physically afraid of the white characters on behalf of the Black characters is powerful and effective. Her work connects the viewer to the anxiety of Black and brown bodies in today's America who still live in a state of physical fear, tension, and anxiety.
- During the film, I mentioned how difficult it would be to act the white parts and say the N-word to a Black colleague, even though it's "just acting." Having overt racism in my body and actions would be physically and emotionally revolting for me.

At this time, we need to buckle our seatbelts.
- My partner of three years was a man who had dated a Black woman prior to dating me. He is progressive, liberal, and anti-Trump. He is the father of a LBGTQIA+ child with mental health issues. He is a man who encouraged and supported me through my every trauma, from divorce and surgery to the deaths of my family members and investing in my business. He supported my writing and was there emotionally, physically, and intellectually for me.
- He said the N-word.
- What?
- Yes. He said the word in a sentence similar to, but not exactly, "They sure do say n– a lot." Yes, he said it just in passing, like when a teenage white bro rolls in his BMW belting out Drake's "Nice for What" or something.
- I interrupted and asked him not to use the word, even in this context. It's just not ever okay with me.

- He said it again. The classic argument came up: they're saying it in the movie. I interrupted again. He said it again. Another classic argument: it's just a word. I interrupted again, and he said it again. Yet another classic argument: you know I'm not racist. Yet I interrupted again, and then the movie ended.

I will quote him here. He said, in front of his teenage daughter, "Now Holly's all mad at me because I said n–."

Was he seeking white solidarity or validation because *of course he isn't a racist?* Was he seeking patriarchal control, challenging me and his daughter to interrupt him in his goading?

He laid out the challenge.

His child excused herself to bed.

I turned to him and said, "Yes. I am angry. I told you it made me uncomfortable you said that word. I told you I felt uncomfortable. I asked you, directly and clearly, to stop, multiple times, and you continued, despite my speaking up."

"I was just being silly," he said.

I had a flashback to that time I told my spouse, "I want to feel emotionally safe" and my spouse said "that's bullshit."

It was déjà vu.

This man was invalidating and diminishing my stated need for comfort over his *intent* to make a silly joke. He was using racism and sexism together to push me into a corner where I felt uncomfortable. When I spoke up, he told me he was a good guy and I was overreacting. He told me I was wrong to be angry and uncomfortable.

He claimed his *intent* wasn't to make me uncomfortable, so I had no grounding to be angry.

But I still felt discomfort, fear, and confusion, and I stated it unequivocally.

I pushed him harder, asking him to apologize.

I could have forgiven him had he said, "I am sorry I made you feel discomfort, fear, and confusion. I made a mistake."

But he said, something like, "I was just playing. Lighten up." Now I was faced with a choice.

Am I supposed to shut the fuck up about it because his *intent* was not to harm me? Should I minimize my own discomfort because he is "just being silly?"

Or should I state my need, reiterate my strong feelings, and ask for a place of emotional safety so we can repair?

Well, I ain't playing this gaslighting bullshit anymore.

But I was also triggered. I lost my shit. I was slightly drunk, disoriented, and awash in confusion and disbelief.

I saw an opening when he said (paraphrasing), "You know I'm not racist. I was just being silly. You know me. It was a silly joke."

I could have said (and in other non-racially charged arguments, had previously said), "Yeah, I know. You're just being silly, sweet lover. Let's just go to bed."

Instead, I said, "Would you say this in front of Selena? Would you say this in front of Michelle? Would you say it in front of your Black ex-girlfriend?"

He dug his heels in. "You're being dramatic. Don't lecture me on racism."

With my brain-on-fire, I felt the argument pivot from the N-word to a power struggle.

I don't know why he was goading me like this. He stepped into his white privilege and racism by the use of the N-word. He stepped into his male privilege and sexism by invalidating my needs and my feelings, telling me my discomfort was not important to him.

I'm not sure why he chose the N-word. I'm not sure why he did this in front of his child.

If he wanted to end our relationship with his codependence, with pushing me away, and his goading-plus-gaslighting behavior, it could have been about literally any topic. But he picked racism.

I mean, I can see him trying one of the older gaslighting tricks like being mad at me for criticizing his parenting or drinking habits by telling me I'm "crazy" or "too critical" or "not on his side." But he chose *racism* as the hill to die on.

To be honest, gaslighting might have worked had he picked any other topic, but in retrospect I thank him for this bold, intersectional outburst. It couldn't have been clearer what to do next.

In a half second, I asked myself: who am I in this relationship? Am I the person who allows someone to make me uncomfortable, minimize my discomfort, persist in the behavior, and then deflect responsibility because they are "just being silly?"

Am I the person who interrupts racism with my words, but then takes off my clothes and snuggles up to the comforts and familiarity of my access to the white men in my life who take care of me and provide for me, even though they also try to control me because they, themselves, are scared?

I had one more thing to say, begging the question: could this person show humility and vulnerability and feel shame and not weaponize it?

"If you would just swallow your pride and apologize, I know we can work through this tomorrow when we're not drunk," I said.

He said he had nothing to apologize for.

I went off the rails.

Imagine this next part being said in a very screechy, "typical hysterical woman" voice:

"You fucking asshole. This is no longer about just the N-word. Yes, it's 'just a word.' N–! N–! There, I can say words, too. Does it make you feel better when I say it?" I yelled while storming through the apartment, collecting my things. "How does that disgusting word land on your ears coming out of my mouth? It's still disgusting and wrong, and you wouldn't stop using it even though I clearly asked you to stop. To stop hurting me and making me uncomfortable.

"But I'm not letting you use the power of that word to confuse things here. This is about me asking for you to respect my feelings and my wishes, and you didn't, about something I care deeply about, and *you know it!*

"If you could just swallow your fucking pride and apologize, then we might get somewhere."

He said…actually, I can't remember what he said. I just remember him standing in the kitchen with his back to me, his soft blond messy pandemic hair that made him look like a little boy, his shoulders, his posture. I will always remember our last moment that way.

He may have said words, but he had his back turned.

He shut me out, unequivocally.

In his mind, his intent—to be silly and provoke me—outweighed my actual feelings of disgust, hurt, confusion, and betrayal. My therapist and I talked about his own pain, depression, and trauma, and how he may have internalized defensiveness and built walls.

His Theory is he is not racist or sexist, he is a "good man," good father, provider, and hard worker. His Ethic is he values unconditional love, empathy, and support. But in his Praxis, he has unconditional love only with himself and was rigid and violent toward me as I challenged his "good man" Theory with my very real pain.

I have bad news for him. His Theory, Ethic, and Praxis need revision. Until he goes into his ancestry and lived experience in an EbonyJanice Moore/Resma Menakem, go-to-therapy-and-experience-true-embodied-vulnerability sort of way, his Theory and Ethic will always be limited, and he will continue to fail in his Praxis.

I obviously left right then. It was after midnight.

I left with tears pouring down my face, horrified I yelled the N-word, loudly and said it at all, and horrified I might have, in my slightly drunk state, actually overreacted. I was horrified this was my real life.

On my way home, I frantically called everyone on my emergency call list. Jessie answered. She was my life preserver.

The next day I told my closest friends. They surrounded me with love, support, and affirmation. They brought cookies and beer and sushi and hugs (even in a pandemic).

I texted him the next day, "I'm here when you're ready to talk."

"I am tired of your drama and the lack of respect. So, we are over," he texted back.

"This is the first I'm hearing about you being tired of me or my behavior, with the exception of when we have been drinking. So, this comes as quite a surprise," I texted.

"So be it," he texted back.

That was that.

* * *

I'm not saying you should end your marriage over the N-word. But maybe I *am* saying you should end your marriage over the N-word, especially in the context of when white men use their combined powers to control you.

This is just one time.

This is one time I stood up for myself as a woman, as Madeline's mother, as a feminist, as a progressive, as a white person who has accepted my identity and owned my history through my work practicing and learning about sexism, intersectionality, and anti-racism. I did exactly what I would applaud my own daughter for doing if the situation was hers.

"You will lose friends over this," said a Facebook post a few weeks ago, referring to a commitment as a white person to potentially lose white friends by living in this Praxis of humanism.

My own not-posted-Facebook-post should read like this:

You will change if you choose this new way of being. At the moment, your best friend and lover goads you into a gaslit, drunken argument about the N-word, and you will be confused and alarmed.

As he pushes out of fear and insecurity to demonstrate his control over you, believing you'll forgive him and reject your own Praxis to keep him in your life, you will feel afraid. But then you will stand up and walk out, and into the arms of your beloved community.

When he doesn't call the next day, or the next, or the next, or the next, you will doubt if any of it was real to him. You will crave and feel loss remembering those many, many affirming moments when he said words your former partner never said

out loud like, "You give me the most love I've ever felt...I love
your openness...I adore you...I am so lucky to have you in
my life...You're beautiful...You're an amazing mother...I am
so happy with you...I miss you endlessly...I love you forever."

You will feel shame and betrayal. You will doubt whether
you ever saw anything clearly, and it will hurt.

You will mourn a friendship and a connection to another
soul who felt close and real. You will cry. You will feel lonely.
You will ugly cry. You will reflexively reach to text him. You
will feel shame again.

I have lost a touchpoint. I have lost physical nourishment
from someone who fed my body as well as challenged my intel-
lect. I have lost the inside jokes and the amped up conversa-
tions about politics. I have lost Netflix and chill, long walks
looking at neighborhood architecture, a shared love of flowers
and gardens, discussing books, lingering over a bottle of wine
on the rooftop, luxurious weekend getaways, easy laughs and
comfortable closeness, and the mutual feeling this time it could
be love forever.

But that night, and his abuse of his privilege and power—
gaslighting, insecurity, sexism, alcohol, depression, racism,
control—was felt in that room and in my body.

He was using his power in aggressive ways, and because I
have grown more powerful, I was in Praxis. I was able to trig-
ger my soul power and walk away. It wasn't pretty. I screamed,
and the N-word came out of my mouth for the first time in
decades. It was embarrassing.

But this is about making a mistake and being offered a
choice to move through shame and grow. He chose to walk
away instead of embrace humility and vulnerability. He chose
to deny everything, put up walls, and stay in his "good man"
theory, alone.

I chose to tell my story, reach out the next day and try and provide him an opening. He reaffirmed his earlier decision, and that's okay.

Forever, I will remember he is also kind and intelligent and empathetic, too. He will always be a central part of this entire story.

He committed a hurtful, racist, and violent act, and he is wrong ←→ He is worthy of love and belonging.

Our partnership was a journey I do not regret. It is a series of decisions, mistakes, moments, and love shared, and ultimately a final choice that determines that, yes, I have lost someone. Over this.

So be it.

So it was.

Time to begin again.

AFTERWARD

INVEST, INVEST, INVEST

———

You never really know whether something is fortune or misfortune. We only know the moment where it changes and alters our sense of hope.

—QUOTE ATTRIBUTION BY ALAN W. WATTS

Nothing is ever created or destroyed, they say.

They say history repeats itself.

That feels right.

You are not special, but you are unique. We are all living, hurting, loving, fucking, learning, failing, and fighting "goddamn *cheetahs*," says Glennon Doyle. Tending to that wounded person inside of us is top priority.

As you dig deep to build a Theory and embody your Ethic, you'll start to feel your strength to practice grow. I know I have.

You'll need guides, teachers, mentors, and will make mistakes. It will hurt. I know it has for me.

One day, you'll have just an extra ounce of energy. You'll feel brave, worthy, loved, and accepted. You'll take a step forward and the extra ounce of strength is still there. You are in a single sunbeam in one moment of your glorious life.

What are you going to do with that extra ounce? Who will you love with that? Who will you invest in? Whose soul will you feed?

Will you insist you must *watch the video?* Or will you cry, send love to your beloved community, and donate again to Black Lives Matter?

Our power and strength as white women with access to white male privilege and to white power structures is an asset. We have opportunity for comfortable, "normal" lives. We take for granted that we are mostly safe.

Now we have a way to channel our privilege and power to connect with ourselves, share openly, and connect in community with others. To end the -isms, we must accept and hold space for them, study our ancestry and lives, reject paralysis and overwhelm, eliminate patriarchal values in our Ethic, and start practicing at the intersections of what we hold to be true and what we believe is right.

To use our privilege, we must be determined and find community. If you can't find it, build it by sharing your story or reaching out to someone who is sharing theirs and thank them. Find your guides and take back your time to invest in this journey.

To be strong, we must heal. Once we are healed, we need to turn back into the pain, hurt, and fear to go fight again.

Sorry I don't have better news.

IT'S RECAP TIME

THE PRACTICE OF SELF-HEALING
- Step 1: Solemn Acknowledgment—Heal your body and soul before you ask them for more.

- Step 2: Learn to Evaluate Your Guides—Feed your soul with the right nourishment until you are well enough to feel fleeting joy.
- Step 3: Dig Your Heels in on the Matriarchal Values— Define your values, commit to them, and be in community with those who share your values.
- Step 4: Learn to Prioritize Your Time—We only live once, right? Take that to heart and commit to living a full, values-driven life.
- Step 5: Commit to Embodied Practice—Feel deeply in your faith and soul before you decide your next action.

Once you've done this once, the fifth becomes the first step. You are in a circle, repeating in practice, over and over and over and over.

* * *

It is at the end of the fifth step we get where Rachel Hollis and Glennon Doyle leave us in their writings. True, they went through trauma and worked hard to heal. They use their powerful voices and writing talents and faith to preach "Heal Thyself."

But now we know we can do two things at once. As we will never be forever healed, we must treat healing as a continual practice of care. Just because we are practicing self-care at one moment, doesn't mean we can't practice another part of our Theory and Ethic the next.

As you follow my weaving tale, you'll see how it is truly impossible to hold the values of the matriarchy in high esteem without running headfirst into the gigantic, seemingly impenetrable wall of racism and sexism and all the other -isms.

It's true we need healing and self-care. It is true we have power and should use it. Do both.

Once you have achieved the second step above, maybe for the third or fourth time in this endless loop, you will begin to build resilience and find more meaningful relationships built on shared values, including vulnerability, empathy, and curiosity, which will lead to a feeling of security and joy.

Then we move on to a different part of practice.

THE PRACTICING OF HELPING OTHERS
- Step 1: Solemn Acknowledgment—Your body and soul are embedded in a patriarchal, racist system, which is just part of our ancestral journey to right now.
- Step 2: Find the Right Guides—Fill your soul with knowledge about what this means, without spiraling into shame and unproductive, privileged actions. Read, work, go to classes, and listen to podcasts. Find the guides who make the journey one of joy and being productive.
- Step 3: Dig Your Heels into the Anti-racist Values and Ethic, and Stand up for What You Believe In. As white women, we *are* the patriarchy, and we must reject it fully to truly build an equitable society.
- Step 4: Prioritize Your Time, and Actively Invest in a Better Future via Continued Practice.

WHAT DO YOU MEAN BY INVEST, INVEST, INVEST?
I thought the bulk of this this book would be about "practical ways to invest in fucking the patriarchy." But it's not.

The book is about the story. I sought to trigger the white lady reader into realizing a new way of being in the world by deeply understanding we *are* the patriarchy. If we want to end it, start the matriarchy, and achieve a world of equality, it starts with getting "woke" to that hard fact right there.

If it works, the daily Praxis becomes simple and more obvious.

In the matriarchal society, we have two forms of labor: love and work.

In the matriarchal society, we have two forms of currency: time and money.

How will you labor and how will you spend?

INVESTING MONEY

Michelle said, when talking about the typical investment of money white people make in the world of antiracism, "A white person who has discretionary income to themselves, invest in a community space or effort in a Black community. They tend to believe they are doing a good thing. But what I rarely hear people say is that person *first* went to the community and asked the community how best they could use an investment."

Lesson: Do what BIPOC/Q people *ask you to do* with your money. Donate to the causes that share your values and are supported by BIPOC/Q people who also share your values. It's that easy. Don't go building another fucking "community garden" in Southeast DC because you just want cheap land. Don't start your own fund and distract and draw resources from the leaders of a movement that already exists. Don't attach strings to donations or complain when their "tone" wasn't what *you would have done.*

You don't actually know what the right steps are because you're centered in the patriarchy, so you have to just believe, stop pulling the invisible strings of control and power your money demand, and just *give into service.*

If you have money, do the research to find organizations and people who share your Theory and Ethic and who are themselves practicing from a place of expertise, joy, hope, or learning.

More often than not, it's not what you would do. That's the point.

Ideas on the Table:

- Donate Money to groups and organizations supporting antiracist work.
- Donate More Money to other groups and organizations supporting work that helps make this world better. When you see a donate button, press it. It always feels better and you'll just go out and make more money, anyway.
- Hire someone who is not white, cis, heterosexual at premium market rate.
- Be open to the concept of, and implementation of, reparations or things that aren't "fair." Understand it will be taxation or higher costs of goods and services and no one will be "taking" your money, but you may have to live with less. Lean into living with less right now.

INVESTING TIME

You know how many times I order from Amazon to "save time?" Too many.

We always say, "shop local," but do we do it?

We know the statistics about how much money spent in the local economy stays (a lot more than if you go to Target), but we continually invest our time in *something easier than* shopping local, finding a BIPOC business, finding a local artisan, tracking down a farm share with humane practices, taking the bus versus driving, and so on.

People think investing in equality is about money, but the truth is we spend money all the fucking time on all sorts of shit based on the privilege of convenience.

Ask yourself: what was the last consumable product I purchased that cost more than fifty dollars? Could you have found it from a local and/or BIPOC and/or Queer and/or womxn-owned and/or et cetera source instead? Did you even try? Can you commit to trying next time?

What was the last product of any kind you purchased? Did you need it? Did you need it with *Prime two-day-free-delivery?* Was it disposable? Was it essential? Was it necessary? Is there an alternate version that is handcrafted, homemade, could be made at home, easier to access without ridiculous environmental impact of transportation costs and shipping boxes and packing bubbles? Could you have found it from a local and/or BIPOC and/or Queer and/or womxn-owned and/or et cetera source instead? Did you even try? Can you commit to trying next time?

Making the investment of time is about more mindfulness around spending habits, product sourcing, and craftsmanship.

We all have to be much more mindful about the decisions we make on a daily basis. We're told that's because of environmental damage—climate change is caused by our pillage of the Earth's resources. While that is true, the damage to human bodies is directly tied to our consumption, too.

As a culture, we're in constant pursuit of more for less.

Think about free shipping. We are starting to learn "free shipping" is just some labor stolen from some human person downstream.[80]

---

80   Neil Ungerleider, "Free Shipping Is a Lie," Fast Company, November 1, 2016.

When we start to value low prices and free shipping over the people packing the boxes and the humans sewing the dresses, what we're doing is devaluing the labor that goes into that product. Our patriarchal-capitalist system is *designed* to squeeze and funnel money to the top. So, are you buying in?

Think about what human hands touched your purchase before it got to the sparkling shelves of the big-box store. You need to consider the following: was your thirty-dollar purse made by child labor in South Asia? Is this a knockoff of an artist's original design? Was *that* designer compensated or was she ripped off? What is that handbag made of? Where will it go once it starts to fall apart?

You need to own those purchasing decisions.

I'm not saying you can't get a new purse or go cruise Target but own that choice. I want you to fucking own it.

This everyday behavior is really hard to change but *try.*

Every bit of change is important. Congratulate yourself for what you *can do*, and then give yourself a little scolding for when you fucked it up, and then *try to do better next time.*

What I'm finding in changing my consumption habits is I love my "things" and the memories they hold. I love the experience of procuring them and the relationships that result. I love making my shopping list, and then going from thrift to yard sale to Etsy, to craft market, to local shop to find it. When I can't, I try and buy more responsibly in "mass production," too.

Look for B-Corps, companies with robust environmental-social reporting, and buy from BIPOC, womxn, Queer-owned businesses.

Everyone is contributing labor or time to help keep our lives and our bellies full, but as we have given to toxic capitalism, mistaking "full lives" for "full closets" and self-care for feel-good quick-fixes, we have all lost the value of art and craftsmanship.

We have separated the makers from the material objects they make, the writers and thinkers from the ideas they put forward. We've relegated some contributions to be invisible, and then the patriarchy can pay them less, not offer them benefits, and steal their labor, health, and life.

We are literally pretending they don't exist.

Not only is this diminishing their humanity and their individual worth in society, but it is diminishing our own humanity, too.

"They" are largely Black and brown bodies and poor white bodies.

How do we stop being just takers? How do we redistribute?

Of course, collective measures are more than necessary, but individuals have a responsibility to own their consumption decisions, too. We need to realign our personal values back toward craftsmanship, art, and the value of human bodies and their labor.

Ideas on the Table:

- Prioritize. Go through your budget and your credit card bills. Take a cursory look and identify one or two unnecessary purchases that could have been *made differently.*
- Research. Again, this is less about money and more about taking the time to be mindful. It's *easy* to run to Walmart or click on Amazon. Instead, purchase from a local, BIPOC, Queer, womxn-owned, community-supporting human being (and their team) whenever possible. When it is a decision you make to do a Target run, *just fucking own it.* You might find you get a few things, and then pass on others because you'll start to see alternatives in real time.

- Evaluate. I'm on the fence about Marie Kondo's "spark joy" mantra, but I am completely invested in the *idea* that your things matter. Get out your useless wedding china and eat your leftovers on it. Use things until they disintegrate because you've used the life out of them. Or share them with someone who needs them.

INVESTING EFFORT

It's possible you go to work some place every day. You get paid for that work, hopefully. Or maybe you "labor" in other ways.

Your own labor can be an investment in social justice, too. Where you choose to work, whom you choose to work for, and how you feel about investing your effort in a system you disagree with, but double down with an investment to help change from within.

All of these things are part of the contribution *you are making to the world.* You want to be paid well, have quality housing and health care, eat well, play well, and feel safe. You work hard for that, and you deserve that. We all do.

If you're investing your career time in some bullshit, toxic, corporate patriarchal activities, start figuring out how to liberate your labor from that cycle.

If you're investing your career time in a traditionally capitalist "squeeze the production" chain, then start figuring out how to liberate your labor from that cycle.

If you're investing your career time in something more nuanced, lean into changing the system to one aligned with the matriarchal values.

You are the only person who must sleep at night with your choices.

In my case, I'm a freelancer. My goal is to hire with social justice in mind (if ever I have money again after the pandemic, am I right?). But I still have *effort* to invest.

"For you right now, in terms of pricing, consider raising all of your prices so you have money to offer your services to people who can't afford to pay them," Michelle advised me. "Become involved in a community and you'll see where you can easily do just a small amount of effort which makes a huge difference for someone else.

"I mean like the graphic design work you did for me at no cost. Yeah, I'm able to carry it around with me as an actual tangible thing I show people around the educational work I do. I didn't have access to the software, I thought I could make it myself, and I couldn't. I was really stressed by that, by looking 'unprofessional.' By you just sharing your talents with me in that way, I have this document now which helps me, which may feel like nothing to you, but that's real investment in me."

As I sat in front of my computer screen, I am so touched by what Michelle said.

Yes, it was *easy* for me to whip up that graphic for her, and in doing so I made something *easier* for her.

But we can't go around doing all pro bono work and still function in our patriarchal capitalist society and still eat, can we? No. So, what else can I do?

"I think it's like just being more intentional about when you are planning things, gathering groups of people, or starting a new committee or something. You have to consider the particular barriers folks have to go through or around to be able to participate fully in your practice," Michelle said.

What she means is it is my responsibility to go out and find more diverse communities and join them authentically.

Then the path will show itself more clearly. This will be a slow, patient journey.

Ideas on the Table:

- Hire a BIPOC, LBGTQIA+ person. Oh, I already said that. Do it.
- Get involved with your policymakers. Understanding the legal structure of your community isn't so hard, but we think it is. Politics is local. Go figure it out.
- Join and get involved in a community of practice that is diverse in a more mindful sense. This not about mentoring or selling or volunteering. It's about authentic networking and *opening your network.* There are people I know and places I have access to because of my privilege being leveraged over a lifetime. I can do some things reflexively, like call my council member or walk into the manager's office, without ever feeling like I am entitled to be treated well. I also know people at the levels of power, leadership, and influence. I know CEOs and executive directors and athletic directors and upper managers and generals and such. Using my existing network, built on whatever structure it was built on, and intentionally opening it up to a broader community is essential. You just never know what introductions you might make that will ignite something huge.
- Learn craftsmanship. Have you ever fixed a broken laptop yourself? Have you ever hung drywall? Have you ever laid tile? Have you ever sewn a dress? Craftsmanship is about "skill in a particular craft." From witchcraft to plumbing, we are all craftspeople or artists creating something. If you're a knowledge worker like I am, then when you try to use your body in labor, it can be an ugly-ass, frustrating experience. If you respect your own inability as a

craftsperson, you'll learn to value those who craft well and pay them for their skills. If you learn a craft yourself, you'll find a new way to spend your time that isn't primarily centered on consumption. Then the next time you start haggling with your contractor over the cost of your bathroom remodel, consider that maybe cheaper is not better. You want the people working with you to feel like you value them, and you show them you value them by paying them for their craftsmanship.

INVESTING LOVE

You are unique and fragile, powerful and helpless, overwhelmed and motivated. Now we know we are all of these things at the same time.

What else? We are a source of love and strength, first for ourselves, and then for our surroundings and our beloved communities.

Being focused on holding space for many things at the same time means you will be vulnerable. You will feel hurt and confused, empowered and affirmed, abandoned and alone, supported and loved simultaneously, and more often.

As I recommit every day to a life of radical transparency and push myself toward balance, patience, and joy, I just feel more resilient, loved, safe, and curious.

As I explore the world with fresh eyes, I want to know more about the people around me, the things they make, and the stories they tell. But I'm doing this in my own unique way, and that's okay.

It's okay not to stand up and storm out and end your relationship when you intervene in a personal or racially charged moment. It's okay if you do end it, too.

Own it, and your beloved community will support you

through it. Own it all. Whatever you do, own it; don't skate through life pretending your privilege has no impact.

"People working on antiracist practices are often in a role of helping white people on their journey and, you know, it might be a very gentle intervention in the beginning because that is what's going to be the most effective," said Laura Wilson Phelan.

When you do act, act out of love, first for yourself, then for your values, then for the person you've just engaged.

"Our objective is to help them along on this journey, and they have to want to be on the journey, too," said Phelan. "So, if you say something that's going to induce fear, shame, or guilt, they're going to come right off that journey and go back to what's comfortable because being shamed or 'called out' is scary."

Going back to "racial comfort," as DiAngelo puts it in *White Fragility,* or as I would say fleeing to patriarchal white comfort, is the definition of privilege, but it's also a perfectly normal fight-or-flight response.

As you engage with friends, loved ones, strangers, colleagues, and acquaintances, Phelan reminds us as individuals, "It all starts with the individual relationship. Oftentimes, it starts with validation. Some of the most challenging things we do and conversations we have are where we don't validate the other person's perspective or experience."

In the ending of my relationship, my lover didn't validate my discomfort with his use of the N-word. He didn't validate my pain and confusion for having to beg for him to end my discomfort, and him persisting. He didn't validate my hurt for having *race* be the stick he used to goad me. He didn't validate my position as a woman in a world who is always on guard, afraid of male bodies, even just subconsciously.

I was hurt, defensive, angry, and afraid. I escaped.

In the ending of my relationship, I didn't validate my lover's silly jokes. I didn't validate him and tell him I know he isn't racist. I didn't tell him he is loved, even though he made a drunken mistake. I didn't validate any of that, and I shamed him in front of his daughter.

He was hurt, defensive, and angry. He withdrew and put up walls.

It could have ended differently, but in that moment, we both felt unsafe emotionally. In that moment, we both needed to protect ourselves more than we needed to validate and support one another. Sometimes that's okay, too.

"I love you, but I love me more," I thought, "and it appears I have more work to do to be a better partner in the future. Do you?"

From interpersonal communication, to self-care, to politics, to religion, to marriage, to racism, ableism, sexism, homophobia, and so on, the skill and strength learned from being able to hold multiple things at the same time delivers the ultimate gift: the power of empathy and curiosity.

It's a gift for yourself, for others, and for the world.

I will fuck up. I already have. I will do it again. I am unafraid to forgive myself, be curious about my failures and shame, and try again.

Investing in Love:

- Find and commit to a practice of embodiment to lead you to your higher power.
- Find and commit to intellectual and physical treatments and therapies to heal from your trauma.
- Find and commit to radical transparency within your beloved community. A shared vulnerability and circle of trust is as strong as the strongest family bond.

- Find and commit to learning about the world. Become a student of the world. Read the news. Read psychology, sociology, history, science. Expose yourself to art, culture, music.
- Forgive yourself. Forgive others. Let go. Accept. Love Again, Harder.

Things are as they are. Looking out into it, the universe at night, we make no comparisons between right and wrong stars, nor between well and badly arranged constellations.

—QUOTE ATTRIBUTION BY ALAN W. WATTS

Things are as they are.

If you've found your connection to your higher power and you're doing this hard work investing in relationships, healing, and learning, then you will stumble and recover more quickly, buoyed by true joy, connection, support, love, and grace.

I am here at the dawn of "woke," feeling afraid and safe. I am connected and isolated. I am powerful and fragile.

Take that first step and invest in the time to drill into your own story and begin your version of this journey of a life lived in play, joy, and Praxis.

APPENDIX

———

CHAPTER 1: FUCKING THE PATRIARCHY

Fernandez, Maria Elena. "Why Shrill Took Aim at 'Sinister' Empowerment Conferences." *Vulture*, February 10, 2020. https://www.vulture.com/2020/02/shrill-season-2-waham-conference.html.

Hollis, Rachel. *Girl, Wash Your Face: Stop Believing the Lies About Who You Are So You Can Become Who You Were Meant to Be*. Nashville: Nelson Books, 2018.

Lyonne, Natasha, dir. *Shrill*. Season 2, episode 6, "WAHAM." Aired January 20, 2020, on Hulu. https://www.hulu.com/series/shrill.

Quarshie, Mabinty. "Is the Women's March More Inclusive This Year?" *USA Today*, January 18, 2018. https://www.usatoday.com/story/news/2018/01/18/womens-march-more-inclusive-year/1038859001/.

Sarmiento, Isabella Gomez. "After Controversial Leaders Step Down, the Women's March Tries Again in 2020." *NPR*, January 17, 2020. https://www.npr.org/2020/01/17/797107259/after-controversial-leaders-step-down-the-womens-march-tries-again-in-2020.

CHAPTER 2: PLEASE DON'T TAKE MY PRIVILEGE

Dederer, Claire. *Love and Trouble: A Midlife Reckoning*. New York: Alfred A Knopf, 2017.

Strand Book Store. "Claire Dederer + Ada Calhoun | Love and Trouble." May 19, 2017. Video, 46:30. https://www.youtube.com/watch?v=6XgkJfGhLyg.

CHAPTER 3: EVERYONE IN THE ROOM, PLEASE BE UNCOMFORTABLE NOW

"Key Spouse Program." Air Force Personnel Center. Accessed October 2, 2020. https://www.afpc.af.mil/Benefits-and-Entitlements/Key-Spouse-Program/.

CHAPTER 6: THE CRISIS IS REAL

Calhoun, Ada. "The New Midlife Crisis for Women." *Oprah.com*. Accessed August 28, 2020. http://www.oprah.com/sp/new-midlife-crisis.html?fbclid=IwAR1fNJ4EfLEC9yEIvCoit_55wr7OW-FZOSnMoaD7rMAzjlR8LdZN7ULonOUc.

CHAPTER 7: GASLIGHT ME NO MORE, RACHEL HOLLIS

Calhoun, Ada. "The New Midlife Crisis for Women." *Oprah.com*. Accessed August 28, 2020. http://www.oprah.com/sp/new-midlife-crisis.html?fbclid=IwAR1fNJ4EfLEC9yEIvCoit_55wr7OW-FZOSnMoaD7rMAzjlR8LdZN7ULonOUc.

Jong, Joy de. "ACN & Donald Trump." December 4, 2014. Video, 2:55. https://www.youtube.com/watch?v=Z9UD3aalrsI.

LaRosa, John. "U.S. Personal Coaching Industry Tops $1 Billion, and Growing." *MarketResearch.com* (blog), February 12, 2018. https://blog.marketresearch.com/us-personal-coaching-industry-tops-1-billion-and-growing.

Laryea, Brittney. "Survey: Vast Majority of Multilevel Marketing Participants Earn Less Than 70 Cents an Hour." *Magnify-*

ing Money, September 17, 2018. https://www.magnifymoney.com/blog/news/survey-vast-majority-multilevel-marketing-participants-earn-less-70-cents-hour/.

McClure, Laura. "The Landmark Forum: 42 Hours, $500, 65 Breakdowns." *Mother Jones*, August 17, 2009. https://www.motherjones.com/politics/2009/08/landmark-42-hours-500-65-breakdowns/.

Turner, Laura. "'Girl, Wash Your Face' Is a Massive Best-Seller with a Dark Message." *Buzzfeed News*, November 9, 2018. https://www.buzzfeednews.com/article/lauraturner/rachel-hollis-girl-wash-your-face-self-help-book.

Wang, Amy B. "Gwyneth Paltrow's Goop Touted the 'Benefits' of Putting a Jade Egg in Your Vagina. Now It Must Pay." *Washington Post*, September 5, 2018. https://www.washingtonpost.com/health/2018/09/05/gwyneth-paltrows-goop-touted-benefits-putting-jade-egg-your-vagina-now-it-must-pay/.

West, Lindy. "'Gwyneth Glows like a Radioactive Swan' – My Day at the Goop Festival." *Guardian*, June 14, 2017. https://www.theguardian.com/lifeandstyle/2017/jun/14/gwyneth-glows-like-a-radioactive-swan-my-day-at-the-goop-festival.

CHAPTER 8: SEEING SINISTER EVERYWHERE

Ambirge, Ash. "#242 – The Art of Trusting Your Most Dangerous Ideas with Ash Ambirge – The Middle Finger Project." *AffordAnything.com*. Interview by Paula Pant. Afford Anything Podcast, February 17, 2020, audio, 1:12.

Avins, Jenni, and *Quartz*. "The Dos and Don'ts of Cultural Appropriation." *Atlantic*, October 20, 2015. https://www.theatlantic.com/entertainment/archive/2015/10/the-dos-and-donts-of-cultural-appropriation/411292/.

Choose Wonder. "Amber Rae." Accessed April 1, 2020. https://www.choosewonder.com/team/amber-rae.

Girlboss Foundation, "Girlboss Foundation." Accessed April 15, 2020. https://www.girlboss.com/foundation.

Girlboss. "The Girlboss Rally." Accessed April 15, 2020. https://www.girlboss.com/rally/.

Girlboss. Website homepage. Accessed April 15, 2020. https://www.girlboss.com/.

HeyMama. "Membership." Accessed April 15, 2020. https://www.HeyMama.co/membership/.

HeyMama. "Our Story." Accessed April 15, 2020. https://www.HeyMama.co/ourstory/.

Sincero, Jen. "Home." Accessed April 15, 2020. https://jensincero.com.

Sincero, Jen. "You Are a Badass DIY Coaching Program." Accessed April 15, 2020. https://jensincero.com/coaching/.

Sincero, Jen. "YouAreABadass." June 16, 2017. Video, 0:23. https://www.youtube.com/watch?v=CxLug7OoKeI.

TheCru. "Our Story." Accessed October 1, 2020. https://www.thecru.com/our-story.

CHAPTER 9: MY WHITE HUSBAND, THE VICTIM OF A TERRIBLE INJUSTICE

Catron, Mandy Len. "The Case Against Marriage." *Atlantic*, July 2019. https://www.theatlantic.com/family/archive/2019/07/case-against-marriage/591973/.

Dederer, Claire. *Love and Trouble: A Midlife Reckoning*. New York: Alfred A Knopf, 2017.

Orenstein, Peggy. "The Miseducation of the American Boy." *Atlantic*, December 20, 2019. https://www.theatlantic.com/magazine/archive/2020/01/the-miseducation-of-the-american-boy/603046/.

Riggio, Ronald E, "How Are Men's Friendships Different from Women's?" *Psychology Today*, October 9, 2014.

CHAPTER 12: SO, YOU WANT A CHECKLIST?

Angelou, Maya. "For Years, We Hated Ourselves." *New York Times*, April 16, 1972. https://www.nytimes.com/1972/04/16/archives/-for-years-we-hated-ourselves.html.

Moore, EbonyJanice. "White Urgency Is Violence." July 22, 2019. Online lecture. Produced by The Free People Project. www.thefreepeopleproject.com/lectureseries.

CHAPTER 13: WHY DOES EVERYONE WANT TO MOVE TO A TROPICAL FUCKING ISLAND?

Dederer, Claire. *Love and Trouble: A Midlife Reckoning*. New York: Alfred A Knopf, 2017.

Strand Book Store. "Claire Dederer + Ada Calhoun | Love and Trouble." May 19, 2017. Video, 46:30. https://www.youtube.com/watch?v=6XgkJfGhLyg.

CHAPTER 14: ASPIRE TO BE AN ELEPHANT

Armbrust, Jennifer. *Proposals for the Feminine Economy*. Topanga: Fourth Wave, 2018.

Marsden, Harriet. "International Women's Day: What Are Matriarches, and Where Are They Now?" *Independant*, March 8, 2018. https://www.independent.co.uk/news/long_reads/international-womens-day-matriarchy-matriarchal-society-women-feminism-culture-matrilineal-elephant-a8243046.html.

CHAPTER 15: THE PROBLEM OF PRIORITIZATION

Knight, Sarah. "Home." Accessed April 20, 2020. http://nofucksgivenguides.com/.

Watts, Alan. *The Book: On the Taboo Against Knowing Who You Are*. United Kingdom: Knopf Doubleday Publishing Group, 2011.

CHAPTER 16: DRINK FROM THE FIREHOSE OF MY FRAGILE WHITE FEELINGS

Brown, Brené and Glennon Doyle, "Glennon Doyle and Brené Brown on Untamed." Interview by Brené Brown. Unlocking Us Podcast, March 24, 2020, audio, 1:05.

Neilson, Sarah. "Is Glennon Doyle's New Memoir 'Untamed' Inspiration or Heavy-Handed?" *Seattle Times*, May 6, 2020. https://www.seattletimes.com/entertainment/books/is-glennon-doyles-new-memoir-untamed-inspirational-or-heavy-handed/.

Waldman, Katy. "A Sociologist Examines the 'White Fragility' That Prevents White Americans from Confronting Racism." *New Yorker*, July 23, 2018. https://www.newyorker.com/books/page-turner/a-sociologist-examines-the-white-fragility-that-prevents-white-americans-from-confronting-racism.

CHAPTER 17: GETTING ALL "WOKE" AND SHIT

DiAngelo, Robin. *White Fragility.* Boston: Beacon Press, 2018.

Kindred Communities. "Our Vision & Approach." Accessed March 31, 2020. https://kindredcommunities.org/what-we-do/our-approach/.

CHAPTER 18: BEING ANTIRACIST AFTER (WHILE) BEING RACIST

Allain, J. M. "Sexual Relations Between Elite White Women and Enslaved Men in the Antebellum South: A Socio-Historical Analysis." *Inquiries Journal/Student Pulse* (2013 5:08), http://www.inquiriesjournal.com/a?id=1674.

Bertrand, Natasha. "The 40 Smartest People of All Time." *Business Insider*, February 27, 2015. https://www.businessinsider.com/the-40-smartest-people-of-all-time-2015-2.

Coates, Ta-Nehisi. *Between the World and Me.* United States: Random House Publishing Group, 2015.

Hughes, Akilah, and Gideon Resnick. "Racism Cont'd." May 27, 2020. In Apple Podcasts. Produced by Katie Long. Podcast, 25:43. https://podcasts.apple.com/us/podcast/what-a-day/id1483692776?i=1000475918844.

Kendi, Ibram X. *How to Be an Antiracist*. New York: One World, 2019.

Silva, Danielle. "From Juneteenth to the Tulsa massacre: What Isn't Taught in Classrooms Has a Profound Impact." *NBC News*, June 18, 2020, https://www.nbcnews.com/news/us-news/juneteenth-tulsa-massacre-what-isn-t-taught-classrooms-has-profound-n1231442.

Spruell, Marjorie J, "Women Can Be Racist, Too" *Democracy Journal*, Winter 2018: 47. https://democracyjournal.org/magazine/47/women-can-be-racists-too/.

Vincent, James. "Google 'Fixed' Its Racist Algorithm by Removing Gorillas from Its Image-Labeling Tech." *Verge*, January 12, 2018. https://www.theverge.com/2018/1/12/16882408/google-racist-gorillas-photo-recognition-algorithm-ai.

AFTERWARD: INVEST, INVEST, INVEST

Ungerleider, Neil. "Free Shipping Is a Lie." *Fast Company*, November 1, 2016. https://www.fastcompany.com/3061686/free-shipping-is-a-lie.

RESOURCES

———

In addition to the many works referenced in the text and the appendix, check out the following sites to help you understand, desegregate, and diversify your information and inspiration:

- Definition of terminology compiled by Forth Worth Independent School District at https://docs.google.com/presentation/d/1YyOSB0LrDp5S720xrvM2rWJik2g-PU3ZE/edit#slide=id.p1
- Anti-Racism Resources – Document compiled by Sarah Sophie Flicker, Alyssa Klein in May 2020 at http://bit.ly/ANTIRACISMRESOURCES
- "Anti-Racism" Page compiled by United State of Women at https://www.theunitedstateofwomen.org/antiracism/

ACKNOWLEDGMENTS

First, I would like to thank Amy Throndsen for committing to reading every draft, giving feedback, and pushing me forward. Without her, I don't know how I could have ever finished.

I'd also like to thank the many people who have supported me and put up with my rants, urgency, heavy-handedness, injury, mistakes, overthinking, and intensity as I've careened through the past eight years, leaving piles of rubble in my wake. Your endless wells of generosity and empathy have helped keep me moving bravely toward radical transparency, repairing my harm, and finding joy.

Thanks also to my immediate family Jared, Jackie, Shawna, Moira, Setsuko, John, and Vickie for always picking up the phone. Endless love to my heart sisters Jessie, Neva, Amy, Herrin (and MOMO et al.), Lara, Celestina, Lindsey, Maggie, Kate, Timmi, Nicole, Angie, and Erica for being my chosen family. Gratitude goes to the women who I interviewed for this book, Michelle, Stefanie, and Laura, for making it feel real. Acknowledgments go to Leandra and Jen for being a huge part of the sequel.

Additional thanks to the small-but-mighty group of beta readers who read and provided feedback on each working draft so I could make it worth reading: Amy, Andy, Annie, April, Ashley, Becca, Dave, Dori, Hannah, Jennifer, Jessie, Karyn, Liz, Maggie, Michele, Scott, and Stefanie.

An additional thanks to the early supporters who purchased during the crowdfunding campaign. First, special thanks to my superhero supporter, Setsuko Gion, who got me over the hill and made the hardcover possible. To those who paid way too much for a paperback: Amal Disparte, Ron and Jamie Collman, Jerrold Martisak, Nicholas Foster, Susan Eubank, Jared Gion (for also buying mom a copy), Jessica DuBose, Lindsy Abendschein, Timmi Claveria, and Amy Throndsen and Scott Hartwell. Finally, thanks to those who bought the paperback and eBook before it was even finished: Aaron W. Hunt, Alice Gouvernayre. Alice Stokes, Amanda Deaver, Amy Treat, Andy D., Angie Sit, Annie Hunt, April Bofferding, Betsy Gouvernayre, Betsy Poos, Brandy Hawkins, Cate Sevilla, Christopher Becerra, Cory Langley, David Hunt, Jr., Dori Spaulding. Dorothy James Jorgensen, Effie Kapsalis, Elizabeth Childs, Eric Koester, Erica Rivers, Erika Toman, Erin Bott, Erin Thompson, Helen Lottridge, Herrin Hopper, Jackie Woodside, Jamie Mitchell, Jessica B., Jenni Chillstrom, Jennifer Hall, Jerrold Martisak, Jerry Holloway, Jessica DuBose, John Gion, Jolene Francis, Jordi Hutchinson, J. Pine, Karyn Soltis-Habeck, Katherine Grobe, Katie Bruner, Katie G. Dow, Kirsten Gunst, K. Myers, Lara Landers, Laura Davis, Lauren Gion, Linda McBride, Lindsey Williams, Marge Piper, Matt Cryer, May Wheelwright, Miranda Franco, Mitch Eisman, Moira Gion, Molly, Nicole D'Ercole, Nina de Keczer, Peggy Jones, Quinnan Picton, Rachael Blumenberg, Rodster Hunt, Sara Cameron-Ragazzo, Shawna Britton,

Sheryl Freedman, Staci Landers, Todd Kepple, Tyson Martin, Vickie Shaw, and Zelda J.

Thanks to the editors and teams at the Creator's Institute and New Degree Press for keeping the trains running on time.

I could not have produced this book or lived this life without benefitting from centuries of largely unacknowledged, unpaid, and stolen lives, labor, and land. I acknowledge my ancestral opportunities and my privilege. I am awed, humbled by, and grateful for all of the warriors who have worked and continue to work to dismantle white supremacy culture and wish them joy, liberation, and peace.

Say their names.

CPSIA information can be obtained
at www.ICGtesting.com
Printed in the USA
FSHW021152271220

9 781636 765600